"*The Behavior Analyst's Guide to Working with* for how behavior analysts can incorporate acceptance and commitment therapy caregivers within their scope of competence. Alyssa Wilson conveys technical content in a conversational and engaging way. I appreciated the emphasis on creating reinforcement-rich environments for caregivers. I will refer to this work often and suggest it to behavior analysts learning ACT."

> —**Kendra Thomson, PhD, BCBA-D**, associate professor at Brock University;
> and clinician-scientist at Azrieli Adult Neurodevelopmental Centre and the
> Centre for Addiction and Mental Health

"The board-certified behavior analyst (BCBA) professional is aware of the practical constraints in reaching the parents of their clients, despite knowing they must. Alyssa Wilson has provided a road map for doing something about this that fits with the current way ABA services are defined, authorized, and delivered. Parents of children with complex health needs facing their own mental health challenges will benefit greatly from this book."

> —**Becky Nastally, PhD, BCBA-D**, owner and executive director of Bloom
> Behavior Therapy, and instructor at Murray State University

"Alyssa Wilson provides a comprehensive account of ACT as a behavior-analytic intervention within the area of parent training and coaching. The chapters build on each other to provide a broad understanding of the components of ACT as behavioral repertoires, and specific guidelines and practical steps to pave the way for implementation. Essential reading for any behavior analyst working with parents, families, and caregivers."

> —**Marianne L. Jackson, PhD, BCBA-D**, professor of psychology,
> coordinator of the graduate training program, and clinical director of
> ABA services at California State University, Fresno

"Alyssa Wilson's guidebook for including mindfulness and acceptance in parent training is full of 'ah-ha' moments. Her scientific, flexible approach emphasizes curiosity, perspective taking, and awareness during behavioral intervention. She shares easy-to-understand strategies that create more positive and joyful family experiences. The tools also help parents cope with everyday challenges. This resource cements Wilson's status as one of the field's primary advocates for kind, human-centric behavioral services."

> —**Robyn M. Catagnus, EdD, LBA, BCBA-D**, adjunct full professor at
> The Chicago School of Professional Psychology, and vice president of
> service excellence at Brightside Benefit

The Behavior Analyst's Guide to Working with Parents

Acceptance & Commitment
Training for Effective
Parental Collaboration
in Treatment

ALYSSA WILSON, PHD, BCBA-D

CONTEXT PRESS
An Imprint of New Harbinger Publications, Inc.

Publisher's Note

This publication is designed to provide accurate and authoritative information in regard to the subject matter covered. It is sold with the understanding that the publisher is not engaged in rendering psychological, financial, legal, or other professional services. If expert assistance or counseling is needed, the services of a competent professional should be sought.

NEW HARBINGER PUBLICATIONS is a registered trademark of New Harbinger Publications, Inc.

New Harbinger Publications is an employee-owned company.

Cover design by Amy Shoup

Acquired by Ryan Buresh

Edited by Jean Blomquist

Indexed by James Minkin

Library of Congress Cataloging-in-Publication Data on file

Printed in the United States of America

25   24   23

10   9   8   7   6   5   4   3   2   1   First Printing

To Simon and his family

Contents

Foreword

I first met Dr. Alyssa Wilson in graduate school in the late 2000s where we shared mentors who emphasized two major themes in behavior analysis: 1) it should always strive for technical precision and 2) it should have a bigger impact in our everyday lives. Greater mainstream relevance requires learning how to address behaviors under complex and "messy" verbal stimulus control, and that is extraordinarily difficult to do while maintaining the precision we expect of our analysis.

This book accomplishes this feat by providing a detailed behavior analytic guide for applying acceptance and commitment therapy (ACT) to the "messy" business of parenting and parent training. Notably, this work offers a novel approach to ACT by organizing the model around a behavior-analytic taxonomy instead of relying on mid-level terms. The behavioral flexibility model is grounded in core behavioral assessment and intervention techniques that all behavior analysts should have in their repertoires, making this book an extraordinarily accessible introduction to ACT for behavior analysts. The model is also informed by recent developments in relational frame theory, including detailed consideration of deictic relations, hierarchal relations, and analogies. This focus on contemporary research makes the book an ideal resource for behavior analysts who are looking to expand their practice to include consideration of more complex verbal repertoires that are often involved in parenting behaviors.

A major strength of this work is the clear focus on the behavioral assessment of ACT parent training. One of the core challenges of using ACT in behavior analysis is ensuring that ACT interventions are guided by ongoing data collection and visual analysis. Dr. Wilson offers clear guidance on developing individualized multimodal data collection systems and provides assessment recommendations for all major intervention components. In addition, the intervention chapters are not metaphors to be memorized or worksheets to be assigned; instead, they are conceptual guides that will empower behavior analysts to design individualized interventions for the families they serve. This detailed consideration of direct assessment of observable behavior and individualized approach to intervention clearly align this book within the scope of practice of behavior analysis.

I believe that this book is coming out at an important moment in behavior analysis. While ACT came from behavior analysis and has been developed within the behavior analytic community for almost forty years, it seems to be gaining broader momentum. The 2022 special issue on ACT in *Behavior Analysis in Practice*, which Dr. Wilson coedited, showcased a wide range of conceptual and data-based applications of ACT in applied behavior analysis, with even more research now in progress. This book provides an ideal entry point for behavior analysts looking to integrate ACT into their professional repertoire when working with parents. My sincere hope is that as more behavior analysts do so, the value of this work to our clients, stakeholders, and profession will become even more evident.

—Michael Bordieri, PhD, BCBA-D
Associate Professor of Psychology
Murray State University

Preface

My clinical exposure to working with parents and families wasn't a straight line. I started exploring acceptance and commitment therapy (ACT) in my clinical practice as a doctoral student, focusing on adults and adolescents with a range of presenting symptoms. By 2014, I began to be asked how behavior analysts could use ACT—not only with clients but also with caregivers or family members, staff, teachers, and others interacting with those clients. I usually tempered my answers to such inquiries, both publicly and privately, with hesitation and skepticism about using ACT with parents or staff members. At that time, I believed there was too much gray area for potentially unethical situations and quandaries to thrive.

People in my support network, however, didn't accept my hesitation and skepticism, and challenged me not to dismiss this new area of practice but explore it and figure out how behavior analysts could do it ethically and without causing any harm. So I took up their challenge. I attended workshops and trainings, expanded my own clinical practice, and began to emphasize parent and caregiver coaching and ACT training.

In 2018, I took my first client where we (a small but mighty graduate student research team and I) used ACT for both client (an adolescent with complex health needs) and parent coaching sessions. I learned a lot from that family, particularly the importance of going at the family's pace and incorporating metaphors or activities that aligned with the family's experiences. We didn't get to complete the intervention, as the client ended up being hospitalized and it was too much for Mom to come into our clinic. Because of this, I initially thought our intervention was a failure. But about a year later, I learned that the mom was telling her new Board Certified Behavior Analyst (BCBA) all the wonderful things she learned from our sessions, including the value of ACT.

I discovered a few things during those early years. First, there were resources for how to provide psychotherapy to parents generally or to parents of children with specific or complex health needs, but nothing was available specifically for behavior analysts on how to use ACT within their parent training.

A second discovery was how desperate behavior analysts and parents/caregivers were to find a better way. Countless behavior analysts told me how hard it was to collect data or to get parents to implement a behavior plan or any other action or behavior they were focusing on during parent training sessions. Rarely did I ever hear a behavior analyst talk about helping parents build better relationships with their children, or rethinking parenting styles and approaches, or dealing with other macro-level family considerations. This isn't to say that nobody in our discipline was talking about such things from a parent training perspective; it's just that those voices were not as loud or as common as the voices pleading for help.

A third discovery, but probably the most impactful, was more of a question than anything else. Throughout my experiences with using ACT and training behavior analysts how to use it,

I started to question whether all the midlevel terms and components (e.g., defusion and self-as-context) within the ACT model were necessary or important. I began to think about underlying mechanisms or intervening variables rather than constructs derived from another level of analysis. By 2019, I presented some of my early pontifications about a reconsidered ACT model, and by 2020, I was committed to articulating ACT using behavior analytic language to help teach other behavior analysts how to use this in their practice.

My experiences in those early days, coupled with my experiences during the beta testing phase of my version of the original ACT model, resulted in the development of this current book. I set out to write this book for behavior analysts specifically, to create a guidebook of sorts to assist with easily adapting and using ACT in parent training or coaching contexts. This book was not established as a copy-paste curriculum, as my own experience with that approach had failed miserably. This is not to say that others may not be successful in that approach; in fact, sometimes they are. It just wasn't my experience. I found using curriculums was fine until the metaphor failed or the parent "didn't get it." Then I needed my own clinical expertise to problem-solve and figure out a different way to present the activity to the parent. I learned that most of my own ACT repertoires were shaped from the clinical experiences where things didn't go as planned. These repertoires were not necessarily derived from a curriculum either, but rather from trial and error. Hence, this guidebook emphasizes helping you to establish your own approach to using ACT and how to individualize your intervention for each parent and family you work with.

I hope this book helps you understand ACT in a way that isn't muddled with midlevel terms or hypothetical constructs. By relying on behavior analytic concepts and principles (including those established through relational frame theory), I also hope that you can ensure that each time you use ACT you (a) stay within your scope of competence, (b) provide effective and evidence-informed interventions that are specifically designed for the parent and family, and (c) feel confident in not only using ACT but also in speaking about what you are doing as a behavior analyst.

CHAPTER 1

Taking a New Perspective
*Person-Centered Approaches
with Parents and Families*

A parent is a person who brings up and cares for another. There are many ways for a person to become a parent (such as reproduction of offspring, foster care, adoption, or family circumstance), and many more ways for that person to parent their child. At any moment in history, being a parent usually aligns with our evolutionary predispositions toward ensuring the child's health and safety. Yet being a parent today also comes with its own unique child-rearing considerations, like developing socially and emotionally, performing academically, surviving a pandemic, and setting limits on social media and other internet-based apps or sites. On top of this comes the challenges of talking to children about school shootings (US specifically) and other socially relevant issues (such as climate change and war) that are discussed in the news. Being a parent of a child with complex health needs—for example, a neurological disorder such as autism or a motor disability such as cerebral palsy—only adds to the pressures of being a parent.

Parents may turn to parenting "self-help" guides and quickly be overwhelmed. A quick Google search in August 2022 showcases the situation: "parenting children" yielded 456 million results, "parenting self-help books" yielded over 73 million results, while "parenting children with special needs" yielded over 87 million hits. Most of these search hits are books, social media blogs, and top ten lists for tips and tricks. But in the context of information overload, how do parents know what is useful and what is just noise?

One way around this information overload is to seek professional help. Parents of children with complex health needs often seek advice or assistance from primary care professionals such as pediatricians. Other helping professionals, such as marriage and family therapists, social workers, psychologists, and behavior analysts, can also advocate and/or assist parents across the range of unique parenting situations and needs that arise.

Children with complex health needs can include a range of chronic, genetic, and/or developmental considerations that impact parents and families differently. For instance, individuals with neurodevelopmental disabilities (NDD; e.g., autism, ADHD, intellectual/developmental disabilities) and their families have unique health and wellness needs that span across medical, educational, behavioral, and mental health systems (Myers et al., 2007). Neurodevelopmental disabilities (NDD) encompass heritable, chronic, and nonprogressive lifelong conditions, including autism and intellectual or developmental delay (Brehaut et al., 2004). Families of children with NDD face unique challenges. For instance, parents of children with autism have been found to experience higher levels of stress than parents of neurotypical children (Costa et al., 2017), often because of the additional care needed. Similarly, parents raising children with intellectual disabilities have also been found to have poor physical and mental health outcomes (e.g., Cohn et al., 2020) and report being challenged by the array of demands and medical necessities that are required for raising a child with complex health needs (Whiting et al., 2019; see also MacKenzie & Eack, 2021).

Given these realities, it is critical for us to consider family needs from a whole-person perspective. This means that the child's presenting problem—such as social communication deficits or property destruction—is not the primary issue or target of services per se. Rather, considering the whole person requires us to also consider the health and wellness of others within the child's family unit.

While most behavior analysts may be called in to cases where the primary client is a child, adolescent, or adult with complex health needs, the primary treatment goal doesn't stop with programming for the client's presenting symptoms. Rather, our work necessarily incorporates training others around the client (from parents and caregivers to direct support staff and teachers) to implement various programs. Given this, the behavior analytic literature is saturated with demonstrations on how to best train other nonbehavioral persons to implement behavioral interventions, and often includes aspects related to behavioral skills training (such as rehearsal and modeling, shaping, active role playing, and corrective feedback (see Sun, 2022, for a review). However, training parents about behavioral principles is just the tip of the iceberg when it comes to establishing thoroughgoing parent training programs.

Parent and Caregiver Training

Before we consider the evidence, it is important to discuss the overgeneralized term "parent training." Karen Bearss and colleagues (2015a) accurately establish how the umbrella term "parent training," in the field of autism particularly, is used as a catchall of sorts to identify education, skills training, and implementation. The authors state that

> [the] ambiguous application of the term "parent training" may be due to the complexity of ASD and the multiple targets of intervention including skill deficits in communication, socialization, imitation, play, and adaptive skills as well as disruptive behavior. Thus, although the term "parent training" is a clear and succinct label for describing an empirically supported treatment for typically developing children with disruptive behavior, the use of this term…calls for clarification. (p. 170)

I have found this to be true across a range of populations, particularly when working on interdisciplinary teams. The overuse of the term "parent training" to describe basically anything we may need to do when working with parents or caregivers can be challenging as we seek to discern strategies that are helpful or necessary to adhere to evidence-informed practices.

To help clinicians distinguish what the training program is targeting, a parent training taxonomy was established by Bearss and colleagues (2015a) that separated programs by way of *parent support* (where the parent is the direct beneficiary of knowledge-based programs) or *parent implementation* (where the parent's skills are targeted for fidelity). Parent support includes care coordination and psychoeducation about accurate disability characteristics. Parent implementation (what the authors refer to as "parent-mediated intervention") includes programs that focus on specific techniques or implementation plans that function as primary or complementary programs to the child's treatment plan.

For example, the Early Start Denver Model (ESDM; Dawson et al., 2010) and Joint Attention Symbolic Play Engagement and Regulation (JASPER; Kasari et al., 2014) target a range of core symptoms like social communication or disruptive behaviors. While JASPER is considered as a primary parent implementation program, ESDM might be primary and/or complementary, depending on how the child's treatment is organized over time (i.e., may begin complementary with parent coaching and become more primary as the child's treatment progresses).

Other parent training treatment packages, such as Behavior Parent Training (BPT; Bearss et al., 2015a), Research Units in Behavioral Intervention (RUBI; Edwards et al., 2019), and Triple P Positive Parenting Program (Sanders, 2012; Sanders et al., 2014) offer variations in parent support and implementation (e.g., Bearss et al., 2015b; Bearss et al., 2018). For example, the RUBI program has been shown to be a feasible and efficacious treatment for helping parents improve their child's behaviors (Bearss et al., 2013; Burrell et al., 2020). Finally, inclusion of parental well-being and strategies directly targeting stress reduction and behavioral flexibility is also beginning to emerge and show promising results (e.g., Blackledge & Hayes, 2008; Hahs et al., 2019; Magnacca et al., 2021).

A recent meta-analysis conducted by MacKenzie and Eack (2022) investigated 37 studies that targeted outcomes of parent training programs. Analyzing intervention strategies based on the taxonomy of Bearss et al. (2015a), the researchers identified 21 (56%) of the studies as parent support interventions that targeted knowledge about ASD symptoms and characteristics, resources, and care systems. The other 16 articles (43%) were parent implementation programs that targeted skills training for social behavior or communication, reduction of excessive behaviors (e.g., Parent-Child Interaction Therapy, Autism Managing Eating Aversions and Low Intake Plan, Functional Behavior Skills Training). Researchers reported small but significant improvements to parenting confidence and mental health following psychoeducation. However, no improvement in parental stress, family and caregiver burdens, or health was found to favor treatment. These results suggest that the existing parent support programs are effective at teaching family members how to better parent their child with ASD, while additional strategies for psychological and emotional aspects of the parent and family of the child are needed.

Whole-Person Perspective: Establishing the Case for Parental Mental Health via ACT

From the evidence collected to date, parent implementation programs are helpful to reduce excessive behaviors and enhance family well-being (e.g., McConachie & Diggle, 2007; Thomas & Zimmer-Gembeck, 2007). While this approach is useful, some have argued that it is limited in scope given the omission of parental psychological and emotional well-being (e.g., Coyne & Wilson, 2004; Gould et al., 2018). This point is underscored by the clearly established association between maladaptive parenting repertoires and levels of parent psychological distress (e.g., Crnic et al., 2005; Fonseca et al., 2020; Lovejoy et al., 2000; Mak et al., 2020; Rekart et al., 2007; Vostanis et al., 2006).

Take the example of stress or the response to an aversive or unwanted situation or stimuli. While most of us experience some degree of stress, parents of children with complex health needs such as ASD report higher levels of stress than parents of neurotypical children (Costa et al., 2017; Singer et al., 2007). Similarly, high levels of parental stress are associated with parental engagement in controlling or coercive parenting strategies, low or negative affect, and avoidance repertoires (i.e., flight, fight, and freeze; Siegel, 2004). Unfortunately, increased stress has a negative relation with parent implementation of interventions (Nock & Kazdin, 2001; Rovane et al., 2020) and is associated with maladaptive parenting styles and lower levels of psychological flexibility (Fonseca et. al., 2020). Parental views on the response effort or burden of their child's behavioral treatment are associated with lower levels of treatment fidelity (MacNaughton & Rodriquez, 2001). Parents of a child with complex health needs also face additional financial burdens (Saunders et al., 2015), further adding to the complexity of what parental "stress" is for each parent and family system. In other words, parents deal with a complex range of psychological and environmental stressors that should be considered when using a whole-person or person-centered approach.

The neglect or lack of inclusion of the parents' psychological experiences represents what Corti and colleagues (2018) describe as

> an obstacle at helping parents to adopt an effective conduct, since parental behavior responds to overt environmental contingencies (e.g., tantrums of the child), and to [subtle] events (e.g., thoughts, images, physical sensations, and emotions). Private [subtle] stimuli may be accompanied by verbal rules, which may influence parental behavior. (p. 2888)

In this way, we cannot ignore a parent's subtle behaviors (such as thoughts, sensations, and urges) as they pertain to and potentially influence how the parent responds across various environmental conditions. Parents may follow a verbal rule (e.g., "We can't ignore our child throwing his food at the restaurant because we will be judged by others") by behaving in a way that produces long-term negative outcomes, such as providing escape as a reinforcer when they allow the child to leave the table or even the restaurant after throwing an item. The fact that the parents reinforce the child's throwing behavior isn't bad or negative in and of itself, as allowing the child to escape something that they don't like or don't want to participate in is not inherently wrong. It is the persistence of rule adherence or following it over time that results in more context-limiting environments and repertoires that are narrow or "rigid." I'll return to this point throughout the book, because it is central to the general understanding of why parent training programs should incorporate parental supports related to behavioral and psychological health and wellness.

Given what we know about the challenges of raising a child with complex health needs, a reasonable goal for us is to accommodate for both parent implementation of behavioral treatment plans as well as to consider the parents' health and well-being within our parent training programs. Doing so may increase the parents' overall chances for successful outcomes, particularly when we consider how the parents generalize the learned techniques within parent coaching or training programs.

Researchers to date have set the stage for how to incorporate parental support within parent training programs—in particular, the target of private or subtle behaviors through acceptance and commitment therapy or training (ACT; Hayes et al., 2011). ACT comprises six components that together influence psychological (or behavioral) flexibility. The overarching goal of ACT is to promote open, nonjudgmental perspectives and actions that align with longer-later abstract reinforcers and other aspects related to overall quality of life. Traditional ACT treatment components—present moment, acceptance, cognitive defusion, self-as-context, values, and committed action—are used together to establish behavioral flexibility (Hayes et al., 2011).

When implemented as an interconnected set of treatment components, evidence to date across a range of training formats (online or asynchronous vs. in home or in clinic), dose of treatment (e.g., 30 minutes once vs. 60 minutes once a week for twelve weeks), and parent training group size (one on one vs. group; e.g., Holmberg et al., 2022) all have found treatment outcomes to favor ACT compared to treatment control (e.g., Gould et al., 2018; Hahs et al., 2019; Andrews et al., 2021; Garcia et al., 2021; Whittingham et al., 2016; Yi & Dixon, 2020). In a recent meta-analysis conducted by Han and colleagues (2020), researchers examined articles published before March 2020 and retained those that incorporated an ACT intervention program for family caregivers (broadly considered across chronic pain, ASD, traumatic brain injuries, cancer, and others). Of the eighteen retained articles the authors drew their results from, four recruited family caregivers who provided care to children with autism, while two recruited those who cared for a child with one chronic condition, including ASD and attention deficit/hyperactivity disorder. Overall, researchers found changes in caregiver report of psychological flexibility–favored treatment (ACT) when compared to control both immediately and at follow-up (i.e., Hahs et al., 2019). However, changes in parental report of cognitive fusion to unwanted or aversive private experiences, values, and mindfulness did not favor treatment.

Other studies not included in the review by Han and colleagues (2020) are worth mentioning here, given their more traditional behavior analytic approach to ACT within parent training contexts. For instance, Gould and colleagues (2018) used a nonconcurrent multiple-baseline design to investigate the effects of brief ACT intervention on parent values-directed behaviors. Three Caucasian mothers with a child with ASD participated (mother ages 35, 37, 52; child ages 2, 4, 12, respectively). During baseline, the researcher met with each parent to identify values and corresponding values-directed behaviors (or the behaviors everyone sees the parent do to get closer to her values) and instructed the parent on how to self-monitor her engagement in values-directed behaviors. After two weeks, none of the parents had engaged in any of the identified behaviors (such as eating dinner together as a family, going for a walk, husband putting child to sleep). In other words, just telling the parents about values and self-monitoring did not result in the parents doing these things.

During the ACT intervention, mothers completed six 90-minute training sessions, with each session targeting one of the interrelated components. Session structure included didactic lecture and discussion, trainer modeling and role playing, homework, and outside session practice. Between sessions, the researcher provided a single prompt via email, recapping the homework goals and providing tips or relevant exercises to the content discussed. After a few ACT sessions, two of the three parents increased engagement in values-directed behaviors, with all three parents maintaining higher than baseline levels of engagement seven to eight months posttraining.

In a telehealth context, Yi and Dixon (2020) developed a sixty-day parent support and implementation program that combined ACT with parental education around general principles of applied behavior analysis. Thirteen families were randomly assigned to either treatment control (ABA online training; N=6) or active treatment (ABA online training alongside a brief 30-minute ACT exposure; N=7). Families in each group received weekly messaging during progress monitoring, while the ACT group received additional messages about ACT-related concepts such as values-driven behavior. Results found higher percentages of online lessons completed overall by parents who completed the ACT lessons (64.29%) compared to the treatment control group (20.5%). Similarly, families in the ACT group completed a higher number of slides per each unique login than families in the control group.

Finally, Andrews and colleagues (2021) combined behavior parent training (RUBI) with ACT to examine the effects on parent stress, implementation of behavioral principles, and the child's behaviors. Four parent-child dyads participated in the study (all Caucasian parents, three female mothers and one transgender father, 35 to 51 years of age, with one child with ASD). Parent implementation was measured as a percentage of skills completed based on common behavioral strategies (e.g., verbally identifying the target behavior to reinforce, delivering the reinforcer, and avoiding talking or responding to the child during challenging behaviors). Parent responsiveness to training was measured as a percentage of objectives demonstrated during either the ACT or RUBI portion of training. Parent-perceived stress, experiential avoidance, and measure of frequency and severity of child's challenging behaviors were tracked using Likert scales. Finally, the child's rate of challenging behavior was measured by rate per minute during targeted routines.

During baseline, all four parents engaged in low levels of behavioral strategies during targeted routines. Following treatment, three of four participants immediately increased percentage of correct implementation on various routines, and all four participants maintained higher than baseline rates during maintenance. Similarly, during baseline, the child's challenging behavior rates were variable across parent-child dyads. During treatment, two of four children reduced engagement in rates of challenging behavior per minute, and three of four children engaged in below baseline rates during maintenance.

Reconsidering Our Approach

Taken together, it appears empirical support of ACT within parent training contexts shows promise. While encouraging, there is still more work left to be done to understand fully the mechanisms that control aspects within an ACT model. For instance, a major finding of the meta-analysis conducted by Han and colleagues (2020) was the lack of changes on process measures targeting parental cognitive fusion, values, and mindfulness. These results support criticisms against the use of midlevel terminology, given that it may cause more noise than answers to clinically significant questions (see also Assaz et al., 2018; Barnes-Holmes et al., 2015). It may not be that there were no changes to parental flexibility across cognitive fusion and mindfulness processes per se, as much as the ways in which authors have conceptualized such constructs using less precise terms or variables that may result in a lack of precision (see chapter 2 for a more in-depth discussion).

Another consideration is the emphasis on parental support programs rather than only targeting parental implementation. Part of integrating effective parental supports is to consider the parent and family system through a whole-person perspective. Beyond implementation fidelity and observation agreement or congruence among others, I have found that most behavior analytic graduate training programs lack an emphasis on training future behavior analysts about skills and worldviews that support our involvement as an active participant in our client's therapeutic environment. In a seminal study, Taylor and colleagues (2018) asked parents to rate their experiences with collaboration in the therapeutic relationship, conveying empathy and compassion, and areas that may contribute to problems within the therapeutic relationship. The authors found that parents were in relative agreement (80–90% agreement) that behavior analysts tended to acknowledge and express their appreciation of the child's strengths and are optimistic about the child's capability and potential progress. However, parents indicated high need for improvement with behavior analysts' demonstration of caring or empathy for the entire family, acknowledgment of mistakes or treatment failures, and demonstration of compassionate care.

In addition to the points and considerations brought forth by Taylor and colleagues (2018) and others, I argue that it is not enough to train behavior analysts how to engage in such soft skills. Instead, a more intentionally established attitude toward how the world is arranged (i.e., philosophical worldview) must be established to move beyond a topographical approach into a functional one. In this way, the exact behaviors we engage in as trainers may be categorized as "empathetic," "compassionate," or even "unconditional positive regard" (see also Rogers, 1957,

1980), but the overall function of the repertoire is what is relevant. In this way, humanistic philosophy and person-centered approaches as applied within a functional contextual framework will establish a more purposeful approach to our own repertoires within sessions.

Person-Centered Collaboration with Parents

Humanistic psychology has a robust history within philosophy, with some historians tracing the origins of humanism back to fifth century BC. Most readers, however, are more likely to be familiar with the American version of humanism from the works of Carl Rogers, Abraham Maslow, and the person-centered psychology of the 1950s and 1960s (deCarvalho, 1991). Humanism has evolved to emphasize both the "philosophical and scientific understanding of human existence that does justice to the highest reaches of human achievement and potential" (Schneider et al., 2014, p. xvii). In this way, humanists are concerned about what it means to be human (i.e., philosophy and science must incorporate all aspects of the human experience), and how understanding as such results in a life characterized by meaning and vitality. Said another way, humanists return to the fundamental question often: Does understanding aspects of the human experience help us get closer to a meaningful or valued life?

Two foundations of humanistic or person-centered psychology include actualizing and formative tendencies (Rogers, 1980). *Actualizing tendencies* are ways in which organisms continue to adapt for survival. In evolutionary psychology, and even in Skinner's (1981) analysis of selections by consequences, we see a similar consideration. From single-celled organisms to birds, monkeys, and humans, all life will organize itself to survive, regardless of how bare or hazardous the environment.

Formative tendencies are ways in which organisms become more complex over time. All life forms start with a single or simple form that over time evolves and incorporates more complex forms. Take as an example a baby's early connections with the world around them through touch and taste. These then evolve in the first few years from crying to babbling to forming sentences, and eventually to writing essays and solving complex logic statements.

These two central tendencies inform what Rogers (1980) defines as growth-promoting conditions (i.e., context-broadening or appetitive environments), namely (1) genuineness, realness, or congruence demonstrated by the therapist or trainer, (2) unconditional positive regard (or the radical acceptance of the client or parent as whatever they are in the here and now), and (3) empathetic understanding (or the therapeutic alliance toward repertoires of empathy and compassion for the client, regardless of the client's experiences).

We may apply this in a parent training context through our philosophical orientation as well as specific skills or target repertoires to practice within sessions. First, we may align a functional contextual philosophy with humanism by arranging our truth criterion (i.e., successful working of the act-in-context) with attitudes of practice (i.e., therapeutic alliance, unconditional positive regard for the parent and family system). Skills for us to consider and monitor include building positive rapport (e.g., using flat affect or hyperfocus on negative child outcomes minimally, placing emphasis on engagement in positive and realistic statements about treatment outcomes and progress, and demonstrating general enthusiasm and general congruence matching the parent).

We may also consider how commitment toward empathy and understanding for the parent may, over time, influence our engagement in compassion for the parents' experience. For instance, empathetic understanding may incorporate a range of therapeutic skills (e.g., active listening, omission of technological behavior analytic terms, and adaption of collaborative communication style) that, when practiced over time, becomes a natural aspect of establishing appetitive training environments.

While programs exist that emphasize the role of specialized treatments focusing on compassion (e.g., compassion-focused therapy, Gilbert, 2014; cognitively based compassion training, Reddy et al., 2013), I will argue throughout the book that we may be equally successful in integrating aspects of compassionate care and compassionate repertoires into our application of humanism within a functional contextual framework. In this way, we may integrate our ACT sessions with person-centered strategies in order to optimize growth-promoting conditions for the parent, child, and family system.

Using the Guidebook

Many interventions developed for parents of children with complex health needs include psychoeducation. This includes key characteristics of the symptomology of the health need, education about behavioral concepts and principles (such as functional relationships, schedules of reinforcement, extinction, skill acquisition, and so on), shaping adaptive behaviors, and supporting their child's adaptive growth. Key features of the training environment are also important, including didactic instruction in addition to role playing and in-vivo practice of principles or techniques (e.g., Ginn et al., 2017; Howard et al., 2018; Iadarola et al., 2018; see also MacKenzie and Eack, 2022). The next step, however, is to make the necessary additions to our parent training tool belt in order to account for parent and family mental health and overall well-being.

Using relational frame theory (RFT; Hayes, Barnes-Holmes, & Roche, 2001) to inform how we approach our ACT intervention may assist us in determining presenting target repertoires and relational networks. It may also assist us in our case conceptualization process when things don't work out as planned or when metaphors fall short in session. We may consider a more technological version of the ACT model originally described by Hayes and colleagues (2011) to incorporate targets of (a) flexible perspective taking, (b) attending to or orientation toward potentially aversive stimuli, and (c) values-based patterns of actions (see chapter 2 for additional details).

Therefore, my goal is to provide you with an easy-to-use ACT guidebook to enhance your existing parent implementation program (using a similar taxonomy as designed by Bearss and colleagues, 2015a). If you are not already using an evidence-informed parent training program in your practice, I encourage you to start there before implementing some of the strategies discussed here. These strategies are developed to be delivered in conjunction with evidence-based practices described above (such as RUBI or ESDM). Once you have a parent implementation program in place, this book will help you fold aspects related to person-centered parent supports into your clinical toolkit by addressing the parents' personal and unique experiences, verbal rules, and overall health and well-being.

This book was developed to guide you on how to incorporate ACT into your parent training or coaching contexts. It was not developed to be used as a curriculum or manualized approach. You will not find worksheets or a designated first/then model here to implement ACT. This book is not designed for a one-size-fits-all approach to parent coaching. Instead, ACT components are organized and discussed in a way to provide a conceptual foundation for target repertoires for acceleration—and perhaps deceleration, as appropriate—that you (as a practicing behavior analyst) must determine, operationalize, and measure. The metaphors and activities provided are given as examples in order to highlight how to start from establishing a general hypothesis and progressing into how to arrange metaphors during parent coaching or training sessions.

The guidebook is presented in three sections. The first section (chapters 1–4) covers foundational topics of applied behavioral service delivery, including an overview of humanistic considerations (chapter 1), theoretical underpinnings of parent supports (chapter 2), and ethical considerations (chapter 3). These chapters are designed to help you reflect on your own training, scope of competence, potential for dual relationships, cultural responsivity for each parent and family system, and other considerations to help you organize your behavior for better implementation. Chapter 4 provides an overview on how to get creative with your data collection systems by incorporating measurement systems that examine the range of parental behavior, including parent-child relationships and family dynamics.

The second section (chapters 5–6) highlights general considerations before you start implementing ACT within your parent training. Chapter 5, Getting Started, provides a thoroughgoing overview of how to plan for and arrange your ACT sessions generally and then specifically with a selected parent or family. Chapter 6, Assessment, presents assessment strategies to use throughout your intervention. This chapter emphasizes the importance of ongoing assessment to determine whether what you are doing is working. Select assessments, such as the matrix (Polk et al., 2016), parent specific assessments, and naturalistic and experimental functional analyses are outlined for ease of replication and application in clinical practice.

The third section (chapters 7–10) discusses ACT components—here and now relational emphasis along with perspective taking, experiential acceptance, and values-based action—for establishing behavioral flexibility. Each chapter is supplemented with clinical applications, where cases are briefly established and discussed to help you learn how to target a particular component within a parent coaching context. A component-based checklist for clinical practice, developed as a tool to guide you before you start targeting the component in sessions, is also included in each chapter.

Flexible perspective taking is separated into two chapters for ease of conceptualization. Chapter 7, Here and Now Relational Emphasis, focuses on training sessions that specifically target here/now relational repertoires. These will help you better assist parents in shifting to here/now repertoires generally and specifically during more intense or aversive contexts. Chapter 8, Flexible Perspective Taking, takes this a bit further and focuses on assisting parents in shifting perspectives from I/here/now to you/there/then or you/there/now, depending on situational variables. Chapter 9, Experiential Acceptance, targets experiential acceptance repertoires as alternatives to conditioned avoidance repertoires, while Chapter 10, Targeting Values-Based Action, focuses on values-based patterns of actions—both the verbally constructed abstract values parents find reinforcing and the patterns of actions that align with the articulated value.

The appendixes provide case examples of two different families dealing with various levels of needs. The content is based on real clients and cases in my clinical practice and research experiences. Some of the specifics related to the location of services and approaches to treatment as well as nuances of the details have been modified to protect the confidentiality and anonymity of both the families and the behavior analysts. I've used a narrative format for readability and context regarding how to arrange the coaching model discussed in this guidebook.

***

I hope this guidebook empowers you to practice ACT while also remaining within your scope of practice and training expertise. Perhaps this book will jump-start a meaningful conversation within our discipline to encourage us to critically examine how we talk about the phenomena that we target during clinical practice. We can include aspects of parents' private or subtle experiences, such as their thoughts or feelings about a situation or an event, but we may need to do so without adhering to dualism or constructs that occur at a different level of analysis. I believe that the proposed model offered here is a first step in this direction.

CHAPTER 2

Humanistic Applications in Parent Training

Science, as a method for understanding how the world works, is not merely concerned with "getting the facts" or describing events as they occur. Instead, science attempts to discover order from chaos, showcasing a unique wisdom and way of thinking about the world that highlight how "certain events stand in lawful relations to other events" (Skinner, 1953, p. 6). When we use science to understand human behavior, we must also adhere to the corresponding *attitudes of science* (such as determinism, principle of parsimony, philosophic doubt or a "healthy degree of skepticism") when analyzing and drawing conclusions from collected data. In this way, we must assume that human behavior is itself deterministic and lawful (Skinner, 1953, 1987). For Skinner, applying science to the study of human behavior meant no longer looking for "cause" and "effect," but rather establishing a "cause" as a "change in an independent variable" and an "effect" as a "change in a dependent variable," otherwise known as a *functional relation* (Skinner, 1953, p. 23).

The application of the science of human behavior (i.e., behavior analysis) has been categorized across four interrelated domains: theoretical or philosophical (targeting the underlying philosophy of behaviorism generally and radical behaviorism specifically), experimental analysis of behavior (highly controlled experiments explored across species), applied behavior analysis (highly controlled experiments with humans specifically in more controlled settings than the natural environment), and service delivery (clinical practice that is guided by research and theory in behavior analysis). These domains showcase how the science of behavior is applied across a unified discipline; from philosophical foundations to provision of service delivery, each domain adheres to the same foundations and attitudes of science and radical behaviorism (see also Cooper et al., 2019).

While such a taxonomy is clear in theory, in practice there is much deviation and dissent among various behavioral camps or *schools of behavioral philosophies* (O'Donohue & Kitchener, 1998). Behavioral psychology writ large is comprised of a plurality of philosophical worldviews that centers human behavior as an independent or stand-alone subject matter (see also Zuriff, 1985). For instance, Watson's early form of behavioral psychology employed a mechanistic and reductionistic philosophy of science, where muscular movements and glandular secretions were selected as the subject matter (O'Donohue & Kitchner, 1998). Mechanistic and reductionistic worldviews emphasize the *parts* that comprise the whole. For example, the answer to the question "How does a person walk?" would be "by bioneurological and muscular movements."

In contrast, Skinner's form of radical behaviorism employed a contextual and pragmatic philosophy of science, where the *parts* are understood by the *act-in-context*. Take, for example, all the parts comprised of the behavior of walking across the street. We may consider biophysiological aspects such as the coordination of muscle movements needed to place one foot in front of the other, to turn one's head to the left and to the right, to "see" the street and so forth, in addition to other aspects, including considerations of the environment (such as the surface of the street, paint of crosswalks, shoes worn by the person), and sociocultural aspects (such as walking in the crosswalk or jaywalking, looking left vs. right for oncoming traffic, and so on). A mechanistic worldview may target the various parts, in order to answer the question "How did the person cross the street?" In contrast, a radical behaviorist would consider the act-in-context, rather than focus on the individual parts, and would focus on all aspects of the context.

Radical behaviorism is often considered the dominant philosophy of behavior analysts (Moore, 2010), and is often associated with the term *applied behavior analysis* (e.g., Baer et al., 1987). While Skinner's radical behaviorism is no doubt pragmatic and contextual, some scholars argue he "maintained enough fragments of mechanistic thinking to confuse not just serious readers, but occasionally even himself" (Gifford & Hayes, 1999, p. 287).

Functional contextualism, on the other hand, as a specific variety of scientific contextualism, considers successful working by the act-in-context rather than by a mechanistic or structural approach (Hayes et al., 1993). Pragmatism is the working philosophical worldview among contextualists, considered across two general tenets: "an absence of absolute foundations and a focus on the situated concrete event" (Gifford & Hayes, 1999, p. 304). Contextual worldviews are holistic in that the "parts," or the act and the context, are not separable (Hayes et al., 2012). Unlike the mechanistic or reductionistic philosophies that emphasize the *parts* (e.g., the muscular and other biophysiological movements of walking), contextualists consider the context *in which the person walks* as inseparable from *how the person walks*. The unit in this example is whole; it includes not only the topography of behavior (i.e., walking), but also the aspects of the environment (i.e., shoes, street surface, sociocultural variables such as crossing in a crosswalk).

While Skinner's radical behaviorism is no doubt contextual, there are nuanced differences and mechanistic influences that separate functional contextualism from a more traditional Skinnerian approach. While historically behavior analysis and functional contextualism have grown from similar starting points, over time the two schools of thought have diverged more than they have aligned, as not all behavior analysts accept the subvariety of functional contextualism (e.g., Marr, 1993; Staddon, 1993; see Hayes et al., 2012, for similar argument) or its empirical applications supported by relational frame theory (see also Gross & Fox, 2009, for a review).

Given the breadth of behavioral worldviews, behavior analysts interested in practicing ACT should consider their own philosophical truth criterion and how their worldview impacts their clinical practice. How we view the world—in terms of emphasizing the parts or the actions as stand-alone variables or emphasizing the act-in-context—will directly influence how we arrange our operational definitions of selected target repertoires, measurement systems, and design strategies as well as what we select as intervention strategies.

To assist with adherence within a functional contextual framework, this chapter will (a) provide a brief overview of the basic features proposed by RFT, (b) establish how RFT influences how we approach our ACT intervention, and (c) establish a revised ACT model that intertwines applied applications of RFT without ascribing to midlevel terminology. The goal here is not to provide a review of published literature per se, but rather to establish basic foundations that are empirically supported so that when we later discuss using assessment and intervention strategies within an ACT framework, we directly relate basic concepts to our selected intervention.

It is important to note here that psychological phenomena discussed within ACT and contextual behavioral science (CBS) are often termed *private events* by radical behaviorists (e.g., Skinner, 1945). Skinner first articulated private events as words used to point to events taking place within the bounds of the skin, and later refined his definition to state that "not all contingencies can be replaced with rules, and some contingency-shaped behavior is beyond the reach of verbal description. Similarly, the most precise description of a state of feeling cannot correspond exactly to the state felt" (Skinner, 1974, p. 192). He was clear in how we may incorporate behaviors (like thoughts or feelings) that occur at a level of analysis that is not subject to direct observation. We may do this by adding corollary repertoires (or behaviors that occur at or around the same time as the event taking place within the skin), either through verbal means like rules and metaphorical language or through direct contingency shaping (Skinner, 1945).

Throughout his career, Skinner (1945, 1974) argued that the social community may generate verbal behaviors in response to the private event. This occurs in four ways: public accompaniment, collateral responses, common properties, and response reduction.

Public accompaniment occurs when an observable stimulus accompanies a private stimulus. For example, a child hits her head on the table, and her father assumes she experiences pain and therefore teaches her to say "That hurts" in agreement with what the father observed. Public accompaniment, however, is limited by "the degree of association of public and private stimuli which will supply a net reinforcement sufficient to establish and maintain a response" (Skinner, 1945, p. 273).

Collateral responses are observable responses, generally nonverbal and unconditioned, that occur with the private event. These are inferences made by the observer, who directly observes the collateral response, not the actual event itself. For example, one person may directly observe a child hitting their head, and another may observe a child holding their head, which may produce the same response in the social community. These may not be established through the same process. For instance, if a child has a toothache and extends their hand to their jaw, makes various facial expressions and noises, a parent may say to the child, "What is wrong with your mouth?" or "Does your tooth hurt?" to orient the child to express their experiences from the private event. The parent does not need to directly see the event itself, but rather uses the observable behaviors emitted by the child as potential cues of an unpleasant private experience.

Common properties, on the other hand, involve a type of stimulus generalization, where the speaker's descriptions or words used to describe the private event are arranged in a way that aligns directly observable events to their private experience. The social community provides reinforcement for the speaker's response in connection with additional proprioceptive stimuli, even though the speaker and community react to different, though closely associated, stimuli (Skinner, 1945, p. 273). For instance, when we teach adolescents about falling in love, some social communities may say, "You know you are in love because you will feel butterflies in your stomach," to generalize the feeling of fluttering in one's stomach. As another example, when your foot falls asleep, you may be inclined to tell your friend, "My foot feels like a soda pop," to generalize the feeling of bubbles to the feeling in your foot. These extensions are taught by the social community and are therefore culturally selected. (However, the soda pop reference above may make some readers in the Midwest of the United States cringe, as the bubbly drink is preferably called "pop" rather than "soda.")

Finally, the principle of transfer of stimulus induction, or response reduction, explains how the social community reinforces the speaker's own behavior about the private event. *Response reduction* is considered to be any response emitted in the presence of a private stimulus that is descriptive of the speaker's own behavior (i.e., the private event), provided that the emitted response is "occasionally reinforced in the presence of the same stimulus occurring with public manifestations" (Skinner, 1945, p. 274). This transfer is not due to identical stimuli, like common properties, nor due to the same magnitude of response, but rather due to similarity in public stimuli or in coinciding properties. The speaker's behavior is carried over from the public to private or covert experiences (e.g., speaking about swimming is reinforced and reduced to imagining or thinking about swimming).

Taken together, we may teach a child to verbally respond to private stimuli not directly observable to the social community through public accompaniment or consequences (i.e., collateral responses), or through reinforcement provision for metaphorical extensions about private stimuli (i.e., common properties) or public stimuli (i.e., response reduction). We may also align our language to clearly describe procedures or steps to take to shape a child's verbal behavior toward private events.

However, the delineation between *private* and *public* establishes a clear case of dualism (or the division of something into two contrasted variables), which can be a fundamental flaw, depending on how the construct is established. The way in which behavior analysts discuss *private events* may establish a causal relationship to begin or occur within the skin (i.e., private stimuli occur within the skin, and therefore cannot be validated through direct observation, only through verbal behavior). When constructed in this way, we may inadvertently use hypothetical constructs (i.e., constructs meant to explain events in terms of unobservable variables; K. G. Wilson, 2001) as intervening variables (i.e., verbal abstractions of observable events and variables, statements that can be tested and measured to establish laws of relationships between variables without adding surplus meaning to the construct; see also K. G. Wilson, 2001).

In contrast, we may shift to a molar multiscale perspective (e.g. Baum 2018) to avoid ascribing to dualism and stay within the same level of analysis as our direct observation. In this way, we may instead discuss environmental events and behaviors that are directly observable to a single person. Let me highlight this difference in an example. Imagine a person dancing in their home when they are alone. By Skinner's definition, dancing would not constitute a private event, even though there is no one else around to observe or witness the behavior. However, from a molar perspective, dancing at home when nobody else is around would be considered a subtle behavior, given that the behavior is only observable to a single person (the same person engaging in the behavior, i.e., dancing). The loci of the initiating stimuli no longer reside "within the skin," but rather in the environment beyond the boundary of the skin.

This same logic can be used to understand conditions where the person engaging in the behavior may not know they are doing it or observe themselves doing it. For instance, I often get asked "Are you okay? You have a concerning look on your face." This happens even though I may not be aware of my facial expression, and I may not agree with the assumption that I am in fact concerned about something. My facial expression may be a subtle behavior, but in this instance, it is only observable by an observer rather than by me, the individual engaging in the behavior. Given these limitations, I will purposely avoid using the term "private events" when possible, and instead use the word *subtle* to discuss behaviors or events that are only observable by a single person (see also Baum, 1995).

Core Features of Contextual Behavioral Science

Contextual behavioral science (CBS) is a scientific and practical strategy of science to connect philosophical assumptions and empirically based knowledge development with technological progress across basic and applied levels of the work (Foody et al., 2014; Hayes et al., 2012). Hayes and colleagues (2012) articulate CBS as

> grounded in contextualistic philosophical assumptions, and nested within multi-dimensional, multi-level evolution science as a contextual view of life[. I]t seeks the development of basic and applied scientific concepts and methods that are useful in predicting-and-influencing the contextually embedded actions of whole organisms, individually and in groups, with precision, scope, and depth; and extends that approach into knowledge development itself so as to create a behavioral science more adequate to the challenges of the human condition. (p. 2)

According to Foody and colleagues (2014), we may think about CBS as the broad application of contextual science across three areas of knowledge. First, CBS provides a clear philosophy (i.e., contextualism) and a connection between philosophy of science to basic and applied scientific studies so that behavior can be predicted and influenced with precision, scope, and depth (Gifford & Hayes, 1999). It is important to note that there have been nuanced debates around different applications of contextualism (i.e., functional vs. descriptive; see also Hayes & Fryling, 2019; Rehfeldt et al., 2020, for recent debate), and while those distinctions are relevant to levels of precision, scope, and depth, they are beyond the scope of this chapter. While I will use the word "contextualism" as a general term for a pragmatic philosophy of science, the descriptive contextualist may criticize my approach because it will certainly lean toward a functional contextual perspective.

Second, the empirical support of relational frame theory (RFT; Hayes et al., 2001) provides the basic contextual variables (i.e., relational, or functional, contextual cues) that allow for prediction and influence of behavior, particularly human language and cognition (i.e., verbal behavior). RFT has a robust body of empirical evidence in support of basic relational units such as mutual and combinatorial entailment and transformation of function (see also Dymond & Rehfeldt, 2000) and more complex relational responding (see also McEnteggart, 2018).

Third, clinical treatments or intervention models (e.g., acceptance and commitment therapy [ACT]; Hayes et al., 2011), based on principles demonstrated and supported by RFT, help to effectively influence psychological health and well-being (Hayes et al., 2012). Within an ACT model that emphasizes workability defined by the act-in-context, behaviors (either overt actions like walking or talking, or more subtle events such as thoughts) can only "cause" events inasmuch as they are regulated by the context as such. In this way, it is prudent to "change the context that causally links these psychological domains [i.e., behaviors]" (Hayes et al., 2006, pp. 4–5).

Basic Mechanisms of Relational Frame Theory

The basic idea of both RFT and ACT is that human language and cognition, or *verbal behavior*, is at the root of human psychological suffering (Hayes et al., 2011; McEnteggart, 2018). This work began with the exploration into instructional control, or what Skinner (1969) came to call *rule-governed behavior* (RGB). Skinner (1953, 1969) defined rules as contingency-specifying stimuli, an aspect of listener behavior, which was different from contingency-shaped behavior where the control of the contingencies did not include verbal elements.

Research in the mid-1980s produced a robust literature base demonstrating many aspects of instructional control in search of determining what it meant for a rule to "specify" something. One such finding was the insensitivity effect to changing contexts. For instance, adult participants who were told a rule for how to obtain reinforcers on a basic computer task were less likely to change their response patterns when the reinforcement schedule changed (i.e., Catania et al., 1989). Further, researchers suggested that verbally governed behavior may be categorized as plys (or rules that describe the implied social contingencies), tracks (descriptions of natural or programmed contingencies), and augments (verbal establishing operations) (e.g., Zettle & Hayes 1982). However, this research agenda stagnated over time, and was criticized for its reliance on mid-level terminology and disconnect with functional relations (see also Harte & Barnes-Holmes, 2022, for commentary).

A functional-analytic definition for specification of a rule was provided in part by Murray Sidman's early work on equivalence (McEnteggart, 2018). Sidman demonstrated that after establishing one or two key conditional discriminations (i.e., in the presence of a picture of a dog, select the word "dog," not "cat" or "duck;" and in the presence of a picture of a cat, select the word "cat," not "dog" or "duck"), new discriminations emerged without formal training (i.e., in the presence of the word "dog," select the picture of a dog, not cat or duck, an example of symmetry).

Sidman's work on equivalence supported the basic type of symbolic relation—to relate to stimuli based on sameness or coordination. Hayes and colleagues (2001) later argued that equivalence was an example of generalized operant behavior, referred to as *relational frames*. For example, a child may learn that a copper coin is a penny while a silver coin is a dime (i.e., coordination, denoted by contextual cue "is a"), and may even learn that they need ten pennies or one dime to purchase candy from the store.

The newly established equivalence repertoire (or frame of coordination) is just the beginning. The child may later learn that while a penny is bigger than a dime, social contingencies establish a dime as worth more than a penny (i.e., comparison relational frames, denoted by contextual cues "bigger than" and "more than"). The child may also learn that they receive more dimes if they complete their chores before the end of the week (i.e., temporal and comparison relational frames, denoted by contextual cues "more than" and "if/then"). More expansive relational networks may later come to have evaluative (i.e., skinny is better than fat) or descriptive (i.e., fat is bigger than skinny) functions that may start to relate to other relational networks (i.e., "Jane is skinny and I am fat, and skinny is better than fat; Jane is therefore better than me"; see also Luoma et al., 2007).

From this perspective, the idea of a relational frame as a generalized relational operant has been used to define and study rule-governed behavior. According to McEnteggart (2018), a "rule or instruction is typically composed of a network of frames of equivalence and temporal relations.... [T]he equivalence relations serve to specify the events in the relevant contingency, with the temporal relations coordinating the rule with the contingency itself" (p. 218). Within this approach, researchers may better understand psychological terms (such as thoughts, feelings, emotions) by identifying the specific stimulating conditions in order to determine why a behavior or response is controlled by its corresponding condition (see also Skinner, 1945, for considerations on examining psychological terms and repertoires).

According to RFT, human language and cognition are the result of arbitrarily applicable relational responding under the control of contextual features. *Arbitrary* in that the symbols, words, gestures, and so on that we use are selected by the social community and do not need to share formal properties (i.e., size, shape, color, etc.). *Applicable* in that the responses are applied in the natural world; they are not something only observed in a lab or highly controlled environment. *Relational* in that the responses are controlled not only by directly conditioned stimulus functions but also by relations between stimuli (i.e., entailment and transformation of stimulus functions). In this way, humans can learn to respond relationally to stimuli that do not share formal similarity.

While symbolic relations of entailment are also demonstrated within equivalence literature (i.e., mutual entailment is to symmetry, and combinatorial entailment is to transitivity), the unique application within RFT is the emphasis on the functional and relational contextual cues that control a history of arbitrarily applicable responding and therefore may perpetuate single or narrowed conditioned repertoires.

Take, for example, the following common presenting problem during parent training (see also figures 2.1 and 2.2). Jimmy is a 12-year-old boy who loves to play video games with his friends online. Jody, his mother, struggles to get Jimmy to do anything around the house; all he does is play video games. Often while Jimmy is playing a game, Jody will interrupt his game play by yelling at him, turning off the lights, or standing in the way of the screen. Upon hearing her instruction (e.g., clean your room, set the table), Jimmy yells back at her, "I will do it when I want to. I'm busy, leave me alone!" He continues to play the game, and sometimes he resorts to throwing things at her. In this example, the aversive event of Jody interrupting Jimmy's video game play (A1) establishes frames of coordination with repertoires aligned with rigid rule following (B1: "I will do it when I want to. I'm busy. Leave me alone.") and elicited conditioned responses aligned with fight-or-flight responses (C1: increased heart palpitations, emotion states like anger, and the like). These relational repertoires establish evocative functions that increase the likelihood of Jimmy engaging in aggressive responses such as throwing (D1: see top panel of figure 2.1).

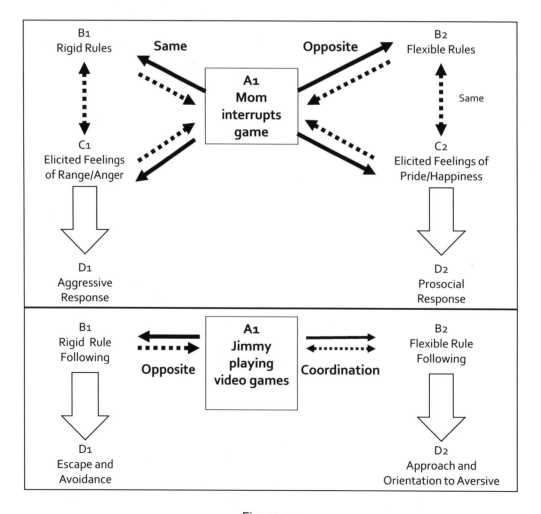

Figure 2.1

The same aversive event that establishes the coordinative relational responses may also be related in frames of opposition with flexible rule following (B2) and conditioned responses aligned with approach or other appetitive responses or feelings (C2), which in turn increases the likelihood of engagement in prosocial responses (D2). In this way, Jimmy's repertoire may function to maintain or support aggressive responses over more prosocial responses. The stimuli associated within either relational frame of coordination (i.e., sameness) or opposition (i.e., opposite) may be altered through derived relations, as the contingency of escape from the aversive event (A1) can influence the extent to which aggressive repertoires will be selected during the next exposure to a similar aversive event.

Similarly, we may analyze Jody's patterns of actions in a similar way (see bottom panel of figure 2.1). To begin, the aversive event is Jimmy playing video games (A1). This event is established within a frame of opposition to her rigid rules about her son: "My son will not sit around all day playing video games" and "I will not allow him to do X without consequences." Over time you notice Jody's patterns of actions align with escape, avoidance, and punitive punishment strategies. For example, you hear her say to him, "Why are you like this? What did I do to deserve this?" and "I can't do this anymore. That's it—no more phone after dinner [or other privilege]!" Transformation of reinforcing stimulus functions may also derive to other stimuli in frames of opposition between Jimmy playing video games and the misalignment to the rigidly held rules and subsequent rule following. The simple repertoire of relating events in this way results in transformation of stimulus function (see also Törneke, 2010, for similar discussion). Taken together, RFT establishes how human language and cognition can lead to human suffering that cannot practically be eliminated. Established conditioned responses are a "reflection of historical learning processes" (Hayes et al., 2006, p. 5), meaning that we may arrange the environment to help inhibit the repertoire, but we are unable to restrict or get rid of the repertoire per se. Rather than targeting the subtle behaviors or events directly, we may consider arranging for transformation of stimulus functions to change the overall function of the events in order to establish flexible relational responding that is adaptive and motivated by delayed and abstract reinforcers.

RFT-Based Acceptance and Commitment Training: Connecting Theory with Practice

While there is considerable overlap between the development and expansive research on RFT and ACT, there is still considerable debate as to whether RFT principles offer adequate description or support of ACT (Foody et al., 2014). However, in my own practice, I have found it helpful to think about the parents' presenting concerns and target repertoires through an RFT analysis, particularly when identifying potential relational networks and stimulus functions that maintain the targeted conditioned responses. This practice must be returned to frequently, as is the case with case conceptualization strategies.

I cannot emphasize enough how important it is to hold our RFT analyses lightly and remember to rely on our direct observations rather than constructs spoken about either by the parent or by other behavior analysts. In this way, while I will return to RFT principles and concepts when discussing the ACT model, these must be practiced idiosyncratically; it is our job to identify functional relations for each client, parent, and family we work with. Functional relations in RFT incorporate clinically relevant behavior that can be understood as a result of the arrangement of contexts, including functional and relational contextual cues, a history of arbitrarily applicable relational responding, as well as respondent-operant conditioning histories and contextual schedules (see also McEnteggart, 2018).

Using RFT to inform how we implement ACT in parent training contexts is critical for three reasons. First, it will help us understand how the presenting or targeted repertoires were established. As discussed, an overextension of human language leads to behavioral inflexibility. This tends to include an overreliance on escape and avoidance repertoires even when doing so produces long-term negative outcomes.

Second, by relying on RFT foundational concepts, we will arrange our language about the target behaviors in ways that align with a contextual worldview and overarching CBS strategy rather than relying on mechanistic or structural worldviews. In this way, we will avoid analyzing subtle behaviors such as thoughts or other psychological phenomena as "causes" of behaviors; instead, we will target subtle behaviors that may align with our treatment goals (i.e., providing parent support or parent implementation training).

Third, using RFT will help us to rationalize why we are selecting a specific ACT component, metaphor, or activity for intervention. This will assist us with adhering to the ethical code of conduct. It will also require us to identify contextual functions and relations in order to create and develop target metaphors that share similar stimulus functions as the target repertoire. In this way, ACT relies on experiential activities, including metaphor, analogy, paradox, and others, to expose parents to novel experiences that may share similar stimulus functions with the targeted presenting issue. In sessions, parents are given opportunities to establish their own self-generated rules (i.e., through experiencing the activity or session, parents establish their own words about how the world is arranged) to reflect upon and establish new rules for navigating the world.

The RFT approach to analogy and metaphor not only establishes the core concept of arbitrarily applicable relational responding, but also establishes the more complex or higher order concept of *relating relations* (Foody et al., 2014). Unlike traditional literary distinctions, analogy in RFT can be considered a "coordination between two sets of stimuli or events not normally coordinated" (e.g., plants and domestic animals), while metaphor is considered "one stimulus or event that is representative of another or embodies it in one or more ways…suggesting that the relationship among the stimuli in a metaphor is more complex than the relationship among the stimuli in an analogy" (Foody et al., 2014, p. 4).

To help illustrate this, take the two analogies modified from Foody and colleagues in figure 2.2. In the left panel, the analogy might be described as "cat is to dog as rose is to tulip," where coordination relations between two other arbitrary coordination relations are established by the contextual relations (Crel) "is to." Each arrow is used to denote the relationship within the simple coordination relation (vertical arrows) and the overarching relationship between networks (horizontal arrows). In this example, there is no transformation of stimulus properties across networks, given that roses are not furry and cats are not flowers. In this way, the stimuli that comprise each network (i.e., animals on the left side and plants on the right side) only share stimulus properties with other stimuli within the network, not across the networks.

In contrast, the analogy on the right side may be described as "son belongs to father as cheese is to dairy product," where two contextual relations (i.e., hierarchical and coordination) are established by contextual cues "belongs to" (hierarchical) and "as" (coordination). Here, vertical arrows denoting hierarchical relationships are marked with different arrows to signal a direction (i.e., son belongs to father, but father does not belong to son). Similar to the previous analogy, transformation of function occurs across relation of coordination, or sameness; therefore, all stimuli share the same stimulus function.

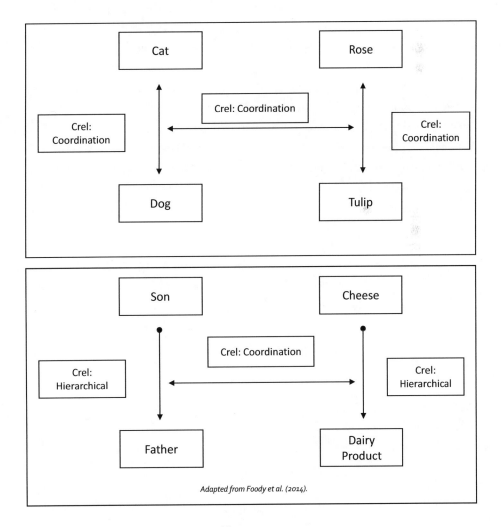

Adapted from Foody et al. (2014).

Figure 2.2

When we apply this within a therapeutic context, we must begin by identifying the verbal relations that support the targeted behavior. Once we identify the functioning relational network (i.e., the target network), then we may construct relational networks that establish a metaphor (i.e., the vehicle). The trick here is aligning the vehicle metaphor to the target network, as the closer our created vehicle network is to the presenting target network (including stimulus properties to align transformations of functions), the more likely the metaphor will be successful. It is important to remember that not all metaphors will work; parents won't always "get" a metaphor, depending on how they are established and how close the common features are between the parents' experience with the target repertoire and the common features in the metaphorical element (see also Törneke, 2017).

For the purposes of illustration, let us explore how RFT-based clinical metaphors may function in an ACT intervention (see also figure 2.3). Consider the parent, a 32-year-old single woman with a child recently diagnosed with ASD. The parent reports that she is consumed with fear and worry about being a bad parent to Ruby, her daughter. The parent reports feeling helpless and worthless, as she does not feel as though she knows how best to parent Ruby. She worries that her lack of parenting will make Ruby's life more challenging. Let us also assume that we have additional details needed to establish functional relationships, but for brevity, we will focus on a simple metaphor that considers the parent's experience: "being a single mom to Ruby is like being forced to juggle in the circus."

The target network is represented on the left and highlights how the parent's fear of failing as a parent is coordinated with her avoidance of any parenting strategy or repertoire. In this way, her avoidance of parenting strategies is in a causal (if/then) relation, given that if she avoids her parenting responsibilities, then she avoids her fear of failure (in the immediate here/now).

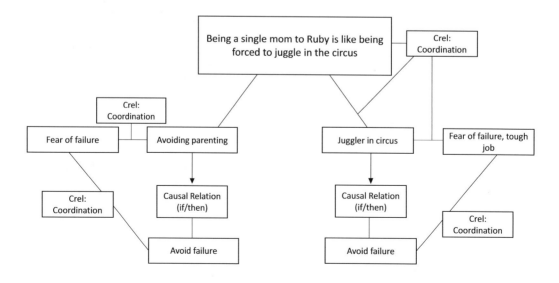

Adapted from Foody et al. (2014).

Figure 2.3

The vehicle network is represented on the right side of the figure and highlights how juggling in the circus (particularly with no formal training) is coordinated with a fear of failure of doing a tough or challenging job (similar to her conceptualization of parenting Ruby). In this way, juggling in a circus is also in a causal relation, in that if she avoids juggling, then she avoids her fear of failure. The success of the juggling as metaphor will be based on the stimulus functions between the parent's experience with parenting Ruby and forced juggling in a circus.

RFT-Based Acceptance and Commitment Training: Reconsidering the Model

From a functional contextual perspective, contexts that broaden a person's exposure to reinforcers or appetitive environments can be selected to recontextualize the identified conditioned aversive that narrows or limits a person's exposure to reinforcers. In this way, we can speak to the goal of ACT as the identification and shaping of flexible patterns of actions (i.e., defusion, acceptance, and committed action components) that align with here and now functional relations (i.e., self-as-context and present moment components) and schedules that produce larger-later abstract reinforcers (i.e., values components).

Midlevel terms may be useful clinically or when training nonbehaviorally trained individuals about intervention strategies. However, given our roots in eating, sleeping, and breathing all things behavior analysis, we can reasonably expect that, as practicing behavior analysts, we will not need to rely on midlevel terms to "understand" ACT per se. Instead, we may return to our agreed-upon attitudes of science and shared disciplinary values, with particular emphasis on pragmatism, the principle of parsimony, and the use of conceptually systematic and technological language. In this way, we may not need to hold on to constructs described via midlevel terms if they (a) do not produce effective outcomes when lumped together (evidence of lack of precision) or (b) produce overgeneralization rather than distinctions (lack of scope and depth). Midlevel terms in this way may not be helpful particularly for a behavior analytic audience already acclimated to the behavioral principles that are believed to support the constructs (see also Dixon et al., 2020).

Given this, this book will provide a novel framework for conceptualizing an ACT model for a behavior analytically trained audience. The model discussed is something I have been developing in both my consultation practice and as part of my research agenda for several years now. Anybody who has attended a workshop of mine since 2018 has seen a version of this conceptualization. While it was a very hard transition for me personally to get away from using and relying on midlevel terminology, as I started to rely more on the behavioral mechanisms rather than on a construct in and of itself, I started to notice a change not only in the clients exposed to the modified intervention strategies, but also in the BCBAs/clinicians whom I was mentoring and coaching to use ACT.

As an alternative to the traditional ACT model, we may return to our behavioral roots and avoid midlevel terminology to instead focus our attention to behavioral concepts and principles.

Major distinctions are therefore made to the words and conceptualizations used across treatment components, and these distinctions are described using a more technological taxonomy (see figure 2.4).

We can consider three primary areas of functioning: flexible perspective or deictic relational responding, attending to or orientation toward unwanted or aversive environments or stimuli, and engaging in values-based patterns of actions. Each of these three target areas can be further broken down into specific target areas and strategies. Flexible perspective taking incorporates helping the parent shift perspectives, with emphasis on shifting and maintaining I/here/now repertoires. Research to date has identified three deictic relational units including I/you relations, spatial here/there relations, and temporal now/then relations (see also McEnteggart, 2018). Relations can be targeted by single relation (i.e., interpersonal, spatial, or temporal), or they can be shaped through practicing shifting across relational networks (i.e., I/here/now vs. you/there/then).

Attention or orientation toward unwanted or aversive stimuli incorporates aspects related to acceptance. The term "experiential acceptance" has been described as a mediating behavior to be an "intentionally open, receptive, flexible, and nonjudgmental posture with respect to

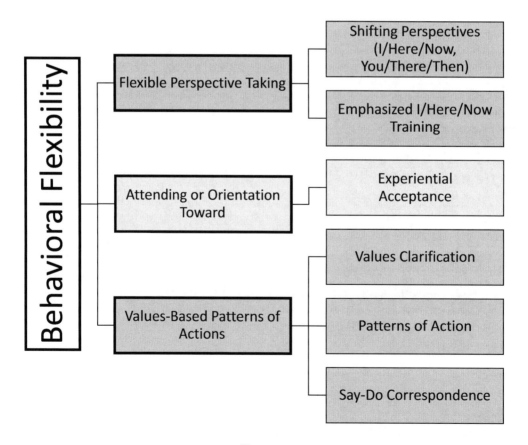

Figure 2.4

moment-to-moment experience" (Hayes et al., 2011, p. 272) or as an alternative repertoire to engagement in escape or avoidance repertoire (Dixon et al., 2020).

Values-based patterns of actions incorporate three general targets. First, values identification and clarification incorporates how the parent identifies, describes, and clarifies aspects of their life that are meaningful or reinforcing. Second, patterns of actions are identified as repertoires that people would see the parent do, and the things only they might experience, that would align with the identified values. Third, say-do and do-say correspondence incorporates the extent to which the parent says they will engage in a specific pattern of action and does, in fact, do so (i.e., say-do) or if they engage in a specific pattern of action and accurately report to you that they have done so (i.e., do-say).

Using this taxonomy, we may begin to reconsider how to align our training sessions, what to target during sessions, and how to conceptualize treatment progress or stagnation. When applied within parent training contexts, we may focus on the parents' engagement of here/now orientation or attention to environmental stimuli (rather than narrowing attention to a single conditioned stimulus), flexibility in response patterns across contexts and relational repertoires (i.e., deictic frames or perspective taking), and engagement in patterns of actions that align with verbally constructed reinforcers. Rather than focus our attention solely on the parent implementation of behavioral techniques or strategies, we may also attend to their verbal rules about their experiences, how those verbal rules may negatively impact their overall quality of life, and how those rules may influence their engagement in values-based patterns of actions.

Conclusion

In my practice, I have found that it is prudent to focus efforts on (a) understanding the parents' whole experience as a human being, (b) developing a collaborative and genuine relationship with the parents and family, and (c) expanding treatment goals to incorporate psychological and behavioral flexibility.

First, our approach to the parents' whole experience as a human being starts with how we identify and consider functional relationships between the presenting concern and other aspects of the parents' life. Here, we may shift our focus to how the parents characterize a vital and meaningful life, not only to help identify what is important to the parents but also to understand what may limit or obstruct the parents' growth potentiality. When we identify networks that are negatively reinforced through escape or avoidance, we don't automatically assume these networks need to be dismantled or recontextualized. Instead, through understanding the actualizing tendency of the parents, we understand that there is functional utility in escape sometimes; what is important is how doing so inhibits the parents from accessing or living their version of a complete and meaningful life.

Second, the collaborative nature of the relationship we establish when working with parents is key to our alignment within a humanistic perspective. Our relationship with the parents we work with must go beyond an "expert-client" dynamic and move into one of unconditional positive regard for the parents and their lived experience raising their child with complex health needs. The relationship we establish should be based on genuineness or authenticity by the therapist and can be applied to a range of training goals, from developing and implementing a behavior plan with their child to coaching or supporting parents through stressful or aversive life events and situations.

Finally, we need to expand our treatment focus beyond parent implementation to incorporate parent psychological and community supports in order to better assist parents in their life. When we consider the expansiveness of what it means to be human (i.e., the central question for humanists), we realize the importance of helping the parents grow across multiple repertoires and relational networks (i.e., perspective of their child, interpersonal relationship with their child and other family members, and so on). This guidebook is the culmination of my quest to establish a behaviorally tailored conceptualization of ACT and infuse it with robust applications of humanistic strategies. In this way, we can be empowered to use RFT as a foundation for understanding the parents and family system in a way that centers on the family's unique experience of the human condition.

CHAPTER 3

Ethical Considerations

Philosophers, psychologists, sociologists, and the like have long grappled with the quandary "Why be moral?" The "why" ranges from variations of pleasing a higher power (e.g., Kierkegaard) and seeking to be serviceable through virtue of doing "good" rather than doing "bad" (e.g., Plato's articulation of the Socratic paradox, and Thomas Aquinas's work during the Middle Ages) to societal gains (e.g., moral societies support moral behaviors and attitudes) and social rules such as "we should be moral because it is right to do so" (e.g., Kant 1785/1959). Moral behaviors are often described with some aspect of what is right or prudent and acceptable, or what are unacceptable or inappropriate ways to behave. Moral repertoires are often culturally selected and defined, and are contextually specific.

For behavior analysts, the answer to "Why be moral?" is likely complex and multifaceted. Unfortunately, ethical considerations around moral repertoires are not a "this" or "that" dichotomy. Contextual features may influence the extent to which a specific decision or behavior is somehow acceptable or not. Various ethical situations will most certainly shape specific clinical repertoires and decisions, and may not only be established based on "right" or "wrong." For example, a behavior analyst who persists with using an extinction procedure even when her client's target behaviors become more severe, intense, and potentially harmful may not always be "right" or "wrong" in doing so. Contextual features—certain levels of staffing ratios, conducting functional analysis, challenging behavior rates below preestablished criterion for terminating intervention, and so on—may suggest that the decision is acceptable or not.

When the question "Why be moral?" is applied to the social sciences, answers are typically contextualized into ethics and considerations of ethical repertoires. Ethics are typically presented in terms of situational contexts, dilemmas, or issues that often leave the person to respond in a way that may be muddled across lines of "right" and "wrong" (Kitchener & Anderson, 2011). From a behavior analytic perspective, ethics have long been considered specific rules about our professional conduct or behaviors. Ethical codes therefore function as rules (or specifying stimuli) that set boundaries around specific behaviors and repertoires that we "ought to do" from repertoires we "ought to avoid." Such rules, and potential aversive consequences from not following the rules, therefore have grave influence over our behavior given various clinical practice situations. According to Freeman, LeBlanc, and Martinez-Diaz (2020, p. 763), behavior analysts make decisions that are grounded by three fundamental questions (emphases added):

- What is the *right* thing to do?

- What is *worth* doing?

- What does it mean to be a *good* behavior analyst?

When taken together, we must seriously reflect on the variables presented in each clinical context in order to articulate clearly and impartially decide the "right" thing that is "worth" doing, and how or whether our behavior aligns with being a "good" (or ethical) behavior analyst. Situational variables include our own unique learning history as well as the client and stakeholders involved; the context of clinical practice and the client and stakeholder presenting behaviors; the goals of what is to be accomplished, and how those goals align with the client and stakeholders; and our scope of competence and scope of practice as practicing behavior analysts, including our accessibility to quality supervision, mentorship, and guidance (Freeman et al., 2020, p. 762).

What makes a "good" decision or clinical skill? This question ultimately situates our behavior into two categories: those behaviors that can be conceptualized as "good" and those that are "bad." Rule-based ethics function within similar dichotomies, where a set of rules can be established to identify moral behaviors from immoral behaviors in order to establish a series of behaviors to engage in (or not) given specific situations (e.g., rule-based ethics, Kant, 1785/1959). While rule-based ethics has a long-standing history in social sciences, including behavior analysis, there may be more to understanding why or how a repertoire is "good" or "bad" or "right" or "wrong." What may constitute a "good" or "right" decision in one context may not necessarily derive a similar outcome when engaged in a different context.

Take, for example, a behavior analyst who uses food as a reinforcer. In the beginning of services, doing so is often considered a "good" intervention strategy, particularly if the client has restricted preferences, minimal vocal-verbal behaviors, and so on. If, however, that same behavior analyst continues to only use food as a reinforcer, that same repertoire may now be considered inappropriate, as they haven't shifted toward broadening the client's preferences or using conditioned reinforcers (like tokens, points, or other tangible items that can be exchanged for a primary reinforcer like food).

In a parent training context, we might categorize a behavior analyst's behavior as "good" if they rescue the parents in the beginning of behavior skills training (BST) by jumping in for the parents and modeling how to implement the particular skill or step. In the beginning of the intervention, doing so may help establish a therapeutic relationship with the parents, and may also limit the extent to which errors of commission occur (doing other behaviors when implementing the behavior plan rather than the ones described in the protocol). But, if the behavior analyst continues to jump in for the parents every time the parents make a mistake or ask the behavior analyst to help and jump in, then the same repertoire may be considered inappropriate.

In both examples, the same repertoire that is considered "good" in one context may be considered "bad" or inappropriate in another. In this way, "good" and "bad" repertoires are not only based on topography or what the repertoire looks like, but also necessarily involve contextual variables such as reinforcement history, current schedules of reinforcement, and discriminative and conditioned aversive stimuli.

Conversely, virtue ethics move beyond "good" and "bad." Instead, they focus on rules that can be formed as commitments and values that a person may hold that align with "being a virtuous person" (Rosenberg & Schwartz, 2019, p. 476). In this way, ethical conduct can be considered outside of a series of topographies of behavior and instead can be considered in relation to their situational or contextual variables and decisions made by a behavior analyst. Rosenberg and Schwartz (2019) propose an ethical decision-making process to help behavior analysts with orienting away from rule-based ethics into ethical decision-making more aligned with virtue ethics. Their original decision-making process (p. 478) has been adapted and condensed here:

1. Why does the current situation trigger your ethical radar? Identify the ethical dilemma as relevant to the BACB ethical code, client and stakeholder, and your personal values or biases about the dilemma.

2. What solutions are there to the dilemma? Brainstorm possible solutions with trusted colleagues, mentors, and other relevant stakeholders as appropriate.

3. What issues, conflicts, or tensions might influence each of the solutions identified in step 2? Consider client safety, dignity, and self-determination; impact on relationships with other stakeholders; and family preferences, values, and cultural practices. If you find the solutions open the door to additional ethical concerns, repeat step 2.

4. Implement the acceptable solution(s) with fidelity and document all actions taken throughout implementation.

5. Afterward, reflect on the results and outcomes of the decision. Ask yourself: *Was the resolution successful? Why or why not? What have I learned that will impact my behavior in the future?*

Within such a decision-making process, the rules of the professional code of ethics are held in accordance with a virtue ethics approach. Said another way, the ethical code is the road we drive on as behavior analysts, while virtue ethics is the direction we are heading in. The ethical code of conduct is the foundation of what we do within our clinical practice. How we approach ethical dilemmas, including integrating novel interventions or populations into our everyday clinical practice, is not a matter of "good" or "bad," but rather based on the relationship between previous decisions we made and the current situational or contextual variables presented.

The above ethical decision-making process can be used whenever we are presented with an ethical dilemma, or when we are asked by colleagues or supervisees to assist with ethical dilemmas. We will be turning to this model again later in the chapter, when we consider the ethical situations that may arise when using ACT within parent training.

BACB Ethical Code of Conduct

All Board Certified Behavior Analysts (BCBA), Board Certified Assistant Behavior Analysts (BCaBA), and Registered Behavior Analysts (RBT) are held to ethical standards as delineated by the Behavior Analyst Certification Board (BACB), state or country licensure laws (as applicable), and disciplinary standards (for those that may be dually credentialed as marriage and family therapists, licensed clinical social workers, clinical psychologists, or other professional roles). While numerous resources discuss codes of ethical conduct across disciplinary lines, this chapter will focus primarily on the 2022 BACB ethical code of conduct.

Four core principles establish the framework for all ethical standards and codes: (1) benefiting others, (2) treating others with compassion, dignity, and respect, (3) behaving with integrity, and (4) ensuring competence (Behavior Analyst Certification Board, 2020, p. 4). These core principles are common within social sciences and human services specifically, and are interconnected and interdependent with one another. For instance, for us to do no harm and maximize benefits for the client (principle 1), we must treat client and stakeholders equitably and with dignity (principle 2), behave honestly and in ways that create professional environments that uphold the ethical standards (principle 3, behave with integrity), and work within our scope of practice and scope of competence (principle 4). Omitting one of those repertoires (for instance, behaving honestly and in ways that uphold ethical standards—principle 3) necessarily limits the extent to which clients and stakeholders can be treated with dignity (principle 2) or if the client has been subjected to undue harm (principle 1).

One principle that is of particular interest for behavior analysts using ACT in their clinical practice is principle 4: ensuring competence. The first consideration within principle 4 is that an ethical behavior analyst must remain within the *profession's* scope of practice. It is not enough for the behavior analyst to practice or use an intervention strategy that they find to be within their scope of practice; the profession itself must also agree that doing so falls within the scope of practice for all behavior analysts. The extent to which ACT is considered within the scope of practice of the profession has been articulated and debated recently.

For instance, Tarbox et al. (2020) and Dixon et al. (2020) both argue how using ACT aligns with the seven dimensions of applied behavior analysis (i.e., applied, analytic, behavior, effective, technological, conceptually systematic, generalizable; Baer, Wolf, & Risley, 1968), and therefore is within applied behavior analysts' scope of practice. However, others argue that research to date on using ACT with populations that behavior analysts commonly work with (including individuals with intellectual/developmental disabilities, autism, and the like) is not very robust, and more research is needed before the profession can adequately decide whether we should be using ACT (e.g., Cihon et al., 2021).

While caution and skepticism are beneficial particularly within applied sciences, the use of ACT within behavior analytic practice can and should be considered as long as (a) our scope of practice aligns with a population that is within our existing practice guidelines or regulation, (b) the educational training history meets a minimum qualification standard to deliver treatment in the region in which we practice, and (c) we uphold our commitment to our ethical code of conduct (see also Dixon et al., 2020, and A. N. Wilson et al., 2021, on similar scope of practice discussions).

The second and third considerations within principle 4 focus on our scope of competence. The BACB (2020, p. 9) ethical code defines scope of competence and maintaining scope of competence as follows (emphasis added):

> *Code 1.05: Practicing within Scope of Competence*—Behavior analysts *practice only within their identified* scope of competence. They engage in professional activities in new areas (e.g., population, procedures) *only after accessing and documenting* appropriate study, training, supervised experience, consultation, and/or co-treatment from professionals competent in the new area. Otherwise, they refer or transition services to an appropriate professional.

> *Code 1.06: Maintaining Competence*—Behavior analysts *actively engage* in professional development activities to maintain and *further their professional competence*. Professional development activities include reading relevant literature; attending conferences and conventions; participating in workshops and other training opportunities; obtaining additional coursework; receiving coaching, consultation, supervision, or mentorship; and obtaining and maintaining appropriate professional credentials.

It is critically important for each of us to consider our own scope of competence as an ongoing and dynamic behavioral repertoire rather than as a static "one and done" topography. Taking a single ACT workshop, attending a single ACT boot camp, or reading everything published on ACT by behavior analysts may not help or establish the individual's scope of competence per se. Rather, active pursuit to develop and maintain our competence is key to practicing any intervention strategy ethically and is particularly important for using ACT in clinical practice.

We can, perhaps, understand this point more clearly by looking outside of an ACT context. Take, for example, implementing an experimental functional analysis (EFA) in your own clinical practice. If you have never conducted an EFA before, you may attend conferences and see presenters showcasing the efficacy and utility of EFA, you may read countless articles on EFA, and you may also attend workshops or trainings on how to conduct EFAs. Yet, even with exposure, you probably would never think of implementing your first EFA without proper supervision or even perhaps without another BCBA there with you (and maybe subsequent analyses, depending upon client behavior).

Why might this be? It might have to do with the overt target behavior that is selected, such as severe physical aggression, property destruction, or even self-injurious behaviors. We know that having a person engage in head banging or severe physical aggression toward others for long periods of time can do serious damage to the client or others, depending upon the topography and environment. Similarly, natural consequences of the target behavior, such as bleeding or bruising, are directly observable in real time, and we may stop or modify the analysis as a result.

It might also have to do with the ethical consequences of harming the client or stakeholders if the EFA is not conducted accurately (i.e., a failure to do no harm as indicated by principle 1 in the code of ethics). If we err when we conduct an EFA, we could face serious consequences, including (but not limited to) injuring a client, caretaker, or paraprofessional staff; loss of practicing credential(s); malpractice lawsuits; and others.

But when we target subtle behaviors, like thoughts or feelings, we may not always see them or have direct access to observe them or their effects. In this way, we do not directly see the potential damage we may inadvertently cause when we use ACT incorrectly or irresponsibly, which may also blind us to potential harm our intervention may cause. Unlike severe aggression or self-injurious behaviors, there are no salient discriminative stimuli (like blood or red marks on a person's skin) to alert us or signal that we need to change environmental conditions. Instead, when we target subtle behaviors, we might be able to see subtle responses (like response-narrowing repertoires or shifting vocal tones), but we must know what to look for.

Given the nature of subtle behaviors, it is critical that we directly assess our level of competence before using ACT with every caregiver/parent, situation, and context. When we include subtle behaviors in a behavioral analysis, it is critical that we set boundaries around the session structure, assessment, and approaches to data collection throughout the implementation of ACT (discussed in further chapters). In addition, setting boundaries is helpful to establishing our competence, in addition to articulating and documenting how much training and mentoring or supervision we received prior to using ACT in our practice.

To help establish whether ACT is within your own scope of practice, consider the following questions (adapted from Dixon et al., 2020, p. 574):

1. Have you worked with the population and target behavior(s) before? If not, what supervision or mentorship will you seek out and receive, and for how long?

2. Does your analysis suggest that ACT might be a useful treatment? Why or why not?

3. Do you have access to the stimuli that you believe control the target behavior? If not, what other disciplines might be better suited to help the client with this behavior?

4. Do you have the cooperation and consent from all stakeholders?

5. Do you have cooperation from the client? (This is ongoing: before every session do you have their cooperation?)

6. Do you have access to a mentor or supervisor? Do you have someone you can connect with to problem-solve or conceptualize your treatment approach/plan with? If not, how will you go about finding someone?

7. What does "in over your head" mean for you and this client? Do you have established boundaries to ensure you do not get in over your head? Do you have a plan on what you will do if you find yourself in over your head?

If you answer no to any of these questions, reflect honestly and without bias on the extent to which using ACT with the client is appropriate. There is no shame in needing additional training, mentoring, or guidance before using ACT. There are, however, serious consequences for getting in over your head when using it, which can be easily avoided by practicing a commitment to being a "good" behavior analyst. Addressing these questions before each client may nudge you closer toward the behavior analyst you want to be and will at a minimum move you further away from doing harm to your client.

Ethical Considerations When Using ACT in Parent Training Contexts

When considering the BACB ethical code and using ACT in parent training contexts, the core principles, in addition to the ethical codes discussed below, remain at the forefront. Just like all clinical relationships, we must ask ourselves, *Is my intervention benefiting my client?* When working with parents specifically, we will narrow our inquiries about our scope of practice and scope of competence, before turning to additional ethical codes that directly relate to using ACT within parent training contexts.

Scope of competence when applying ACT within parent training contexts is similar to using ACT within clinical practice. The only difference here is the emphasis on parents and parent training contexts rather than direct implementation with a client per se. We can use the same set of questions adapted from Dixon et al. (2020, p. 574), but can further modify them to fit a parent training context:

1.   Have you worked with parents before?

    a.   If yes, in what capacity? How does your work history compare to the current parent you may work with?

    b.   If not, what supervision or mentorship will you seek out, and for how long?

2.   Why do you think ACT might be a useful treatment for the parent? What data do you have to support this decision?

    a.   What other methods have you tried to use with the parent? If none, why do you think ACT will be effective?

    b.   What repertoires does the parent currently have? How may ACT be helpful for the parent?

3.   Do you know why the parent is not adhering to the treatment plan?

    a.   If yes, have you tried other behavior analytic interventions with fidelity? If they didn't work, why do you think that was the case?

b. If not, figure out why this may be prior to moving forward with ACT implementation.

4. Do you have access to the controlling stimuli that evokes the treatment nonadherence? Do you know what the controlling stimuli are? What assessments can you do to establish your knowledge here?

    a. If you do not have access, what other disciplines might be better suited to assist the parent?

5. Do you have cooperation from the parent to use ACT during parent training? (This is ongoing before every session.)

    a. What safeguards will you put into place to ensure the parent knows what to expect?

6. Do you have access to a mentor or supervisor who has used ACT for parent training?

    a. If yes, how often will you meet with this person? What will your supervision meetings consist of? Will the supervisor watch you conduct an ACT session, or talk about it after the fact?

    b. If no, how will you go about finding someone?

7. What does "in over your head" look like for this parent?

    a. Do you have established boundaries to ensure you do not get in over your head?

    b. Do you have a plan on what you will do if you find yourself in over your head?

If you answered no to any question, reflect on it and consider alternative treatment strategies.

If your answers suggest that using ACT in parent training contexts is within your scope of competence, the next step is to consider how to arrange the training environment to avoid multiple relationships (code 1.11) and coercive and exploitative relationships (code 1.13). The BACB outlines each of these ethical issues (italics emphasis in original):

Code 1.11: Multiple Relationships—Because *multiple* relationships may result in a *conflict of interest* that might harm one or more parties, behavior analysts avoid entering into or creating multiple relationships, including professional, personal, and familial relationships with clients and colleagues. Behavior analysts communicate the risks of multiple relationships to relevant individuals and continually monitor for the development of multiple relationships. If multiple relationships arise, behavior analysts take appropriate steps to resolve them. When immediately resolving a multiple relationship is not possible, behavior analysts develop appropriate safeguards to identify and avoid conflicts of interest in compliance with the Code and develop a plan to eventually resolve the multiple relationships. Behavior analysts document all actions taken in this circumstance and the eventual outcomes.

Code 1.13: Coercive and Exploitative Relationships—Behavior analysts do not abuse their power or authority by coercing or exploiting persons over whom they have authority (e.g., evaluative, supervisory). (p. 10)

We must critically examine the extent to which our use of ACT within a parent training context puts us into multiple relationships—or not. If our primary role is to work with the child, and now we start to use ACT with the parents, this could open the door to multiple relationships. For instance, if we use ACT within our parent coaching sessions and doing so creates an environment where parents believe they are the client instead of their child, we inadvertently establish conflict of interest and multiple relationships.

Perhaps the easiest way to avoid multiple relationships is to have a different behavior analyst conduct the parent training sessions. This approach would clearly separate the roles of both behavior analysts (e.g., Behavior Analyst A works with the child, while Behavior Analyst B works with the parents to implement the behavior plan as designed by Behavior Analyst A). If a parent shares sensitive content with Behavior Analyst B, a conflict may be avoided given that the behavior analyst does not work with the child. As long as the content is not shared with Behavior Analyst A, there would be no conflict across multiple relationships.

Having two behavior analysts on the family's team may not work for all funding sources, agencies, or family needs. Therefore, in situations where the same behavior analyst is to work with the child and the parents, the simplest way to avoid multiple relationships is to establish clear rules and operating procedures during the informed consent process (see also ethical code 2.11 on Obtaining Informed Consent, BACB, 2020). The informed consent process should be conducted before using ACT with the parents and can be a way to highlight how you will take appropriate steps (including documentation of steps taken) around protecting against a dual relationship (see also chapter 5). For instance, appropriate steps may include these:

1. Clearly establish that the use of ACT is designed to assist with implementing a behavior plan, not to help a parent with their own idiosyncratic subtle behaviors (like anxiety or worry about their child's behavior or diagnosis).

2. Clearly outline what the goal of ACT is.

3. Clearly establish boundaries around how the behavior analyst will use content shared during ACT sessions. (This also aligns with avoiding coercive relationships.)

4. Provide a parent with a list of resources for mental health services, and/or take time during the first few sessions to help the parent find mental health services that align with their financial and insurance needs.

We must also be aware of coercive and exploitative relationships (code 1.13). While this code is clearly written in relation to supervision or exploitation of persons under a behavior analyst's control, this can easily be considered and applied to parents, particularly when the same behavior analyst is responsible for both the child and for conducting parent training.

Take, for example, a mom who is working with a behavior analyst on a parent training program. The mom shares with the behavior analyst that she wants to be a good mom and is willing to do whatever she can to make sure her son becomes the best version of himself. She also tells the behavior analyst that "being a good mom" means doing anything and everything that will benefit her son, even if it is hard for her. The behavior analyst later uses this to motivate the mom to use the behavior plan, by telling the mom, "Remember, you said you wanted to be a good mom, even if it is hard for you. Not implementing the plan might be easy for you, but it isn't good for your son. Will you implement the plan now, even if it is hard for you? You want to be a good mom, right?"

While on the surface, this may topographically seem okay, if we look a bit closer, we can see shades of coercive and exploitative relationships. Take the statement "not implementing the plan might be easy for you, but it isn't good for your son." Does this statement show empathy or understanding for the mom's situation? Does this statement motivate the mom to engage in a behavior to access reinforcement-rich environments, or does it motivate the mom to remove an aversive (i.e., negative reinforcer or potential punisher)? When combined with the last statement—"You want to be a good mom, right?"—we see a bit more about how these phrases may come to serve an aversive function. If you notice that the mom implements the plan only after the analyst makes similar statements, this may be a sign that the mom is behaving to escape an aversive (the analyst's verbal statement) and may concomitantly reinforce the mom's self-generated rules about the environment—"Even the behavior analyst thinks I'm not a good mom." Are there different ways for the mom to "be a good mom"? Are there conflicting values for the mom, depending on the environmental circumstances and arrangement?

The point here is that we must be intentional in how we attempt to motivate the parents we are working with, particularly when they tell us about their subtle and private experiences. We may consider a parent's values or value statements in ways that we believe are motivating. But when we unpack how those statements function in the environment, we may see how those motivational statements may become a conditioned aversive, therefore opening the door for coercive environments.

Ethical Decision-Making Strategies for Using ACT in Parent Training Contexts

When taken together, it becomes clear that using ACT in clinical practice is within the scope of practice for behavior analysts, yet it is up to each of us to determine whether and how it aligns with our scope of competence. In addition to considerations of the four core principles (i.e., benefiting others; treating others with compassion, dignity, and respect; behaving with integrity; and ensuring competence; BACB 2020), it is clear that key ethical codes should be directly considered prior to using ACT in parent training contexts. To help us ensure that we practice ethically, let us return to Rosenberg and Schwartz's (2019) decision-making process and consider how this process can be applied within an ACT and parent training context.

Multiple relationships. To begin, let us start with how you will avoid multiple relationships when using ACT. If you have a second behavior analyst to work with the child or to implement ACT with the parents, then congratulations; this situation should not trigger your ethical radar! If, however, you are the primary behavior analyst who will oversee both the child and the parent training, then this *should* trigger your ethical radar. To address Rosenberg and Schwartz's (2019) second decision point, consider solutions to the multiple relationships' dilemma: How can you use the informed consent process to provide written documentation to the parents about your plan to control for multiple relationships? What steps will you take, how will you arrange the environment, and how will you inform the parents about these steps? What is your plan if the parents disagree with your approach? What boundaries will you set for your ACT sessions?

To address Rosenberg and Schwartz's (2019) third point, how will your solutions align with parental preferences, values, and cultural practices? How will your solutions align with the core principles to do no harm and to ensure client and parent dignity and self-determination? Next, implement your solutions and document all actions taken throughout implementation.

Finally, to address the final decision point, reflect on the results and outcomes of your decision and implementation successes (and failures). Was what you did successful? Why or why not? How will you adjust your plan for the next time you use ACT in parent training contexts?

Coercive and exploitative relationships. Now, let us turn to how you will avoid coercive and exploitative relationships when using ACT with parents. To begin, consider ways in which an ethical dilemma may arise when using ACT. How could you use the parents' values statements to potentially coerce them into implementing your plan? What personal values do you hold regarding this ethical dilemma that can influence how you respond throughout your ACT sessions?

To address Rosenberg and Schwartz's (2019) second decision point, how can you arrange your ACT sessions to make sure you avoid engaging with the parents' value statements in an aversive or coercive way? What potential environmental structures or rules can you set for yourself when implementing ACT that may assist you in avoiding aversive or coercive relationships with the parents? If you do find yourself engaging in coercive or exploitative relationships, what steps will you take to rectify the ethical dilemma? What boundaries will you set for your ACT sessions if you find yourself engaging in coercive or exploitative relationships?

To address the third point in the decision-making process, how will your solutions align with parental preferences, values, and cultural practices? How will your solutions align with the core principles to do no harm and to ensure client and parent dignity and self-determination? Next, implement your solutions and document all actions taken throughout implementation. Implementing these steps before a potentially coercive relationship begins should be the gold standard of using ACT with parents. However, it is never too late to adapt your practice should you find yourself engaging in coercive repertoires. When you implement these steps, be sure to document all steps you take, including how you share this information with parents.

Finally, to address the last decision point, reflect on the results and outcomes of your decision and implementation successes (and failures): Was what you did successful? Why or why not? How will you adjust your plan for the next time you use ACT in parent training contexts?

Conclusion

To return to the original question—"Why be moral?"—we can see that the answer to that question is necessarily dependent on the contextual variables. The BACB provides us with a series of rules that are developed to govern behavior that categorizes repertoires into "ethical" and "unethical" dichotomies. Ethical categories are often equated with "good" behaviors, while unethical categories align with "bad" behaviors. However, when we take ethics beyond a rule-based approach, we can start to see how various situations may call for different topographies or repertoires that may not always align with "good" or "bad" but may consistently align with "ethical" rather than "unethical." In this way, this chapter provided an overview of how to use virtue ethics to help you consider how to be committed to engaging in repertoires that align with contextual situations rather than simply establishing repertoires to practice "good" behavior analysis.

When we use or implement new treatment interventions or treat novel populations, we may need to adjust out of a "good" or "bad" dichotomy. Using a virtue ethics approach, we can consider broader repertoires that "do no harm," while also using an intervention strategy that we may still be in the process of mastering. Similarly, when we consider using novel or emerging supportive treatments, perhaps adjusting out of a similar good/bad dichotomy would mean that we commit to practicing within our scope of competence by way of additional oversight (like mentorship or formal supervision), proactive attempts to mitigate ethical issues (like potentials for dual or multiple relationships), and continued active reflection (especially when solving ethical issues, to determine whether and how the resolution was successful).

In this way, we can use ACT to enhance our clinical practice, particularly with parents and caregivers. While the scope of practice and competence issues when using ACT in behavior analytic practice may evolve over time, we can ensure that we follow the science in how we consider alternative approaches to engage parents and enrich the parent-child relationships during parent training. We can do this while using an emerging supportive treatment, by adhering to our ethical code and staying within our scope of competence.

CHAPTER 4

Data Collection Strategies

Ask any behavior analyst "What is the one thing that all behavior analysts *do* in clinical practice?" and you'll more than likely get some variation of this response: "collect and analyze data." I often teach graduate students and aspiring behavior analysts that our measurement approach and corresponding design strategy is the heart of what we do as behavior analysts. If we don't have valid and reliable data to support our clinical decisions, then we are no longer working within our scope of practice. If we don't have valid data, it is impossible for us to effectively conduct behavioral service delivery. While on the surface, this is an agreeable tenet within behavior analysis, in clinical practice sometimes data collection is often messy, inconsistent, and imperfect.

Behavior analysts have an ethical responsibility to collect and use data (BACB, 2020, 2.17) to make data-based decisions. While we may all agree that collecting data is a *necessary* component of quality behavioral service delivery, how to collect data and what to collect data on is sometimes not as clear. This is particularly true when we investigate and incorporate subtle behaviors into our data collection approaches or incorporate new intervention strategies (e.g., ACT) into practice. Given this, it is critical that we consider data collection and measurement systems prior to implementing ACT within parent training contexts. This is often easier said than done, particularly when we consider the multiple repertoires, environments, and persons involved.

Behavior analysts who begin using ACT in their clinical practice often tell me that they struggle with figuring out how to collect data or what to collect data on. Should they consider directly observable events only, or is there room for other dimensions, such as self-report of behaviors that occur at a different level of analysis? In parent training contexts, this issue is compounded when creating data collection systems that are valid and arranged in ways to consider subtle behaviors or parental behaviors not directly observed by others.

The approach I've taken in my own clinically focused research (e.g., A. N. Wilson et al., 2021; Kasson & A. N. Wilson, 2017; A. N. Wilson et al., 2015), clinical practice, and supervision of or mentorship to other BCBAs has been twofold: (1) always select socially valid primary dependent measures that are directly observable, and rely on these first during data analysis and data-based decision-making, and (2) select flexible and valid measurement systems that align assessment to the selected intervention strategy, in order to better directly assess differences between responding (as appropriate). As such, the goal of this chapter is to highlight these experiences and lessons learned in order to assist readers with arranging flexible data collection and measurement systems to better examine subtle and directly observable behaviors. This chapter will also consider a new way to approach data collection, measurement, and design selection when using ACT in your practice. My goal is to look at ways we might layer our measurement systems to establish a valid and reliable representation of the whole person or family system, including important functional contexts and functional relations.

Data Collection Considerations in Clinical Practice

Data collection is a critically important aspect to any behavior analytic intervention. However, data collection in and of itself is only half of the issue: the extent to which the data collected is trustworthy is equally important. To determine the trustworthiness of data, we must consider measurement validity (the extent to which the measurement system yields information on what the system is supposed to measure), reliability (the extent to which the measurement system consistently measures what it is supposed to measure), and accuracy (the extent to which the collected data aligns with the observed value) (see also Kazdin, 2013; Johnston & Pennypacker, 2008).

Trusting the data. To establish the trustworthiness of a measurement system, we must (a) target socially valid behaviors that are measured across observable dimensions (i.e., duration, frequency), (b) ensure that the measurement system occurs under conditions that are relevant to the behaviors or the concerns about the behaviors, (c) avoid measurement bias (nonrandom measurement error as a result of overestimation, underestimation, or observer bias), and (d) consider internal and external threats to the selected measurement systems (see also Kazdin, 2013; Cooper et al., 2019, chapter 5). Attention is often focused on ensuring accurate, valid, and reliable measurement systems or dependent variables in behavior analytic research, particularly given the goal within behavior analysis to demonstrate how changes in the dependent variable are functionally related to the environment (Baer, Wolf, & Risley, 1968). For most of us, including directly observable behaviors within this approach is ingrained from the beginning of graduate school and reinforced daily within clinical practice. However, including subtle behaviors or behaviors that may only be directly observable to one individual, while adhering to rules around validity and reliability, can become a challenge.

Regardless of dimension or operational definition of a target behavior selected, our goal is to demonstrate functional relationships between environmental conditions and changes in a dependent variable. Perhaps the most effective way in which we can accomplish this is through single-subject designs. Single-subject design (SSD) is intended as a tool for clinicians to use in a way that helps us visually analyze the effects of one or more independent variables on one or more dependent variables. The primary goal of each SSD is to help us increase our believability that our intervention or independent variable is causing the change we are measuring.

Various design strategies (i.e., adapted alternating treatments, multiple-baseline or multiple-probe, component or parametric analyses, reversal, and withdrawal designs, to name a few; see also Kazdin, 2013) can be used to substantiate the believability of the intervention through visual analysis to confirm prediction, verification, and replication. Variations in SSD types assist us in a variety of ways depending on the goal of treatment, environmental barriers, or limitations of what we can or cannot manipulate. For example, not all interventions can be withheld or removed, such as skill acquisition and similar forms of instructional control. Similarly, not all designs may be feasible to help establish a functional relation, given the lack of verification and replication within the design. Therefore, it is critical for us to think creatively about how to embed SSDs into our clinical practice and, when using ACT, in parent training contexts.

Using single-subject design. Visual analyses are employed with each type of SSD to compare patterns of a dependent variable across phases or conditions, where the intersection of time (i.e., abscissa or horizontal axis) and a unit of measurement (i.e., the ordinate or vertical axis) indicates how much a specific dependent variable or behavior occurs at a point in time. Effects of various environmental conditions and/or treatment interventions can then be compared across level (the convergence of values of data on the vertical axis within environmental conditions), trend (the degree or direction of the data path), and variability (the extent to which the data path produced is consistent/fixed or random/stretched; see also Cooper et al., 2019, chapter 6). Each design type will yield different design logic, or the extent to which prediction, verification, and replication of observed data paths are to be configured and applied. It is imperative that we consider the current environmental variables, target behavior(s) of interest or concern, and feasibility when selecting a design. (See figure 4.1 for an example of important features of SSD and visual analysis.)

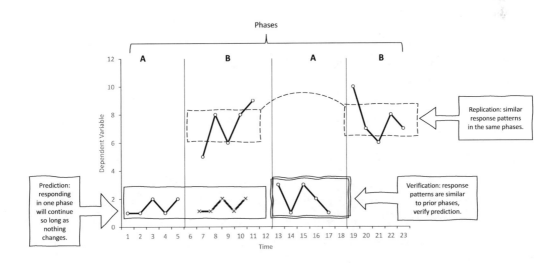

Figure 4.1

The goal of SSD is to assist us with answering this fundamental question: *How do I know what I am doing is working or causing the changes in the behavior(s) I am measuring?* Single-subject designs can also assist with answering a range of additional questions such as: *How does this design help me establish a functional relation between the dependent variable and the independent variable? Or how will I use visual analyses to conclude that I am using a functional intervention?*

For instance, if the goal is to help teach the parents a new skill (e.g., take three deep breaths before using the intervention plan), I may select a design that could help me determine whether the breaths are helpful at increasing consistency with implementation. If I was concerned about how often the parents engaged in deep breathing, or how many breaths the parents took (e.g., three vs. five), I may use a changing criterion design. If I wanted to determine whether the parents used the new breath skill across different environments or settings, a multiple-baseline design may be more suitable. The goal is to use a design that best fits your setting and selected behavior(s) as well as establishes the extent to which your intervention is causing the change you are observing. Which design you use is up to you.

Selecting and defining behaviors.
In addition to the type of design employed, we must consider the selection of the target behavior(s) and corresponding alternative behavior(s). We target behaviors that are considered socially significant, not only behaviors that are of concern to a small group of stakeholders. When considering parent behavior, it is critical to include behaviors that not only are important to us as practicing behavior analysts (like implementing a behavior plan with fidelity), but that are also important to the parents (like spending more quality time with their child or engaging in self-care strategies) and the parent-child relationship. We should always work in collaboration with the parents to identify target behaviors and data collection systems throughout intervention in order to ensure parental buy-in and the provision of human-centered provision of ACT.

When selecting behaviors, it is equally critical to consider response classes or large networks of behavioral topographies that share similar functions rather than chase topographies. Chasing topographies occurs when multiple topographies are selected for data collection, sometimes with different measurement systems, even though each topography shares a similar function (e.g., escape or avoidance).

For instance, take the example of Rio, father to his 5-year-old son, Joey. Rio reports having low motivation to spend time with his son and not really knowing things about Joey. He is often observed to leave the room whenever Mom enters and begins to interact with Joey. Rio tells the behavior analyst that Mom is better at teaching and interacting with Joey anyway, that he'd just get in the way, and it is better for everyone if he leaves the room. Dad is routinely observed attempting to interact with Joey, but as soon as Joey whines or turns away from Dad, he turns to the analyst to say either "See, this is what I'm talking about; it's always like this with him" or "This is what I have been telling you would happen," and "Okay, well that didn't take too long. Okay, where is your mother?" before walking out of the room.

When considering which behaviors to target and how to develop a measurement system for the selected behaviors, we should consider the dimensions of behavior, the properties of data, the extent to which the behaviors are directly observable, or whether the behavior produces a physical change in the environment, prior to selecting a measurement system. Let us turn to these considerations next.

Data Collection and Measurement Systems

According to Johnston and Pennypacker (2008), there are three fundamental properties of data: repeatability, temporal extent, and temporal locus. *Repeatability* is the extent to which the behavior can be considered by the frequency or rate (i.e., the number of times the behavior occurs within a specified amount of time or unit of measurement). *Temporal extent* is the time between an environmental event and the first occurrence of a behavior (i.e., latency) or the duration of a behavior. Finally, *temporal locus* is the time between two behavioral events (i.e., inter-response time, or IRT). These properties are important to consider as the overall goal of your parent training: what do you want the parents to do at the end of your training? Understanding your treatment goals can be useful to identify and establish one or more of these properties across two measurement systems: continuous and discontinuous.

Continuous and discontinuous measurement systems. *Continuous measurement systems* collect information about behavior(s) throughout a predetermined observation period, often to include event recording (such as frequency or count), duration recording (the length of time a behavior occurs), latency (the time between an environmental event and the first occurrence of a behavior), and inter-response time.

Discontinuous measurement systems, on the other hand, collect information within an observation period when the behavior of interest has an opportunity to occur even if the measurement system does not occur. Common discontinuous measurement systems include interval recording where observation periods are split into equal intervals and data collection is based on the extent to which a behavior occurs or not. There are three primary or common interval recording techniques: whole-interval and partial-interval recording, and momentary time sampling.

In *whole-interval recording*, a specific brief amount of time is set for an observational period, and the interval is denoted if the target behavior is observed throughout the entire duration. Whole-interval recording procedures often underestimate the overall occurrences or percentages of intervals in which a behavior occurs, with longer intervals often resulting in higher levels of underestimation. Whole-interval recording could be applied within an ACT parent training session, where a 30-minute session is divided into six 5-minute intervals. At the end of every interval, a yes or no (or a + or a -) would be tracked contingent on the parents engaging in a selected or targeted repertoire throughout the entire interval (yes) or not (no).

In *partial-interval recording*, a specific amount of time is set for an observational period, and the interval is denoted if the target behavior occurs at any point throughout the interval. Partial-interval recording often provides overestimations of behavior occurrences for low-frequency behaviors alongside underestimations of high-frequency behaviors. However, partial-interval recording is beneficial when collecting data on multiple topographies of behaviors at the same time (e.g., A. N. Wilson et al., 2021) and when combined with other measurement systems. Partial-interval recording is a low-stakes way to start collecting data within ACT sessions, given the flexibility of the measurement system. In an ACT parent training session, using the same interval sequence (i.e., a 30-minute session divided into six 5-minute intervals), at the end of every interval, a yes or no (or a + or a -) would be tracked contingent on the parents engaging in a selected or targeted repertoire at least once during the interval (yes) or not (no).

Finally, in *momentary time sampling*, a specific amount of time is set for an observational period, and the interval is indicated if the target behavior is observed at the end of the interval. Momentary time sampling procedures are beneficial in complex environments, given the focus of behavior at the end of the interval, and can be used with other data collection procedures (e.g., Kasson & Wilson, 2017). As such, momentary time sampling is similar to partial-interval recording and is a low-stakes way to start collecting data. In an ACT parent training session, using the same interval sequence (i.e., a 30-minute session divided into six 5-minute intervals), at the end of every interval, a yes or no (or a + or a -) would be tracked contingent on the parents engaging in a selected or targeted repertoire at the end of the interval (yes) or not (no).

Measurement selection. Each type of measurement system and data collection property is critical for any behavioral service provider. It is up to us to determine which property and measurement system is selected, often as a consideration of the target and alternative behaviors of interest. For instance, if a target behavior is a low-frequency behavior, we may wish to select a continuous frequency measurement system to ensure an accurate reflection of the occurrence of behavior, given that we will have few opportunities to determine functional maintaining relationships, and low-frequency behaviors are more likely to be tracked through more sensitive and continuous measurement systems. However, if the target behavior is a high-frequency behavior, continuous frequency systems may not yield accurate outcomes (i.e., it is harder to accurately count how many times a person engages in a behavior that occurs at high rates). Similarly, if the target behavior doesn't have clear start and end topographies, frequency count may also yield invalid or unreliable data if two observers didn't agree, for example, that there were one or two instances of behavior. Finally, if the behavior doesn't occur in a way for multiple people to directly observe it (i.e., subtle behaviors, thoughts, feelings, and so on), then alternative measurement systems such as self-report, Likert scales, and psychometric surveys may be the best option for reliable data.

To highlight these points, let's return to the example of Rio and Joey. Let's say we observe Rio engage in a low-frequency behavior, where he yells at Joey to "Knock it off" or "Why can't you just stop?" But, given that it is low frequency, over the course of working with Rio for six months, we've only seen the behavior five times. Use of discontinuous measurement systems may not be appropriate given the relative rate of occurrence (or how often Rio has been observed yelling at Joey). However, use of continuous measurement systems, like frequency or duration (depending upon how long the episodes last), might be more efficacious for our intervention given how often the behavior occurs.

Similarly, let us say we decide to target Rio's engagement in child-driven play with Joey, and we arrange our parent training sessions to incorporate 20 minutes of parent-child play. We want to help Rio stay committed to playing whatever (and however) Joey wants to play, through targeting Rio's breathing/relaxation exercises taught during ACT sessions and use of positive affect and positive or neutral statements. Selecting continuous measurement systems may be useful for Rio's specific topographies or repertoires, such as the number of instances Rio completes the relaxation exercises or the number of instances Rio uses positive affect or statements.

Selecting discontinuous measures may also be useful, particularly for those repertoires that we are looking to accelerate or increase. Using a whole-interval approach may not be appropriate for measuring both play and breathing/relaxation repertoire concurrently, considering that each repertoire may be incompatible with the other. Partial-interval and momentary time sampling, however, may be useful alternatives. For instance, we might use a 5-minute interval schedule and track whether at any point during the interval Rio engages in positive affect or relaxation repertoires. Similarly, a momentary time sampling procedure could be established where, using a 5-minute interval schedule, positive affect and statements would be tracked and recorded if, at the end of the interval, Rio was engaging with Joey using positive affect and statements (i.e., if yes, score with a + or 1 in the interval and calculate percentage of intervals at the end of the session or observation period).

Data collection systems for directly observable behaviors are one thing, but what about behaviors that may not be directly observable to multiple people? What about thoughts, feelings, and other subtle behaviors that may be important to collect data on but may not be directly observable? When considering behaviors that may not be directly observable, we should first determine whether the behavior produces a physical change in the environment. If it does, then perhaps a permanent product can be targeted for data collection. If it does not, consider whether there is a corollary repertoire that occurs at the same time or close to the same space-time as the subtle behavior. If still not, then indirect measures like self-report, psychometric assessments, and related measurement systems should be considered.

Let us return to the example of Rio, who reports low motivation to spend time with his son, Joey, and often leaves the parent training session when Mom enters the room or when Joey cries or whines. The behavior analyst working with Rio has a few options to consider. They could select each of the specific topographies they observe Rio engage in with the same measurement system, including his vocal utterances (and whether they are positive or negative affect statements), walking out of the room, or moving away from the child.

To ensure a functional class of behaviors, the behavior analyst would want to identify under which environmental conditions each of those topographies occurred and, perhaps most importantly, determine whether each of the topographies resulted in the same environmental change (or whether they shared the same function). With the information provided, we can make a reasonable hypothesis that each topography may share an escape or avoidance function, in that an aversive stimulus (either the child's behavior or the task of interacting with the child) is removed (i.e., Rio physically leaves the room) or the onset of the stimulus is delayed contingent upon engaging in one of the topographies (i.e., verbal utterances to Mom and the behavior analyst).

The behavior analyst may also consider Rio's level of motivation and could use a 5-point Likert scale before each parent training session to gauge Rio's self-reported level of motivation to play with Joey. In this way, we select data collection systems that span across Rio's repertoires—both those that are directly observable and those that are more subtle (i.e., Rio's thoughts, feelings, motivation state, etc.).

Considering a New Approach

When taken together, using ACT with parents doesn't change how we approach data collection and measurement systems. Instead, the question is how to select and arrange a measurement system that will accurately and reliably produce meaningful data for both directly observable behaviors as well as subtle behaviors. The inclusion of behaviors that may not be directly observable to multiple observers is a common barrier for most when considering using ACT in their practice and particularly when using ACT within parent training contexts.

Perhaps one way through such a barrier is to reconsider our approach to data collection and measurement systems. What if how we have come to think about data collection and measurements systems is actually part of the barrier to using ACT generally and particularly within parent training contexts? I have found that it is the rigidity in our own thinking about data collection systems that precludes us from establishing creative, flexible, and reliable data collection systems that the complex natural environment calls for.

What if there was a way for us to stay within our comfort zone as behaviorists, regarding our disciplinary commitment to targeting directly observable behaviors (as observed within the same level of analysis), while at the same time making space for targeting subtle behaviors in a way that is reliable and valid? What if it wasn't about data collection systems that are "good" or "gold standard" and those that are "bad" or "for other disciplines"? Instead, what if it was about the validity and reliability of a *spectrum of measures and data collection systems* that could be used collectively and cohesively that only together would establish a completed "work of art"?

What if that approach was more in line with how an artist approaches a mixed-media abstract painting than how a chemist approaches creating a new pharmaceutical drug? What if approaching data collection as a mixed-media artist approaches a painting helped align both directly observable behaviors with subtle behaviors in a way that didn't abdicate our behavior analytic philosophical roots in empiricism, parsimony, or abjection to mentalism? Let us turn now to how we may think about such an approach, and how we may engage our work like a mixed-media artist in order to ensure that our data reflects the whole person we are working with.

Multimodal Data Collection Systems: A Layering Approach

Mixed-media artists often approach each piece of work by layering various media—paint, gesso, fabric, paper, and other materials. As the artist continues to layer each medium on top of the previous medium, the work of art unfolds. But mixed-media work isn't only about layering; it is also about removing or taking away material. The mixed-media artist dances between adding on and taking away, adding on, taking away, adding on, and so forth. The final product is often multifaceted, so much so that the first layer (or even the third or tenth layer) may not be directly visible to the audience. At the same time, the final product isn't about a single layer but rather the piece as a collective whole.

How then can we approach data collection like an artist creating a work of art? What if considering the whole person, including both directly observable and subtle behaviors, could be accomplished if we reconsidered our data collection approach—moving it away from a static perspective to a more fluid perspective? Perhaps by layering various types of data collection and measurement systems, we may better reflect the whole person sitting in front of us. A layered data collection approach may assist us with adding or removing data collection systems as needed, ensuring a contextualized data collection approach. All of this works together toward our goal of answering this question: How do I know that what I am doing is working?

A layering approach can be considered across various media: the fundamental property of the data collected (i.e., repeatability, temporal extent, and temporal locus, as discussed above), the target behavior(s) selected for data tracking, and the measurement systems selected. Regardless of the layering approach considered, it is critical to acknowledge the potential threats to internal validity by using multiple measures. The proposed data collection approach—selecting multiple measures across various dimensions of behavior—can be helpful for identifying or checking the validity and reliability of the measures. And yet, if we take a "let's track everything including the kitchen sink" approach when selecting multiple measures, we run a greater risk of finding something even if there is *nothing* to be found—that is, the more measures we include just to check to see what changes may actually increase our type 1 error rate. As a result, it is prudent to ensure the measures that we select align directly with the targets the parents identify as relevant and important, in addition to being linked to at least one component of the intervention (Bloom et al., 2006, pp. 307–309).

It may be equally prudent to arrange selected measures and measurement systems into a hierarchy of sorts, to denote primary variables of interest. For example, in Rio's case, the direct observation measures of Rio's engagement with Joey and the use of positive affect should be considered a primary variable, given the presenting challenges and concerns raised by Rio and supported by direct observation. However, Rio's subtle behaviors, like his thoughts and feelings, may be equally important to either Rio or the behavior analyst attempting to establish behavior-behavior relations. In this way, the behavior analyst may use multiple measures, including continuous and discontinuous data collection systems as well as a form of self-report or rating scale.

Layering by Types of Data Collection Systems

Layering by type of data (see also figure 4.2) can be considered across the continuum of proper-ties of data. Each data collection approach represented in the triangle is considered across rec-ommended use—from the bottom of the triangle supporting highly recommended data collection systems to the top of the triangle supporting minimally recommended systems. From a strict behavioral orientation, direct observation either obtained by the behavior analyst or by training others to collect data is the hallmark of quality and competent behavior analytic prac-tice. All approaches to data collection must include some aspect of direct observation, even if the person who is experiencing or engaging in the behavior is the one recording the informa-tion (i.e., direct observation of subtle behaviors through self-report).

Self-report and other forms of individualized rating scales are common measurement systems for behaviors that may not be directly observable or for behaviors that may occur in environments to which we may not have direct access for observation. Self-report is often con-sidered by using both quantitative approaches (i.e., tracking the number of times a behavior occurs, the duration of the behavior, etc.) and qualitative approaches (i.e., Likert scales). Likert scales typically involve asking the individual a specific question about their experience—for example, "How believable are your thoughts?" or "How intense was your urge/craving to do a specific behavior?"—and then aligning their response to a scale (e.g., 0 = not applicable, 1 = not at all believable, 2 = somewhat believable, 3 = very believable). These approaches can be helpful to achieve reliability of parental report, when used consistently over time in conjunction with other data collection approaches.

Other measurement options are psychometric surveys or assessments, such as the Parental Acceptance Questionnaire (6-PAQ; Greene et al., 2015), Valued Living Questionnaire (K. G.

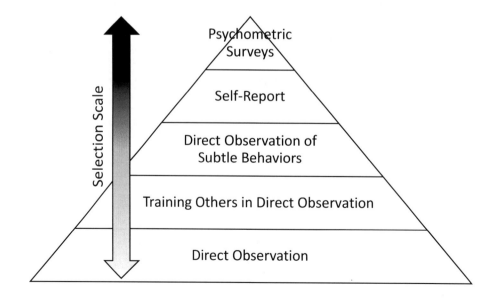

Figure 4.2

Wilson et al., 2010), the Mindfulness Attention and Awareness Scale (Brown & Ryan, 2003), or Everyday Psychological Inflexibility Checklist (EPIC; Thompson et al., 2019). Obviously, this is not an extensive list but rather common psychometric tools that have been validated.

While psychometric tools are available, and heavily relied upon in other human service disciplines like social work and clinical psychology, behavior analysts often shy away from these tools because of their lack of direct reliability and omission of directly observable behavioral properties. This is why psychometric tools are listed at the top of the triangle in figure 4.2—not only to signal their availability but also to suggest that they should be used sparingly.

Layering by target behavior(s). Another consideration is to layer data collection systems by target behavior(s). In an ACT context, this can be considered the response topographies engaged in by the parents that align with experiential avoidance or topographies in conflict with the parents' value systems (e.g., minimal adherence to implementing a behavior intervention plan). To layer these target behaviors is to consider not only the topography of a behavior or response class considered "maladaptive," but also to consider how those response patterns align with the various ACT components (i.e., I/here/now repertoires, values-based patterns of actions, acceptance vs. avoidance repertoires, etc.). For instance, nonadherence to a treatment plan may be selected as the target behavior. If we layer other behaviors, we may also include present moment repertoires (such as I/here/now repertoires and relaxation skills), values-based patterns of actions (such as asking for help and completing the homework assigned following parent training sessions), or acceptance (such as approaching aversive stimuli, e.g., their child's engagement in tantrums or property destruction, by implementing aspects of the behavior plan).

There are many ways to consider layering data collection and measurement systems. For simplicity, I will discuss these approaches as single systems and multimodal (including simple and complex) data collection systems.

Single-system data collection. Single systems include one type of data property (i.e., repeatability, temporal extent, or temporal locus) collected either within sessions or between sessions. For instance, we may target how often a parent provides access to a toy after her child demands (or requests) the toy. Doing so would constitute implementation of a single-system data collection where one behavior (provision of a reinforcer, or the toy, following appropriate request) is tracked through a continuous measurement system (i.e., frequency count). We may add to this single-system approach by tracking whether the parent ignores the child's tantrum (i.e., extinction schedule) in addition to the provision of a toy following the child's request for the toy (i.e., reinforcement FR1 schedule). This would also be an example of a single-system data collection approach given that both data collection procedures rely on repeatability (i.e., frequency) and use the same measurement system (continuous) during sessions.

Multimodal data collection systems. Multimodal data collection systems include additional properties of data, measurement approaches, and when the data is collected (i.e., between and/or within sessions). *Multimodal simple systems* include two or more data collection strategies targeted either between or within sessions. We may use multimodal simple data collection systems if we target parent implementation of differential reinforcement of the child's requests for the toys (two behaviors considered here: provision of reinforcement, or the toy, and ignoring child maladaptive behaviors to access the toy), and we may add to this by targeting parent provision of noncontingent or response-independent reinforcers on a 10-minute schedule. Each of these measurement systems can be strategically implemented either during the training sessions (i.e., within session) or in between training sessions (i.e., between sessions). We would consider this approach a multimodal simple data collection approach if we were only targeting a few behaviors in one context.

When multiple data collection strategies are targeted across two or more dimensions (such as during and between ACT sessions), *multimodal complex systems* are targeted. Complex systems incorporate additional target behaviors and measurements, across directly observable and self-report measures. If the same behavior analyst took the same data approach as described above, but now asked the parent to collect data on her implementation of both differential reinforcement and noncontingent reinforcement provision between sessions, a multimodal complex system may be functioning. The main difference across these various data collection systems is the extent to which we can layer by adding and subsequently removing or adjusting various data or measurement systems. The ability to layer and determine which property and measurement system is sensitive enough to identify behavioral changes across the whole person is key to determining the extent to which ACT is effective as an intervention strategy, particularly when targeting subtle behaviors that may not be directly observable to multiple observers.

Multimodal data collection systems address the *when* (between sessions or during sessions), the *what* (subtle or directly observable behaviors), and the *how* (data properties and measurement systems; see also figure 4.3). Between-session data collection occurs outside or in between sessions and is not necessarily environmentally specific. For instance, if parent training sessions take place in the home, between-session data may be collected both in the home in between sessions in addition to at the park or at a friend or family member's home. Within-session data collection occurs during the training or intervention session, usually from the start of the session to the end. When selecting the type of data to track, it is critical to consider the overall goals of sessions, the extent to which the behavior of interest is directly observable (either through corollary behaviors or through direct observation), or whether the behavior occurs at a level that is not necessarily directly observable to multiple observers (i.e., subtle behaviors).

When thinking about behaviors to select, when to collect data, and how to arrange a measurement system, any behavior that can be measured between sessions should also be measured within sessions at some level of analysis (using as weak or as empirically validated measurement systems as appropriate). Take, for example, a parent who struggles to implement a redirection procedure when her child screams for a toy or a snack. We may target redirection implementation both within session (tracked through direct observation) and between sessions (tracked

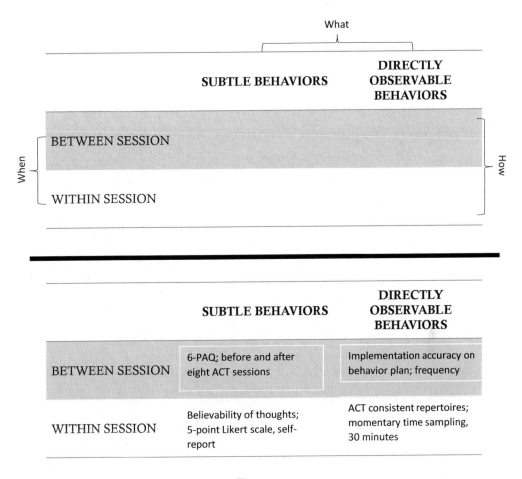

Figure 4.3

through parent self-report). However, it is important to also ask the parent about subtle behaviors that may arise after the child screams that may limit her implementation of redirection. In this instance, we may also track the parent's thoughts or other subtle behaviors between sessions through parent self-report and completion of a Likert scale (i.e., how believable were your thoughts to give in to your child when they screamed, using a scale from 1 = not at all, 3 = somewhat believable, to 5 = extremely believable). Similarly, we may want to target the parent's ACT-consistent repertoires using either a continuous (i.e., frequency) or discontinuous (i.e., partial- or whole-interval recording) measure between or within sessions. In this way, we have a plethora of data properties and collection approaches to select from in order to assess the effectiveness of their intervention across multiple contexts and situations.

When using multimodal data collection systems, it is imperative to consider potential barriers to data collection across subtle behaviors and directly observable behaviors. Prior to creating any measurement system, always ask yourself these questions:

- Who will be responsible for collecting data? If the parents, how will I train them to ensure accurate data collection?

- Can I reliably collect data on a subtle behavior while also delivering a training session?

- How complicated does the data collection system need to be? Will frequency or duration suffice? Will interval recording result in more accurate data?

- How reliable and valid will this data be? How will I trust it after it has been collected?

Using figure 4.3 can help you with visualizing the data collection and measurement approach prior to collecting any data. Filling out each section will assist you in determining what is important information to gather, and then when, how, and who will collect it. The figure can also help with visually identifying what *not* to do clinically. If you are not dually credentialed (i.e., BCBA plus clinical psychologist, licensed clinical social worker, marriage and family therapist, etc.), and you notice that you are planning to only target subtle behaviors through indirect measurements (such as self-report or psychometric surveys) without any inclusion of directly observable behaviors, that is your cue to stop and think critically about what you are doing. Ask yourself, *How am I keeping aligned with my behavior analytic roots, my ethical code of conduct, and my scope of practice and training history? Why aren't I collecting directly observable behaviors?*

When you notice more focus on indirect measures and subtle behaviors without directly observable behaviors, kindly go back to the drawing board and reassess; see whether you can add a directly observable behavior to measure either between or within sessions to supplement the targeted subtle behaviors. See whether you can pick up corollary behaviors or repertoires that align with the targeted subtle behaviors. We should never omit directly observable behaviors, given our scope of practice and competence. (See also chapter 3 on ethical considerations.)

How to Arrange Session Structure to Ensure Data Collection

While we rely on data to make clinical decisions, it is striking how many practicing behavior analysts I encounter who do not always take data, particularly when they start using ACT in their practice. I have conducted countless ACT workshops and consultation follow-up sessions where behavior analysts come back and report that they do not know what data to collect, how to collect it, or how to use data to analyze their intervention approaches. This could be a result of a range of factors, from the property of the target behavior itself (i.e., subtle behavior that may not be directly observable to multiple observers) to our own rules around how taking data during an ACT session is "too hard." If you find yourself reacting in a similar way, here are some quick tips and recommendations for arranging your ACT sessions to ensure accurate and valid data can be and is collected.

Consider the type of measurement approach you will use. Before you begin any ACT intervention, consider the approach you will use. Will you start with single-system data collection and build it over time into a multimodal system? Will you start with a multimodal simple system by targeting within-session data collection first? When considering which approach to take, consider the environment and the target behavior(s). Who will be taking the data, you or one of your supervisees (i.e., behavior tech or assistant behavior analyst, or Registered Behavior Tech)? Will you be having the parents take data between sessions? If so, make sure you build in time to train the parents on how to collect the information and how to conduct validity checks throughout the data collection period.

Think about session arrangement to enable data collection. Next, think about how you will arrange your session to ensure you collect some type of data, whether it be a fundamental data property (i.e., repeatability, temporal extent, or temporal locus), self-report data, or a measurement collection system (i.e., continuous or discontinuous). Are you a data collection ninja, so multimodal complex systems are not that complicated for you? Or are you a data collection apprentice early in your experience and you juggle taking data with intervention implementation? Take a moment to reflect openly and honestly on your data collection experiences, and what you want to use your data for; doing so will help you find a "sweet spot" where you can start with data collection.

One of the things I often hear when training behavior analysts is how data collection becomes increasingly challenging when they are implementing an independent variable or intervention strategy that they are not confident with yet. In an ACT context, often this is reported as "I can only focus on either implementing ACT or taking data; I can't do both" or "I don't really need to worry about what I am doing in the ACT session, so I won't take any data during that time."

Start small. If you also find yourself having similar reflections or experiences, consider identifying a small or single approach to collecting data when using ACT. For instance, perhaps the entire ACT session can serve as a single interval, where at the end of the session you may track the parent's engagement in deictic (I/here/now) relations, by responding to a Likert scale of 1 = not at all, 2 = somewhat, to 3 = more than 90% of the session. At the end of your session, you would identify on the scale whether the parent was engaging in the deictic relation. Or, you may also ask the parent to complete a similar Likert scale at the end of the session, to respond to questions such as "How confident or comfortable were you with X (where X can be whatever the target was from the ACT session)?"

Is this type of data collection the best possible way to measure this parent's engagement in I/here/now relations or other behavioral repertoires? Probably not. However, it will guide your behavior toward data collection as a starting point. From here, you can start to build in more frequent intervals (i.e., 10 minutes to 5 minutes to 1 minute) and more directly observable behaviors that can be measured by frequency, duration, or temporal locus.

Consider how data collection systems align. Finally, consider how the data collection system aligns with other data systems already being collected for the child or parent behavior(s). In this way, you will want to ensure that the information you gather, either between- or within-session data collection, can add to or supplement the data already being collected. Consider the mixed-media artist and approach the additional data collection systems similarly. Is the data you are going to collect adding value to what you are already collecting? How will the additional data supplement the overall picture or whole-person analysis of the intervention? Most importantly, how will you know whether the ACT intervention is effective?

Conclusion

When taken together, this chapter proposes an alternative approach to considering what, how, and when to collect information about a range of behaviors using various types of data collection approaches. When we consider how to collect data like a mixed-media artist, we may start to approach data collection as an art form that can ebb and flow as needed for each client, parent, and family system. In this way, just like painting or other art forms, we may find flexibility in creativity and an openness to exploring and considering new measurement systems or types of data. It will become easier to collect data across various topographies and dimensions, in addition to between or within sessions. Evoking such creativity, particularly when considering a simple or complex multimodal data collection system, will have other broadening effects, including how we conceptualize the parent's behavioral repertoires outside of session and outside of target and alternative behaviors.

Always ask yourself these fundamental questions when considering data collection and measurement systems, particularly when targeting subtle behaviors:

- How will I determine whether what I am doing is effective?

- How will I use visual analyses to identify changes in data patterns?

- How will changes in data patterns correspond with my intervention or environmental manipulation?

- How will I show evidence that, when and only when my intervention is in place, behavior change occurs?

- How can I make sense of the collected data, knowing that the world is often messy, uncontrolled, and imperfect?

Approaching data collection like a mixed-media artist gives us flexibility to adapt to the messy world around us. Using multimodal data collection systems helps us add to and subtract from our data collection approaches. This better supports us as we seek to effectively determine that the intervention we are implementing is the variable that is causing the change we are observing. While direct observation is the gold standard in behavior analysis, we can make room for other types of data, such as self-report, to supplement the direct observation data. Regardless of what other behavioral data is collected, direct observation must be included in any behavior analytic clinical approach to ACT. When using multimodal data collection systems, it is not enough to collect data just to see whether one of the measures shows change. It is possible to conclude that the selected intervention was effective if only some of the measurement systems show change over time (Bloom et al., 2006, p. 309).

Finally, remember that single-subject designs are not reserved only for clinical research—they were designed for clinical practice. Using any single-subject design can be helpful to interpret the effects of an intervention through prediction, verification, and replication. We can use single-subject designs to show that our intervention is what causes the change in the dependent variable. When using ACT with parents, it is critical to be able to show that the intervention is effective. Single-subject designs are like the canvas for our mixed-media artwork.

CHAPTER 5

Getting Started

Behavior analysts eager to use ACT may be tempted to take a training or two and then immediately jump right into using it in their practice. As a result, they may skip steps within the process such as developing rationales for treatment selection, assessment and data collection considerations, or case conceptualization strategies. For instance, new clinicians may return from an ACT skill-building workshop and immediately use a matrix with their client the next day, skipping over necessary steps to ensure scope of competence and ethical delivery of intervention. Similarly, they may struggle with influencing behavior change following parent training, and may argue (as I've heard many say) that "the behavior skills training didn't change the parents' implementation of the plan, so maybe if I use ACT they will change," without any further exploration or examination into the nuances of the parent-child context, relationship, environment, behavior plan, and other important factors. They may not explore the extent to which the parents' omission of various aspects of a behavior plan is the result of treatment integrity or treatment nonadherence variables prior to implementing ACT. They may not examine the training environment or the number of times they provide parents with appetitive rather than corrective—and potentially aversive—stimuli.

While such an approach to using ACT in practice may be supported within the literature, it is the omission of various case conceptualization steps that may hinder new clinicians from implementing a treatment model like ACT. Therefore, this chapter will provide guidance on where to start and what to consider when infusing ACT into behavior analytic parent training and coaching contexts.

The first place to start before implementing ACT is to examine environmental variables that establish and potentially maintain specific topographies or repertoires across a variety of contexts (e.g., parent observation in the home or clinic). To this end, the following ten steps have been established to facilitate preparedness prior to using ACT with the parent: identify current parent training components, identify parental target repertoires, operationalize parental needs and behaviors, identify and establish functional replacement behaviors, determine how to use ACT, create metaphors and experiential exercises, determine session framework and how to run ACT sessions, return to case conceptualization often, and determine how to arrange your own behavior during ACT sessions. Let us examine each of these steps more closely.

Step 1: Identify Current Parent Training Components

As discussed in chapters 1 and 2, research suggests that targeting positive parent-child interactions, practicing program components with their child, and targeting discipline consistency have large effects on parental treatment adherence outcomes (Kaminski et al., 2008). Similarly, behavior analytic research on parent training programs have found that exposure to basic foundations and core behavior analytic principles like reinforcement and punishment also increase parent treatment adherence (Yi & Dixon, 2020). When considering these outcomes in your own parent training programs, critically evaluate the parent training programs you've used with the parents to date, asking these questions:

- What type of parent training do you currently practice—treatment implementation, parental support, or a combination of both?

- Do you already start your parent training sessions with basic foundational knowledge of core behavior analytic principles, like reinforcement, extinction, and punishment?

- Have you arranged the environment in a way to increase the probability that the parents will use the developed treatment plan?

- Have you arranged the environment specifically for the parents by identifying their motivation for treatment adherence?

- Have you held training sessions—both one-on-one between the parents and yourself or another trainer, and sessions that require parents to practice with their child?

If you have not considered some of these situational variables, consider starting here first.

Step 2: Identify Parental Target Repertoires: Treatment Adherence and Beyond

It is also critical that you determine parental target repertoires early in the process. While parent training tends to be focused on treatment adherence and behavior plan implementation, it will be important to consider other aspects that influence each parent as a whole person beyond their adherence to a treatment plan. Consider the parent-child relationship: the parents' overall health and well-being (e.g., Do they have chronic pain or illness?), ecological environment (e.g., Are the parents doing everything for everyone in the house and leaving little time for self-care?), and similar issues. During parent training, you can target many different repertoires that reach beyond treatment adherence.

That said, treatment adherence is often the primary reason why you may be brought in to work with parents. Therefore, it is important that you differentiate between treatment integrity and treatment adherence before you begin assessment or ACT intervention strategies. *Treatment integrity* can be considered as the precise delivery of a treatment or behavior plan by the parents. If there are ten steps in a behavior plan, then the parents would need to engage in those ten steps, often in the same order, at each opportunity. *Treatment adherence*, on the other hand, is the consistent implementation of a treatment or behavior plan by the parents. Treatment adherence deals with the parents' continued implementation of the treatment or behavior plan rather than their completion of each step or behavior within the treatment plan.

It may be helpful to consider treatment integrity and treatment adherence outside of a clinical context. Take, as an example, a chef teaching a group of commis chefs (i.e., chefs in training) how to bake a cake. The chef may give the commis chefs a recipe that details step-by-step how to bake a specific cake. The chef may also require the commis chefs to observe how to complete each step and may provide opportunities for the commis chefs to practice before being responsible for baking a cake for a customer. For the most part, the commis chefs must follow the recipe in order for the ingredients to eventually become a cake. If they omit the leavening, the cake may not rise; if they add sugar before putting the cake in the oven, the sugar will not be mixed in correctly; if they add additional seasonings or substitutes, the flavor profile of the cake will not be consistent; if they set the oven to 175°F rather than the prescribed 350°F, the cake will not be done baking after 30 minutes. In each of these steps, the emphasis is on the order of the steps required to produce the chef's cake at the end. In all the examples provided, we would say the chef has weak treatment integrity if he observed any of the commis chefs engaging in these errors of omission or commission.

Treatment adherence would be considered how often or how many times a week or month the commis chefs bake the cake. If commis chefs were instructed to bake a cake every day of the week, but they only did so on Monday and Friday, then we would say the chef has weak treatment adherence (since the commis chefs only baked a cake two out of seven possible days). The commis chefs could bake three cakes on Monday and four cakes on Friday to get to a total of seven cakes, but given that they did not bake one per day, they would not have met the requirement of baking a cake every day. The error is adherence to *when* the cakes are made rather than *how* the cakes are made.

When you think about this within your clinical practice, consider variables that may signal deficits or strengths across treatment integrity or treatment adherence issues. Table 5.1 provides a handful of variables to consider, but it is not an exhaustive list. However, you may use these as a starting point to identify parental repertoires that align with treatment integrity deficits or treatment adherence deficits before designing an ACT session.

Table 5.1: *Parental Treatment Integrity (I) and Treatment Adherence (A) Considerations*

CONSIDER	Y/N	NEXT STEPS
Can the parents implement all the steps in the plan? (I)		
Do the parents know when to implement the plan? (I)		
Are there environmental stimuli to evoke implementation? (I)		
Are there any implementation barriers such as response effort, magnitude and related parameters of reinforcers, reinforcement/punishment schedules? (I)		
Do the parents implement the plan without consultant present? (A)		
Do the parents implement other plans as prescribed? (A)		
Are there environmental barriers limiting the implementation of the plan? (I/A)		
Does the parents' verbal behavior about the plan correspond to the plan? (A)		

For example, if a parent says to you, "I didn't have time to run your plan this week; I was just too busy," this might be an indicator for you to consider how the environment is currently arranged and whether additional modifications are needed to increase parental implementation (e.g., visual reminders when to use the plan, additional skills training to help the parent engage in the new skills when contacting aversive stimuli). Similarly, if a parent says to you, "I thought I knew how to do it, but when I tried after you left, I wasn't sure. We ended up just doing what we normally do rather than do your plan wrong," this too would be an indicator for treatment integrity skill building. Returning to training sessions with the child may be all that is needed to increase parental implementation.

However, when a parent states, "I feel like you are taking away my right to be a parent. You keep telling me I can't parent my kids the way my parents raised me" or "I didn't use that reward system this week, because my child doesn't deserve rewards," this would indicate a treatment adherence deficit. There may be something else that is getting in the way of the parent implementing the plan—perhaps the parent's rules derived from their lived experience. In the latter two examples, the parent's thoughts and feelings may be limiting or impeding the implementation of the behavior plan and not necessarily a deficit in how to implement the plan.

Step 3: Operationalize Parental Needs and Behaviors

After identifying appropriate repertoires to target during sessions, the next step is to consider how to set up ACT within your parent training work. What makes you consider using ACT for this parent or parents? What are the repertoires of interest (e.g., the behaviors that don't seem to align with treatment goals, parental commitments to doing the work with their child, helping the parents find alternative coping strategies to reduce their stress, etc.)? What are the strengths of the parents (i.e., the behaviors that align with treatment goals that are beneficial for both the parents and the child)?

When considering the "why" here, it is critical to operationalize or define the overall goal of working with the parents. Is the goal to train them how to use a specific behavior intervention plan in a specific setting or for a specific behavior? Is the goal to train them on expanding their repertoire toward a more flexible approach to parenting in general? Or is the goal to help the parents establish a more meaningful relationship with their child? Remember, parent nonadherence to a treatment plan is an important aspect for parent training, but it is far from the only or most important aspect of training. Addressing aspects related to the parental and family system will help establish person-centered goals.

After considering parental target repertoires, it is equally important to consider shaping alternative behaviors or repertoires that are flexible and include multiple topographies rather than single responses. Research has shown that repertoires that include multiple topographies are more likely to be resistant to extinction (i.e., Diaz-Salvat et al., 2020) and therefore are more likely to persist even without provision of immediate reinforcement. Ask yourself these questions: *What are the conditions under which this repertoire exists currently with the parents? What conditions are needed to shape or maintain this repertoire?* If you can't establish these, consider targeting them first during assessment.

Parent-child engagement.
A common parent training focus is on the parent-child relationship, and how the parents engage with the child. For some parents, it can be challenging to engage with their child, particularly if their child is nonvocal or communicates in different ways than their siblings or age-matched peers. Similarly, it may be challenging for parents to fully show up to their teenager's emotions or feelings about something they consider mundane or irrelevant. And for still others, it may be challenging to remain neutral when interacting with their child, particularly when called to do so outside of the privacy of their home. Parent engagement is a broad, overarching operant that encapsulates anything the parents may do that increases the child attending to, and interacting with, the parents and other environmental aspects shared by the parents. Among other things, repertoires may include parenting style, parental responses to child behaviors, and parental affect or tone with the child. Such repertoires can be considered as starting points to help parents enhance their relationships with their child/children.

Parental nonadherence.
Most plans you create are implemented by individuals like parents and caregivers who have no formal training in behavior analysis. When parents don't adhere to implementing a child's plan, a myriad of outcomes can occur—from inadvertently reinforcing a target behavior on a variable schedule (e.g., sometimes the parent may give in and give the toy back to the child or remove a demand to clean their room when the child cries, and at other times crying does not gain access to those events) to using variable punishment schedules (e.g., the parents may adhere and avoid using reprimands when the child cries, and sometimes the parent will reprimand the child when they cry). In either instance, the child learns that sometimes crying will get them what they are looking for, like an item or escape from a household duty, and other times crying will get them into trouble (i.e., reprimand). In both cases, the parents' nonadherence to implementing the plan will inadvertently impact the degree to which the child engages in more adaptive and functional repertoires rather than crying.

The topography of nonadherence is more nuanced than the sole repertoire of "not implementing the plan correctly." For example, parents may completely reject behavior analytic strategies and therefore only adhere to medication regimens or nutrition plans (i.e., avoiding specific foods, eating at specific times throughout the day, etc.), but fail to require their child take their medications daily. Similarly, parents may believe that they need to reprimand their child because "withholding attention" won't teach them anything and may withhold their attention for other behaviors beyond what is targeted in the intervention plan.

When considering parental nonadherence, it is critical to consider whether part of the parental repertoire of interest aligns with errors of commission or errors of omission. *Errors of commission* occur when parents do something that should not have been done or behave in a way that deviates from the implementation plan. For instance, if a plan states to block a child's throwing behavior, and the parents block the child from throwing yet also reprimand the child in the process, doing so would be an error of commission. The parents' behavior is aligned with engaging in a behavior that is not outlined in the treatment plan and therefore should not have been done.

Parents may also add additional steps or variables into a treatment plan without discussing with or getting agreement from the behavior analyst first. For example, if parents believe the child must be told what they are doing is wrong, they may say things like "Your brother doesn't behave this way" or "You know, you won't be getting anything if you continue to act this way." Similarly, parents may start to take privileges away if the child doesn't change their behavior. While each varying topography will yield a similar outcome (i.e., poor treatment adherence), some may require a different or unique approach during training.

Errors of omission, on the other hand, occur when parents do not execute one or more aspects of an implementation plan. For instance, if the same plan is used (to block a child's throwing behavior), the parents may or may not block the child's throwing behavior. Here, there may be a range of environmental variables that precluded the parents from engaging in the implementation plan: Was the child too far away from the parents to realistically expect them to block the throwing? Did the parents see the child before the throwing occurred? Or was there subtle behavior (e.g., fear of hurting the child) that prevented the parents from blocking the child's throwing?

Implementation drift is another nonadherence issue that can sometimes occur when parents are observed following the plan with a high degree of accuracy, and over time begin to revert back to old patterns of behaviors that do not align within the intervention plan. Often implementation drift occurs following a period without direct consultation or training. Common examples include when parents are trained to fade out a prompt hierarchy for washing hands and continue to fade prompts even though the skill of washing hands is not consistent (e.g., soap is still on the child's hands, and the parents move on to the next step in the process rather than prompt the skill of washing the soap off).

Another example of parental nonadherence is when parents follow the plan when the behavior analyst is present, yet they do not implement the plan between sessions. Here, parents will adhere to the intervention plan with a high degree of fidelity during sessions and may even express to the behavior analyst how comfortable or confident they are with implementing the plan. However, when the parents are alone and are expected to continue the intervention plan, they engage in repertoires other than the targeted implementation repertoire. The behavior analyst may notice that, during sessions, the child's target behavior rarely occurs, yet between sessions the behavior occurs at higher and stable rates. Data collection can be helpful in identifying potential parental nonadherence, particularly during sessions when the behavior analyst is not present.

Parent identification of subtle behaviors. When considering parental implementation errors, another variable to consider is the extent to which subtle behaviors (i.e., thoughts, feelings, etc.) may influence parental responding. Subtle behaviors can and should be directly targeted during the assessment phase of the process, and they are important to consider when beginning to operationalize parental nonadherence. Take the following example: A BCBA is working with Mary on implementing a response-interruption and redirection procedure. Whenever her child engages in skin picking, Mary is to block the picking and immediately present a series of high-probability demands that involve actions with the hands (e.g., sit on your hands, wiggle your fingers, put your fingers in the sandbox, etc.). Mary can complete all steps in the behavior plan with the BCBA during role-plays but fails to complete the majority of the steps during sessions with her child. When Mary is asked what she experiences when the child starts to skin pick, she reports that her heart races, and she thinks about how she now must do something about it. She reports that it is hard to think about what the child can do with her hands, and that all she can think about is to say, "Stop picking your skin."

This example with Mary highlights the potential role of subtle behavior that should be considered during the operationalizing phase. We do not have direct access to observe Mary's increased heart rate (without the use of a heart-rate monitor), nor do we have direct observable access to Mary's thoughts about what to do or what to say or not say. We can, however, observe corollary response patterns (see also chapters 1 and 2) or behaviors that occur at the same time as the reported subtle behaviors. Mary reports that these subtle behaviors occur at the onset of the child's skin picking, which gives the behavior analyst a clue as to when to start to observe Mary. Upon closer attention, Mary is observed pacing around the room before the child skin picks, and during the time in which the procedure should be implemented, Mary's behavior changes to include more mumbling or low talking, heavy breathing, walking in and out of rooms, or fidgeting with hands, fingers, feet, legs, or body (swaying back and forth when standing). These topographies can be brought into the assessment and training phases for further operational refinement and subsequent analysis.

Something to consider when we start to include subtle behaviors into our analyses is the boundary we establish with each parent and the goals of our work together. In my experience, when we start talking with parents about what they think or feel and we show up to their answers in nonjudgmental ways, we begin to establish ourselves as conditioned reinforcers. This may lead to the parent sharing more about their experiences beyond their implementation of a behavior plan or engaging their child at the park. As the professional relationship develops and a therapeutic relationship is cultivated, the parents may begin to share more and more about other tangential experiences or subtle behaviors with us. As the parents share, it is critical to remember that, unless we are trained and licensed to do so, we are not conducting psychotherapy and therefore should not be using ACT as a talk-therapy approach (see also chapter 3). In this way, we will consider the context around the content of the subtle behaviors, or why the parents are sharing or disclosing the information.

Operationalizing parent repertoires that will be targeted during training sessions should be aligned with the overall goals of our work with the parents. After target and alternative behaviors are identified and operationalized, a data collection strategy should be identified (see chapter 4). Without the data collection strategy, it will be impossible to determine how to use ACT. Once a measurement system is decided upon, configure how to use ACT and what ACT sessions will look like.

Step 4: Identify and Establish Functional Replacement Behaviors

Identifying and establishing a functional replacement behavior prior to using any type of exposure-based activity will increase the effectiveness of your ACT sessions. Functional replacement behaviors can be simple, like deep breathing, or more complex behaviors, like communicating to another parent the need for a break and physically walking out of the environment. While this will be covered in detail in later chapters, particularly those emphasizing deictic repertoires, the main point here is to highlight that without appropriate and functional replacement behaviors already in the parents' repertoire before starting any exposure-based intervention or activities, you are setting up the parents for failure.

Step 5: Determine How to Use ACT

Once you identify and operationalize parent behavior, next consider how you will use ACT in your work with the parents. In what way do you plan to use ACT in your sessions with the parents? Do you plan to use ACT language to help increase parental motivation toward treatment adherence? Do you plan to use ACT along with other behavior analytic strategies like behavior skill training? Or are you going to have specific ACT sessions, where you will use ACT-related metaphors and exercises to help parents adhere to various treatment plans? Answers to these questions will influence both how you arrange your ACT sessions and also how you will conceptualize how ACT will influence parental behaviors.

Similarly, considering session duration and frequency will assist in the development of the best approach for using ACT. For instance, it would be helpful to know how many sessions you will have with the parents each week or month, the total number of sessions the parents can afford or can access (depending on the funding source), and how long each session will be (e.g., 15 minutes vs. 30 minutes vs. 2 hours). Session duration and frequency will likely be determined based on the funding source, so it is important to consider (a) who the funder will be for the sessions (e.g., commercial insurance providers, governmental funding sources, private pay, etc.), (b) funder policy and what is covered for parent training initiatives, and (c) funder annual limits (if applicable). Each funder and each parent will have a unique benefits package and opportunity for parent training sessions, which is important to consider when determining how to use ACT in sessions.

Examining the parent and family situational context in its entirety can help you determine how best to use ACT. I like to think about three ways to use ACT in a parent training capacity: (1) using ACT as a trainer (i.e., longer time commitment and more emphasis on ACT rather than other intervention strategies), (2) using ACT as a coach (i.e., shorter time availability, smaller dose of ACT in combination with other intervention strategies), or (3) a combination of the two (i.e., combination of ACT with other intervention strategies with use of multiple session types and doses). Various factors, such as clinical service delivery model, time allocated for parent training services (usually based on funding source), and clinician scope of competence within ACT, to name a few, may determine which approach would be more appropriate. At the very least, you determine how to use ACT in sessions, based on the parent and family-specific contexts.

Step 6: Establish Metaphors and Experiential Exercises

As established in chapter 2, from an RFT perspective, metaphor and analogy are ways of relating relational networks. The key to establishing clinically relevant metaphors is to align the target network (or the network established from the parents' experience) with the vehicle network (or the created network). For instance, a parent may report to you how challenging it is for them to be a single parent. They frequently report feeling exhausted, having too much to do in a day, not having enough time to do everything, and feeling like they are constantly on the move—doing something for their children or for work but never for themselves. We may establish this network as a target network of coordination (i.e., single parenting *is* hard, *is* not having enough time, *is* being constantly on the move, *is* feeling exhausted; the Crel here is in italics for clarity). We may establish a potential metaphor by aligning similar stimulus features within another network in order to establish a vehicle network. For instance, I may say to the parent, "It sounds as though being a single parent for you is like being forced to work a job you don't really like, but the job is all day every day, and there is no paid time off or vacation time or even sick time. Does this sound like your experience?" If the parent agrees, the vehicle network may share enough stimulus functions that the two networks can be related via coordination. If the parent does not agree, then the vehicle network may not share enough functions.

If you plan to use an ACT curriculum, the metaphors will be established already, but this does not necessarily mean you don't need to think about the metaphors you will use. Not every parent will experience a metaphor in the same way, so it is critical that you consider the parents' presenting problem, lived experiences, and the target behaviors prior to selecting a metaphor.

If you plan to create your own metaphors, consider metaphors that describe either physical or abstract features of the parents' experience. Metaphors that target or describe physical features are based on formal similarities between the targeted network and the vehicle network. Here's an example:

> Bobby <u>is very slow to do just about anything</u>, <u>it takes him forever</u> to get dressed and get out the door for school. Bobby **is such a sloth**.

Here the underlined portions of the base or target metaphor represent the parents' direct experience with Bobby. The vehicle metaphor is bolded (i.e., is such a sloth) and aligns with the shared stimulus features (i.e., moves very slowly).

According to Stoddard and Afari (2014), we may establish functional metaphors through five easy steps: (1) identify the target behavior, (2) identify the function of the target behavior,

(3) identify the contextual cues and inflexibility processes, (4) identify the targeted ACT component, and (5) identify stimuli with the same functional relations to use within the metaphor. This process will help you establish hypothesized functions from which to build your metaphors and is also helpful to come back to when problem solving or when developing case conceptualization.

Step 7: Determine the Session Framework

Once you have determined how you plan to integrate ACT into your parent training, your next step is to consider the session framework. The following section is tailored for using ACT as a stand-alone intervention within parent training (i.e., ACT trainer). First, establish ACT phrases, questions, or statements to embed into various session structures. For example, questions such as "What are you noticing right now?" or "What is showing up for you?" may be helpful to prompt parents through an activity or BST training protocol.

Regardless of how you decide to use ACT in your practice, it is important to first consider the modality of your ACT sessions: Will you modify a curriculum? Will you use some of the assessment and treatment exercises in this guidebook? Will you create your own client-specific metaphors? Having a game plan before you start will help you develop what you will need during the "doing" portion of the ACT session: Do you need manipulatives? Data sheets? Worksheets for both you and the parents? Are you going to incorporate the child in the session? If so, does the child need manipulatives or worksheets?

Once you determine the modality, consider the session framework. While the session framework can certainly change across sessions and should be flexible and adaptable to meet the parents' needs, in general an evidenced-informed framework aligns with three phases: set up, do, and reflect (see figure 5.1).

Set up. When setting up the session environment, it is crucial to support an appetitive environment throughout ACT sessions. Appetitive environments produce an abundance of reinforcers that are available contingently as well as noncontingently, or free of needing to engage in a specific behavior before accessing a reinforcer. Appetitive environments often support more flexible repertoires given the abundance of reinforcers that are continually being accessed (as opposed to aversive environments that tend to narrow response patterns). To arrange an appetitive environment, it is important to understand what motivates the parents, things that are important to them, topics they enjoy discussing, and so on. How will you set up an appetitive environment with the parents? What reinforcers will you provide contingently and noncontingently? How will you ensure that your ACT sessions omit the use of coercive control? How many times are you providing a range of reinforcers to the parents and child during each session, and how might this be adapted over time to shape parent-child relationships? For some parents, it may be necessary to have an initial discussion to determine what an appetitive environment would look like for them.

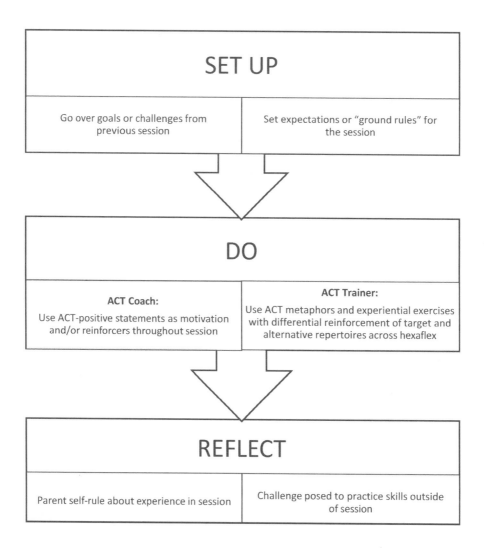

Figure 5.1

Building rapport with parents should also be an ongoing process throughout the duration of the work you do with them. Rapport is often established in clinical practice with children, where positive or appetitive stimuli (such as preferred items, activities, praise, or social connection) are paired with the behavior analyst prior to starting any work task or intervention (e.g., Shireman, Lerman, & Hillman, 2016; McLaughlin & Carr, 2005). When working with parents, however, we should consider rapport as a dynamic process that includes not only pairing preferred activities with ourselves as their behavior analyst but also other considerations such as the therapeutic alliance or working relationship. As a response class, rapport should incorporate (but is certainly not limited to) active listening, effective communication, compromise, and collaboration (rather than authoritarian communication approach), humility (or admitting mistakes), focusing on parent strengths (rather than deficits alone), and celebrating every gain no matter how small or insignificant (see also Taylor et al., 2018). Throughout your work with parents, you always want to create environments that will evoke and support a trusting, empathetic relationship between you and the parents.

After determining how you will arrange your training environment, set up some ground rules for sessions. Establishing guidelines or "rules of play" for sessions can help set expectations for both you and the parents (and child, as appropriate). When going through consent and overview of the work ahead, consider discussing what the sessions will look like (i.e., 10 minutes at the start of every parent training session once a month, or 30-minute biweekly one-on-one parent training sessions) and what the parents should expect during those sessions (e.g., emphasis on mental well-being or psychoeducation). Other inquiries should target what you will do with the information disclosed during sessions: what gets shared with the insurance funder, and what stays between you and the parents?

Do. One of the most common questions I get from new clinicians is "How many activities should I run during sessions?" Generally, we want to avoid hopping across too many metaphors or activities, while ensuring that we cover each component equally throughout the intervention period. The number of specific exercises should be derived by the session length, goals of the session, and parental strengths and target responses. Three may be too few for a 60-minute session, whereas three may be too many for a 15- or 30-minute session.

Each ACT activity or exercise should always be aligned within a behavioral skills training model, which provides the parents with some level of rationale or instructions to follow before moving into modeling and rehearsal. All ACT-related activities should be something that the parents can directly relate to and put into practice, preferably that same session. No activity or topic of discussion should be included *only to reflect upon past experiences*. Remember, we must stay within our scope of practice guidelines during training sessions. For instance, rather than talk about a metaphor or talk only about past experiences and memories (akin to more traditional psychotherapeutic or "talk therapy" approaches), we will focus our actions and intervention strategies on parental engagement in alternative repertoires across vocal/verbal and motor/physical repertoires.

Reflect. Finally, in the remaining 5 to 10 minutes of the session, it is helpful to bring the session to a close by having the parents reflect on the session: What did they experience? How was this activity or exercise helpful or different from before? Ask the parents directly to state what they learned from the session in order to help them establish or generate their own self-rules from their own experience. Avoid giving the parents a rule in order to ensure that the rule they establish is based off their own experiences rather than your own.

Posing a challenge for the parents to practice the targeted skill between sessions is another way to motivate parents to practice the newer repertoires and is established as a way that does not force or require completion. Challenges should not be high-effort tasks. Instead, they should be low-effort tasks tailored specifically on the session content and activity in order to motivate the parent to use the skill learned or acquired during session before the next ACT session.

Step 8: Conduct ACT Sessions

Before starting your ACT sessions, it can be beneficial to set up guidelines to ensure you stay within your scope of practice as a behavior analyst. To assist with this task, table 5.2 provides an overview of ACT "dos and don'ts." This is certainly not an exhaustive list, but it can be a good starting point. Having a list of things *not* to do can be as effective and profound in clinical practice as a list of things to do.

Table 5.2: *ACT Session Consideration List*

DO	DON'T
☑ Obtain active and ongoing consent.	☒ Provide psychotherapy unless trained.
☑ Create individually tailored ACT plans aligned with behavior analytic training components.	☒ Present a metaphor or exercise repeatedly to prove a point or get the parent to understand an ACT concept.
☑ Engage in active, ongoing case conceptualization following each session. Review these before each subsequent session.	☒ Give cookie-cutter ACT exercises that are not aligned to parent experience.
☑ Conduct ongoing functional assessment.	☒ Conduct functional assessment only before starting ACT.
☑ Focus on shaping broad, flexible repertoires.	☒ Shape single responses.
☑ Target functional replacement behaviors prior to exposure-based activities.	☒ Tell parents what their experience is or should be.
☑ Use ongoing reliable and valid data collection systems.	☒ Collect only data when it is convenient.
☑ Use language that parents understand.	☒ Use ACT terminology with parents.
☑ Arrange appetitive or reinforcing environments.	☒ Use coercive control.

Perhaps most importantly, you will want to ensure active and ongoing parental consent to participate in your intervention. This includes both informed consent prior to any ACT session, as detailed in chapter 3, and consent prior to each ACT exercise. For instance, parents may be hesitant to fully engage in a challenging topic or exercise, but when asked if they are willing to do so, the question alone gives them the opportunity to escape *or* lean into something that is hard (or aversive). When the parents withdraw their consent to participate in an exercise or session, we must always honor their request.

It is also critical that, unless you are trained to use psychotherapy or other forms of talk therapy, you should avoid doing it at all costs. When using ACT with parents, use active behavior-shaping techniques and approaches (i.e., behavioral skills training, functional communication training, shaping, etc.) rather than rely on talking through concepts only (i.e., "talk therapy").

At the same time, it is critical that we avoid telling parents what their experiences or subtle behaviors should be or negate their experiences or subtle behaviors. Telling parents "Don't feel that way" or "You shouldn't think that" only degrades the therapeutic alliance. Similarly, rather than telling the parents rules or statements about what they should get from the ACT session, allow them to reflect and inform you with their own words. Doing so establishes a safe environment for the parents to process their experiences as well as feel supported and validated about their experiences and subtle behaviors. It also provides an opportunity to lean in and engage in new repertoires that align with the parents' value systems, instead of behaving as we want them to.

When it comes to delivering the ACT session, it is critical to ensure we stay within our scope of practice and competency by providing function-based interventions. This necessitates assessment (and reassessment), data collection, and ongoing case conceptualization to ensure our intervention is functional. Even if we are modifying a curriculum-based ACT model, we need to be sure to individually tailor all ACT exercises and metaphors to each parent we use them with. Stock metaphors can be very impactful for parents, but it is important to adapt and ensure that the activities, follow-up questions, and discussion around the metaphors align with the parents' experiences and current situation.

Step 9: Return to Case Conceptualization Often

Active case conceptualization before and after each session is critical for ensuring that a functional intervention continues to be implemented throughout parent training. Case conceptualization should include identifying functional variables that reinforce parental nonadherence as well as identifying conditions under which parental treatment adherence is more likely to occur. Similarly, case conceptualization may also result in reassessment or ongoing functional assessment to identify functional relationships between environmental stimuli and parental treatment adherence or nonadherence. Because some of the potential target behaviors during parent training may include subtle behaviors that are not directly observable, it is critical to conduct ongoing functional assessments to ensure functional interventions (see also chapter 6).

Step 10: Arrange Your Own Behavior

Finally, and perhaps most importantly, consider how you will arrange your own behavior during session. As stated, ACT sessions are more likely to be successful if we establish appetitive (i.e., reinforcing) environments, where our clients contact more appetitive than aversive stimuli, even when we ask them to engage with aversive stimuli. To better establish appetitive environments, we must also consider the language we use during sessions. Most psychologists who train others how to use ACT in their practice often stress the importance of avoiding ACT language with clients (e.g., Luoma et al., 2007; Polk et al., 2016; K. G. Wilson, 2021). For instance, asking a parent "What do you value?" or "Can you accept the hard stuff right now to make a values-based decision?" may be counterintuitive and in opposition to taking an ACT stance.

If the goal in ACT is to allow the client or parents to experience contingencies and establish their own self-generated rules based on those experiences, then giving them words and terms to "equate" or describe their experiences can inhibit tracking (rules that are established based on how the world is arranged) or increase the likelihood of pliance (rules that are established based off of social consequences). If we arrange our words and language in a way that does not just replace the parents' rigid rules with our own rules, then we can establish environments that support the parents' whole experience.

Final Considerations

As you look toward using ACT in your parent training programming, I offer a few final considerations to explore and come back to. First, regularly check in with parents throughout your work together, as their resources, time commitments, and competing contingencies will change. Each parent and family system will have their own idiosyncratic challenges, commitments, and life situational contexts. Some parents may change employers or need to work multiple jobs to support the family. Other parents may welcome a new child or family member into the home or lose a family member following a change in marital status or death. Any life event, no matter how small or insignificant to us, will have direct consequences that will compete for the parents' time, resources, and energy. Consider building in regular check-in times throughout your time with parents, as informal or formal as you see fit (see also Taylor & Fisher, 2010, for similar discussion). Check in with parents on their commitment and willingness to continue with the parent training format, and what (if any) changes would assist them on their journey.

Conclusion

Taken together, this chapter highlights various processes and considerations to determine before moving into assessment and treatment. It is critical to remember that ACT can be a useful tool to support behavioral-based parent training programs, particularly when addressing parental treatment nonadherence. Determine which behaviors or repertoires are a result of treatment integrity or treatment adherence and can be accomplished using the same principles and approaches as those applied with the child. And yet, adherence is only the tip of the iceberg when it comes to potential parental repertoires to target. Once identified, the next step is to assess the selected repertoires.

CHAPTER 6

Assessment

Across the helping professions, assessment or evaluations of the presenting problems is essential to providing functional intervention strategies. Assessment is a critical feature of case conceptualization strategies, and functions as an information-gathering tool about a presenting problem. The primary goal of any assessment is to collect information about the environment and the presenting problem in order to establish functional relationships. The extent to which behavior-behavior or behavior-environment relationships are established rests on the validity of the approach or methods applied, the operational definitions and measurement systems used to identify the problem behavior(s), and the correspondence between the assessment and the natural environment (i.e., considering environmental factors such as setting and motivational situations when considering information gathered). Assessments are useful tools throughout the life-span of the clinical intervention, despite common clinical lore centered on assessment as only a first step clinical tool.

Assessments are essential in behavior analytic practice for at least two reasons. First, assessments can provide clinicians with a wide range of information about a selected target behavior, including (but not limited to) the frequency of behavior in the natural environment, environmental conditions that are likely to evoke engagement in the behavior, varying dimensions of target behaviors (such as rate and duration), and other factors. Second, assessments can provide clinicians with ongoing information particularly when they are used throughout a behavioral-change program (see also Kazdin, 2013, p. 95).

As behavior analysts, we use assessments to uncover functional relationships that maintain current levels of observed behavior(s). One of the core features of applied behavior analysis is the reliance on establishing functional relationships. A *functional relation* is the effect an independent variable (or aspect of the environment) has on a dependent variable (often behavior emitted that is directly observable). Said another way, functional relationships are identified when a known aspect of the world, like a stimulus object, person, or event, influences the extent to which a behavior or repertoire occurs or does not occur. Functional relations can be observed through repeated observations of the world within which the person is interacting.

The goal of assessment strategies within a parent training context should therefore include identifying what (i.e., stimuli) and how (i.e., repertoires including inflexible perspective taking, escape or avoidance, etc.) the parents respond across various environmental arrangements or contexts. Determining what stimuli or environmental situations evoke engagement in experiential avoidance, rigid rule following, inconsistent say-do correspondence, and so on is the main premise of any function-based assessment strategy and is equally critical when developing ACT interventions.

For instance, consider the parent who tells you that dealing with their child's behavioral outbursts is too hard and makes them feel like a terrible parent, so they just give in and hand the child the iPad. The parent even acknowledges that doing so goes against the behavior intervention plan, but when they give the child the iPad, the outburst stops. The *what* here is the child's behavioral outbursts (i.e., aversive stimuli), while the *how* is the parent handing the child the iPad. After the parent hands the child the iPad, the outbursts stop (i.e., removal of aversive stimuli). In this way, and only when *repeatedly observed as such*, the parent's repertoire of handing the child the iPad may be functioning on a negative reinforcement schedule in the form of escape from the child's outbursts. The emphasis here is on the repeatability of the observation.

What an assessment looks like, or the methods or approach taken during an assessment, is dependent on not only the presenting problem or targeted response class, but equally upon the approach and inquiries arranged by the behavior analyst. Each assessment selected for each parent-child context should be considered based on the quality of the empirical outcomes provided following implementation.

According to Kazdin (2013), there are two primary themes in considering quality of assessments: flexibility and rigor of the assessment. For Kazdin, *flexibility* involves "a broad range of options well beyond selecting frequency, interval, duration, and other measurement strategies.... [T]he flexibility is reflected in the conditions in which behavior is assessed and how to evoke or obtain the behavior so that it can be observed and altered by the intervention" (p. 120). Said another way, flexible assessments are developed in ways in which the environmental conditions are established to test variables that may evoke behaviors. The flexibility of an assessment is reflected by both the range of conditions and the stimuli selected prior to conducting the assessment. Furthermore, flexibility may also reflect how data is collected or the ways in which data is collected, from unobtrusive (like permanent products such as video recordings, written journal logs, computer trackers, etc.) to obtrusive (like direct observation and experimental analyses).

Take, as an example, the flexibility of a preference assessment. There are many different approaches to select from when conducting a preference assessment (i.e., multiple stimulus without replacement, DeLeon & Iwata, 1996; paired stimulus, Fisher et al., 1992; free operant duration-based assessment, Roane et al., 1998). Preference assessment conditions can be varied by time of day or preceding setting event (i.e., before or after mealtime may yield different observations of behavior toward food items), stimuli (i.e., tangible things, physical activities or behaviors, edibles, etc.), and environmental settings (i.e., school or home).

The flexibility of stimulus parameters is endless, yet other aspects of the assessment's flexibility may have harder boundaries. For instance, a preference assessment will never produce outcomes useful to identifying a reinforcer, only a hierarchy of a limited grouping of items. A reinforcer assessment will produce such outcomes, but only for stimuli considered "preferred." This distinction is critical when considering how to use preference assessments to inform synthesized analyses, as ongoing assessments can be used to enhance case conceptualization.

Assessment *rigor*, on the other hand, involves the extent to which the components of the assessment (i.e., operational definitions, measurement systems, design, interobserver agreement, and treatment fidelity measures reported) align with current standards within the discipline. For example, consider the same preference assessment discussed above. The rigor would be weak if the stimuli were placed in the same physical location at the start of each trial (i.e., book always placed on the right side regardless of stimulus options presented on the left side of the client), as doing so may result in a selection bias based on physical location rather than the stimuli itself.

Conversely, the rigor might be strong if the same multiple stimulus without replacement (MSWO) assessment procedure was replicated every day for a week to establish a hierarchy of stimuli that could be rotated as preferred options during intervention. At the very least, observations made during any assessment must have corresponding data collection systems that not only pick up on the behavioral change following exposure to an intervention or some environmental modification but also do so with empirical evidence or data (see also Kazdin, 2013).

When considered within a parent training context, the assessment strategies selected must be couched in the larger goal of treatment, the context under which the current target behavior occurs or doesn't occur, and the long-term approach to data collection and measurement systems. It is important to note that there isn't a single assessment approach that is right or wrong per se; rather, it is the type of evidence collected and analyzed over time that is considered to be of quality (or not). The goal of assessment is to collect information about the target behavior(s) in order to establish an understanding around environmental variables that may be maintaining (i.e., reinforcing) the behavior(s).

As such, this chapter does not seek to provide the "right" way or "wrong" way to conduct an assessment before using ACT. Instead, I will highlight how to approach assessment as a mixed-media artist—that is, how to both select flexible and rigorous evidence-informed assessments and focus on identifying function rather than content, concept, or form (see figure 6.1). Two pathways for assessments will be discussed: assessing parental problem or target behaviors generally (i.e., using response cost with accuracy, providing praise to child noncontingently, etc.) and specifically within an ACT model (i.e., approaching previously established aversive stimuli, escaping aversive stimuli, and say-do correspondence between vocal value statements and emitted behavior(s)/repertoires).

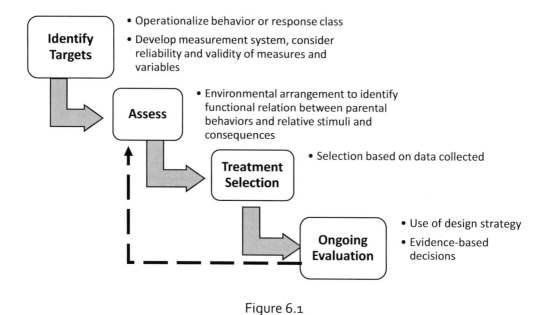

Figure 6.1

Basics in Conducting Assessment

The process of conducting assessments is idiosyncratic and sometimes straightforward. Most assessments include determining what (i.e., target and alternative repertoires), when, where, and why (i.e., functional relationships between repertoires and environment). Given that there are many different ways to answer why a behavior or repertoire is occurring, it is critical to consider fundamental aspects of the assessment process. Let us take a closer look at each these parts now.

Identify target and alternative repertoires. Before conducting any assessment, you will need to identify a target and/or alternative behavior or repertoires. Once selected, you can determine the *what* and the *how* for each repertoire. In parent training contexts, consider the parent-child interactions and relationships, parental engagement in both target and alternative repertoires, and the setting or context under which the selected behaviors will naturally occur.

For defining parent treatment nonadherence, the first step is to ask yourself these questions: *What does nonadherence look like for these parents? Do they engage in rigid rule following so the rules themselves support or reinforce the parents' engagement in nonadherence?* Considerations for operationalizing parent treatment nonadherence include rigid rule following aligned with escape or avoidance reinforcement schedules, accuracy in say-do or do-say correspondence between the behavior plan and their implementation of the behavior plan, or other corollary responses occurring when the parents report experiential avoidance situations (i.e., engaging in other parenting repertoires beyond the behavioral intervention plan to escape an unwanted situation or context). Identifying the parents' say-do correspondence between what the behavior intervention plan is and what they physically do in session may be helpful to further determine potential barriers or skill deficits.

Let us explore this further in another example. Say that a parent tells you what the behavior plan is: "I am working to help Sue regulate herself when it is time to get into the car. First, I will remind her that if she walks to the car nicely and gets inside by herself, we can listen to her music on the way to wherever we are going. I will walk behind her to the car, staying within arm's length. When Sue gets into the car without hitting me, I will celebrate with her, giving her extra love, and put on her favorite music. If she hits me, I will not provide any attention in the moment and will not turn on her favorite music during the ride."

This parent may have a high degree of say-do correspondence when completing role-play and rehearsal sessions with you, meaning they adhere to the plan most of the time. Yet, in the moment with Sue, the parent may engage in moderate or lower levels of adherence than her verbal report would suggest. In similar examples, it is important to not only rely on parental report but also to follow up with some level of direct observation to establish say-do correspondence patterns.

Determine functional relationships of target repertoires.
After operationalizing one or more target behaviors and establishing dimensional qualities (i.e., frequency, duration, etc.; see more in chapter 4), you will determine environmental conditions that may be establishing or evoking the targeted repertoires and then collect information about those repertoires across indirect, direct, and experimental means. Functional behavior assessments (FBA) comprise indirect and direct approaches for gathering information to determine aspects of the environment that are responsible for influencing a target behavior (e.g., Sugai et al., 2000). They are a critical assessment strategy to use when attempting to provide function-based intervention strategies. This step is discussed in detail in the next section.

Interestingly, experimental functional analyses are considered part of applied behavior analytic research standards, but in clinical application, behavior analysts do not always conduct experimental analyses, particularly the specific approach set forth by Iwata and colleagues (1982, 1994). Oliver and colleagues (2015) surveyed certified behavior analysts on their graduate training exposure and subsequent clinical use of functional assessment procedures. Of those who responded (5.8% response rate; 78% female), 54% reported descriptive assessments to be as useful as functional (i.e., experimental) analyses, while behavior analytic educators and professors reported targeting descriptive assessments more than experimental analyses within graduate education programs.

While behavior analysts may not be relying on experimental functional analyses in clinical practice, research to date on the predictability of descriptive assessments is mixed, with some evidence showing moderate predictability outcomes (e.g., Martens et al., 2019; Pence et al., 2009). This is important to consider when building functional assessments, particularly within parent training contexts. At the same time, it is important to consider experimental analyses to test a hypothesis about a specific condition or potential functional relation rather than as a specific methodological or procedural approach.

Determine data collection and measurement systems. Next, you will want to consider your data collection strategy to ensure that you connect what you collect during your intervention with your assessment (see also chapter 4). When we return to the analogy of the mixed-media approach in relation to our assessment strategy, we may consider both self-report and direct observational measures in a way that allows for high degrees of reliability and validity in the data being assessed.

Each assessment you select must meet a series of established criteria. Consider these questions:

- Does the assessment you select align with the target behavior or repertoire of the parents?

- Is the sensitive assessment enough to show change in a specified behavior?

- Is it rigorous enough to minimize skepticism of the outcome—that is, is the assessment valid?

- Is the assessment selected flexible for use across multiple repertoires, contexts, and/or skills?

- What do overall scores or outcomes on the assessment suggest?

- How obtrusive is the data collection system of the assessment?

- Does the assessment put the parents, child, or others at risk for harm? If yes, what is the plan to mitigate and/or stop the assessment?

Answers to these questions will help you determine which assessment strategy is best for the specific parent-child context you are working within.

Return to assessments often throughout intervention. Finally, plan when you will reassess after a period of exposure to the intervention. This can be a simple probe session considered in combination with other long-term strategies such as maintenance effects. Best practice guidelines support returning to assessments at least twice (once before and once following termination of the intervention). However, more frequent assessments can be beneficial to assist with problem solving stagnating treatment effects, and/or changing functional repertoires.

While each assessment will need to be contextualized for your specific practice setting, including funding source, identifying functional relationships and designing reliable data collection systems are the most reported barriers to implementation I come across when working with behavior analysts. Given this, the next section will highlight common strategies you can use to identify functional relationships in a natural environment (e.g., indirect, direct, and naturalistic experimental assessment strategies). This section highlights assessment options available, and how they may be applied within a parent training context generally speaking and specifically within an ACT framework. It is up to you to align your assessment with the overall goal of your parent training and to adjust each assessment approach to fit the needs of the parent and family.

Indirect Assessment Strategies

Indirect assessments, such as interviews and standardized surveys, can be useful during the information-gathering phase to identify potential environmental stimuli that occur before and/ or after the targeted repertoires. Information gathered here can be conceptualized and tested in direct assessments, such as descriptive observation and conditional probability calculations. The culmination of these steps can help inform an experimental analysis where you directly manipulate an aspect of the environment in order to measure response patterns across two or more conditions (i.e., control and test). Indirect assessments take an information-gathering approach to determine potentially context-limiting or context-broadening environments and corresponding target repertoires. Oftentimes, such assessments incorporate self-reporting of past experiences by the client or parents. It is important to remember that this data shouldn't be the only information you collect; rather, this is only a first step in gathering information that will be used to inform the next phase of the assessment process.

Common indirect assessments include some aspect of an interview, either open-ended or through selective questions or statements (i.e., psychometric assessments). Behavior analysts who received limited training during graduate school on conducting interviews—not only with caregivers and others who implement a behavioral change plan but also with the person experiencing the behavior change plan—should consider further supervision or training exposure to evidence-informed approaches to conducting interviews. Going through a series of questions on a task list is not the same as interacting with parents and asking questions as the conversation progresses. Reading off a series of questions during an intake interview just to check a box may not be beneficial for your long-term work with those parents. The intent of the interview is to gather meaningful information about the parents and family system to better establish a functional intervention.

Interviews that are geared toward the parents' lived experiences, their relationships with their child(ren), and the contexts that support their own behaviors are important aspects to consider when collecting information. For example, you may ask questions related to the specific presenting problem or targeted repertoires, the more universal or general aspects of the parents' lived experiences, the family systems and dynamics, and/or the sociocultural variables. These types of questions will help bolster correspondence of parent responses.

Before conducting the interview, consider the variables or environmental contexts that will be important given the selected target and alternative repertoires:

Parental Physical, Emotional, and Behavioral Health

- Are there any physical, emotional, or behavioral health concerns for the parents? Other adults in the household? If yes, are these being treated elsewhere?

- If taking medication, are there any side effects that impact their day-to-day life or specifically their parenting?

- How is their overall quality of life?

Family Context and Cultural Considerations

- What are the current cultural considerations for the family? How do these influence the decisions made for caregiving?

- What type of parenting style did their parents have? How does this influence their parenting style?

- Who are the caregivers for the child? How is their relationship with the child?

- Who are the primary caregivers, the ones that make decisions for or about the child?

- What is the current household context? Any extended family members residing in the household? How are household chores or duties delineated or distributed among family members?

- What is the quality of the parent-child relationship?

- What does compassionate parenting look like for the family?

- What does discipline for the child look like? Is it the same across all children in the family or particular to each child?

- What have the parents done in the past to address the child's maladaptive or concerning behaviors? What has worked and for how long?

- What have the parents done in the past to address their own parenting approach or style? What has worked and for how long?

- What does the family and/or what do the parents want to get out of their work with the behavior analyst?

Parenting Behaviors

- How do the parents respond when the child engages in maladaptive behaviors?

- What type of affect or tone do the parents use naturally when interacting with the child? How does this change when the child engages in maladaptive behavior?

- Do the parents help the child through use of prompts (i.e., verbal or minimal guidance), or do the parents jump in and complete the task or step for the child?

- Do the parents "parent from the couch," or do they get close to the child and gain their attention before giving instruction?

Keep It Fun

- What do the parents do for fun? Do they have any hobbies?

- What are the parents' favorite pastimes or family rituals (e.g., family game night, Taco Tuesdays, etc.)?

- What do the parents do to relax or wind down at the end of the day?

- What are the parents' favorite foods? Do they like to cook?

- How do the parents and family celebrate special occasions like birthdays or holidays?

- What would a perfect day for each parent look like?

Information collected during an open-ended interview can be used to refine operational definitions for potential target and alternative repertoires. This information can also be used to assist with identifying appropriate self-report and/or psychometric questionnaires to be included as part of the layering approach to data collection.

Individualized and standardized rating scales. Rating scales can be useful to collect information about a specific target or alternative behavior/repertoire. Scales can be designed specifically for each parent (individualized) or based on generalized standards (psychometric questionnaires). Self-report is often dismissed as an inaccurate and inherently biased form of data and may be rejected entirely by some behavior analysts. However, when working with individuals who can, with a relatively accurate degree of say-do correspondence, report their own experiences and histories, asking the individual directly about their experiences may be a reasonable place to start, while also being an unreasonable place to end.

Often self-reported measurement systems use Likert scales to quantify otherwise subjective dimensions (i.e., intensity or severity, believability, importance, etc.). Likert scales can be a useful tool to supplement an open-ended interview with quantitative data. Similar measurements can be adapted directly to the parents or client in front of you, by asking a specific question related to the referring problem. For instance, asking parents to rate how close they behaved in accordance with the things that are important to them using a 5-point Likert scale (0 = not at all, 3 = somewhat consistent, 5 = completely consistent) can be a useful way to collect repeated measures through self-report data.

Standardized or psychometric questionnaires are heavily relied on in most psychology circles yet are used more sparingly in behavior analysis. For instance, Newsome and colleagues (2019) reported 80% of experimental studies published in *Journal of Contextual Behavior Science* through 2016 (the hallmark journal for contextual behavioral science research, including RFT and ACT) employed only a single measure, while 99% of published articles used a nonbehavioral measure of self-report (i.e., psychometric questionnaires).

In contrast, a quick glance at mainstream applied behavior analytic journals, such as *Journal of Applied Behavior Analysis* or *Behavior Analysis in Practice*, would yield very few published articles that include a single nonbehavioral measure of self-report. It may be helpful to consider how to reasonably include standardized forms of measurement as supplemental forms of evidence to create a multimodal approach to data collection and subsequent analysis of effectiveness, particularly when we consider subtle behaviors that are only directly observable to the parents. While it is beyond the scope of this chapter to provide a thoroughgoing overview of all the potential psychometric assessments available, it is critical to consider whether the measure has adequate reliability and validity. It is also critical for us to use these tools with caution and never to consider a psychometric tool as a primary dependent variable.

Descriptive Assessment and Direct Observation

Direct assessments can be a useful step in information gathering to verify and refine stimuli that are identified during indirect assessments. Descriptive assessments often involve an aspect of direct observation, where we may or may not start to modify the environment to test the extent to which a target behavior is observed. Information gathered during interviews or through self-report can be conceptualized into a potential hypothesis about why the target behavior is occurring and then tested through direct assessments. The culmination of these steps can help inform an experimental analysis where we directly manipulate an aspect of the environment to measure response patterns across two or more conditions (i.e., control and test).

Descriptive assessments, when implemented correctly, attempt to identify naturally occurring reinforcement conditions. Through direct observation, we collect data on events that occur before and after a target behavior or repertoire. Following observations, response-dependent events (i.e., an event given engagement in behavior) and response-independent events (i.e., engagement in behavior with unknown or unobserved event) can be identified and categorized across themes and patterns within the observational data. Conditional probabilities can be useful to determine more objective patterns (e.g., Vollmer et al., 2001), where the conditional probability of an event given a specific behavior is either independent (low overall observation rate of behavior) or dependent (higher overall observation rate of behavior).

There are alternative ways to consider direct observation assessments as well as how to consider natural observation as a means of assessment strategy. For instance, skill assessments targeting various behavior analytic intervention strategies such as differential reinforcement (i.e., providing social praise to the child after they ask for help while withholding social praise after the child throws the toy at the parent) will help determine whether implementation errors are deficits in treatment integrity or treatment adherence.

Similarly, demand assessments could be considered to determine the parents' threshold for treatment implementation accuracy (or the schedule under which the parents stop adhering to the implementation plan, and switch back to engaging in target behaviors that do not align with the plan). Two specific assessments, the "matrix" (see figure 6.2) and the "parenting triangle," will be discussed in detail, given their particular relevance to most ACT parent training contexts.

ACT matrix. Arguably one of the better known functional assessment strategies within the ACT community is the matrix (Polk et al., 2016). The goal of the matrix is to identify potential functional relationships between what the parents do and the stimuli and environmental context that shapes or supports those behaviors. The matrix was originally developed to be very broad and flexible in terms of populations and client symptoms. At its core, the matrix is a series of four questions centered around stimuli (things that are important) and repertoires (things the person does), juxtaposed against things that are experienced only by the person (subtle behaviors):

- What is important?

- What experiences get in the way of what is important?

- What do you do when experiences get in the way?

- What do you do when you align yourself with what is important?

The matrix can be used to help identify functional relationships between the parents' engagement in treatment nonadherence and environmental contexts or conditions. When applied within a parent training context, we can adapt these four questions in the following way:

- What do you do when you align yourself with the goals of your child's behavior plan (i.e., identify goals and steps of the behavior plan)?

- What is important to you about your child's behavior plan?

- What experiences get in the way when you are implementing your child's intervention plan?

- What do you do when you notice these experiences?

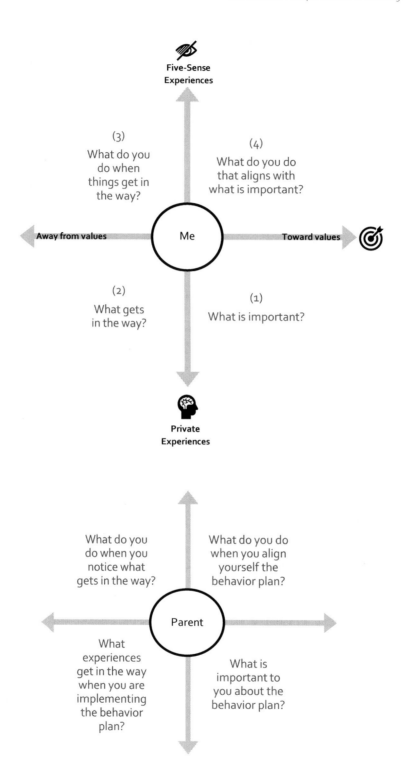

Five-Sense
Experiences

(3)
What do you
do when
things get in
the way?

(4)
What do you do
that aligns with
what is important?

Away from values   Me   Toward values

(2)
What gets
in the way?

(1)
What is important?

Private
Experiences

What do you
do when you
notice what
gets in the way?

What do you do
when you align
yourself the
behavior plan?

Parent

What
experiences
get in the way
when you are
implementing
the behavior
plan?

What is
important to
you about the
behavior plan?

*Matrix adapted by Polk and colleagues (2016) in general (top panel)
and adapted to fit a parent training context (bottom panel).*

Figure 6.2

By changing the focus of the second quadrant of the matrix (identification of values) to the parents' values around the behavior plan, we can ensure that the conversation stays within our scope of practice while collecting information about potential functional relationships between environmental stimuli and parental engagement in treatment nonadherence, as perceived by the parents themselves.

In either application of the matrix, the outcomes are both the same: the identification or verification of stimuli or environmental contexts reported as experiences that impede the parents from implementing the plan. The information gathered can also be used to inform the parenting triangle assessment discussed below.

Parenting triangle. The goal of the parenting triangle assessment is to help the parents articulate their own parenting as it relates to three aspects: *limit setting* (or the removal of privileges and other punishment-based parenting strategies), *planned ignoring* (i.e., interacting with the child while avoiding any discussion around the specific behavior), and *provision of rewards or reinforcers* (i.e., providing high-quality rewards and reinforcers to the child without requiring a specific response) (see figure 6.3).

To begin, consider discussions with the parents across the three aspects of their parenting style, similar to the approach taken in the matrix. Ask the parent what each style looks like in their own day-to-day experiences, and how they use or don't use the approach or style. This discussion can help identify self-rules held by the parent as well as potentially appetitive environments and specific activities or items that may be reinforcing to the parents as well as the child (at least from the parents' perspective).

When using the tool represented in figure 6.3, the metaphor of "flipping your triangle" can be used to think about parents' heavy reliance on limit-setting approaches compared to only sometimes or sparingly using rewards or reinforcers. During the intervention, you may visually show the parent what "flipping one's triangle" may look like when we flip to using rewards and reinforcers more than limit-setting approaches. In this way, our parenting triangle flips to heavy reliance on provision of reinforcement-rich environments with only selective use of limit-setting or other punitive parenting strategies.

This activity can be used as an assessment strategy to determine the parents' rules and personal selection around their approach to discipline and parenting in general. As an information-gathering tool, you would ask questions about what each of the strategies looks like for the parents. For instance, you may start by asking the parents about how they approach discipline with their children: Do they set limits with things (i.e., 30 minutes of TV at a time, or no video games after 7 p.m., or lights off at 8 p.m., etc.), and if so, what does that look like? If their child engages in a behavior they consider inappropriate, what happens? How often do they provide reinforcers or rewards to their children? How often do they provide those things noncontingently? When asking these types of questions, it is important to avoid invalidating the parents' responses. Instead, write down their initial responses even if that means writing or categorizing them in a different area of the triangle (Polk et al., 2016).

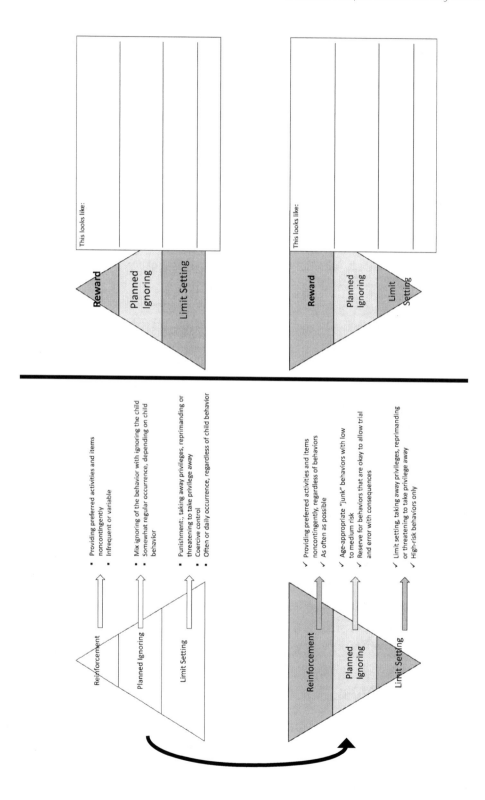

Figure 6.3
Example of parenting triangle. Implementation guide is represented on the left panel,
and the right panel is provided to the parent.

Rehearsal and real-play. Behavioral skills training (BST; Sarokoff & Sturmey, 2004) should be considered when assessing parental progress. Another assessment is to use role modeling and "real-play" to actively track the parents' implementation of the plan over time. One way to do this is to consider the parents' baseline performance of the targeted skill as the assessment; this essentially establishes whether the parents have the skill in their repertoire or not.

Considerations for Experimental Analyses

Experimental analyses are often considered when a handful of identified environmental conditions are intentionally arranged to test the extent to which the condition reliably evokes a target behavior. While evoking target behaviors may be needed to reliably determine functional relationships, variations of the relative dose and/or exposure to punitive or aversive stimuli may not be needed at the same rate across all parents, settings, or selected target repertoires. For parent training contexts, modified versions of more "traditional" experimental analyses will be needed.

The clinical utility, necessity, and ultimate risk/reward ratios of exposing the parents to potentially punitive and aversive stimuli is a major factor to consider when using ACT both generally and specifically as it relates to using the model within parent training contexts. It may be the case that a synthesis of descriptive and experimental analyses may be needed when determining functional relationships within parent-child contexts. It may also be the case that the experimental analyses may be as simple as asking the parents specific questions related to environmental contexts and noting their engagement in repertoires. Similarly, experimental analyses may also arrange the environment in a way to observe what the parents say or do so you can therefore notice functional relationships as described by the parents (i.e., the matrix).

Certain assessment details useful from the functional behavior assessment literature will certainly be different when assessing a target behavior of head banging compared to intrusive thoughts or other subtle behaviors. Other procedural details, such as the consistency of reinforcer magnitude across conditions or the order of conditions to control for motivation effects, may need to be retained given our reliance and inclusion of assessments that are not only flexible but also rigorous (to account for high degrees of validity and reliability).

ACT Component Assessment Considerations

Another potential consideration for assessment is around the parents' repertoires related to the ACT intervention strategy itself, such as metaphor selection and development for individual parent-child contexts and ACT-specific repertoires such as here/now repertoires (i.e., present moment), tolerance repertoires (i.e., acceptance), and say-do correspondence between behaviors engaged in and stimuli/environments accessed (i.e., values-based actions). The following section highlights assessment options but is not intended to indicate which ones to use for all parents. As with the previous assessment considerations provided, it is critical for you to think about how each assessment would align with the overall target goals of the parent training program, the approach selected for data collection and analysis, the idiosyncratic family dynamics and cultural considerations, and other applicable factors.

Here and now relational emphasis. The primary focus in this component is on the extent to which repertoires aligned with here/now relations are emitted, particularly in the presence of aversive stimuli. Direct assessment considerations should target here/now repertoires that are commonly practiced during present moment content exposure during ACT. For instance, "Soles of the Feet" (SoF), the procedure detailed by Singh and colleagues (2003), can be used as an assessment by reading aloud the steps and observing the parents' response (see also chapter 7, Here and Now Relational Emphasis). Other assessment considerations could include observations across various environmental conditions (i.e., appetitive and aversive) to determine whether or how well parental repertoires align with here/now stimuli and context.

Flexible perspective taking. The primary focus of flexible perspective taking is to determine both say-do correspondence between naturally occurring environment and parental verbal report of environment and the extent to which correspondence is disrupted or in alignment with observations. Direct assessment approaches should align with stimuli identified to be potentially aversive and/or part of what the parents seek to escape or avoid.

Desensitization assessment, whereby aspects of potentially aversive stimuli are exposed to the parents, can be conducted across feature, function, and class of the aversive stimuli. For instance, aversive stimuli—for example, when the child engages in aggressive outbursts like throwing toys—may only share function (i.e., say-do correspondence) but not feature (i.e., verbal behavior about the aggressive outbursts is not the same as the child's aggressive outbursts themselves). Flexibility assessments may help you assess the extent to which parents' rules around their parenting style align with the environment and/or their identified parenting values (e.g., a parent who often reports, "I want my child to know that I will never hurt them. I don't reprimand or discipline them because that would traumatize them and hold them back from being who they are."). Information collected during the parenting triangle activity may also be useful during flexibility assessments, especially when considering how the parents identify their own parenting style.

Acceptance. Here, the primary focus is on the extent to which repertoires aligned with approaching aversive stimuli are emitted. The inverse of such a repertoire would be engagement in repertoires to access escape and avoidance from aversive stimuli. Essentially, either the parents approach or escape an aversive stimulus. Ask yourself these questions: *Do the parents "accept" or approach difficult situations or contexts with flexible or broadening repertoires? If so, what do the repertoires and contexts look like? If not, what is being escaped or avoided (i.e., the stimuli or situation)? How is avoidance accessed—that is, what does this repertoire look like?* Direct assessment considerations should include descriptive ABC analyses particularly in the presence and absence of an aversive stimulus (i.e., something that the parents report wanting to escape or avoid) in order to validate parental report as identified during indirect assessments. Stimuli identified during indirect assessments that suggest potential aversive functions can also be used in stimulus avoidance assessments to determine aspects of the environment the parents seek to escape or avoid. Ethical considerations, including the risk/reward ratio of the assessment and potentially aversive stimuli, must be considered prior to conducting the assessment. Similarly, use of progressive ratios can also be used to determine the breaking point (e.g., A. N. Wilson et al., 2015) at which the parents may resort to previous parenting techniques or other forms of nonadherence to treatment implementation.

Values-based patterns of action. In this component, the primary focus is to identify what is important to the parents, in terms of their parenting style and relationship with the child, and whether the parents engage in behavior that aligns with their values. Direct assessment can incorporate say-do correspondence between what is important to the parents and the actions or behaviors they engage in. Similarly, descriptive analyses can be used to help determine or validate behaviors that parents engage in.

Conclusion

Conducting assessments should be an ongoing process; they are not simply the first step to engage in prior to starting treatment or intervention. It is a common misunderstanding that assessments are only completed in the beginning of behavior analytic services; rather, assessments should be conducted as often as needed to ensure that you are providing (or continue to provide) a functional intervention. Assessments can be a helpful case conceptualization strategy when you hit a wall within parent training: when the parents' behavior seems to plateau or fails to achieve higher implementation standards or goals, and when an intervention fails to produce effective or quality behavior change.

When applied within parent training contexts, this may mean that, to some degree, you assess for functional relationships between parents' engagement in treatment nonadherence and environmental events at each session. These assessments can and should be returned to later during parent training to assess the extent to which the target (i.e., treatment nonadherence) and alternative (i.e., behavioral flexibility) repertoires change over time. Doing so will assist you with case conceptualization and provide evidence to inform further treatment modifications and/or targeting new repertoires.

Checklist for Clinical Practice

Use this checklist to help you target experiential acceptance repertoires within parent training contexts:

☐   I have operationalized target parent repertoires (i.e., rigid and/or flexible rule following or adherence, say-do or do-say correspondence, experiential avoidance, and corollary responses, etc.).

☐   I have selected at least one dimension of behavior to assess (i.e., frequency, duration).

☐   I have developed at least one measurement system that is reliable and valid to track parental repertoires.

☐   I have selected flexible and rigorous assessments that align with the targeted repertoires.

☐   Before beginning each assessment, I ask for the parents' consent and provide information to the parents about the assessment prior to implementation.

☐   The indirect assessment strategy selected will inform direct/descriptive assessments.

☐   The selected direct/descriptive assessment is reliable and valid.

☐   If I use the matrix, I don't rely on reading verbatim off my notes or a handout. Instead, I lead the discussion with the parents, avoiding any corrective feedback or direction for answers.

☐   If I use the parenting triangle, I avoid telling the parents what their parenting style should be, and I do not pass judgment on their answers. I use the information provided to understand potential environmental situations or contexts that may hinder the parents' engagement in treatment.

☐   I have considered the use of synthesized experimental analyses, including the risk/reward ratios of the situation. I have written down my rationale for including these assessments (or not) in my case notes/files.

☐   I have considered ACT-specific assessment considerations. I have written down my rationale for including these assessments in my case notes/files.

☐   I have a plan to return to the selected assessments throughout intervention, particularly as a case conceptualization strategy.

CHAPTER 7

Using ACT in Clinical Practice
Here and Now Relational Emphasis

This chapter highlights how to train flexible here and now (or here/now) repertoires within parent training contexts, and how to connect these repertoires to other ACT components. Interventions have been selected from my personal experiences in clinical practice, research, and supervision of other behavior analysts working with parents. The theoretical orientation toward use of here/now emphasis over other mid-level considerations is discussed first in order to establish a conceptual foundation before moving into how to use here/now interventions within parent coaching contexts. Intervention strategies have been selected due to their supporting evidence to date, minimal response effort required for implementation, and successful outcomes when used in my own practice.

I will use the phrase "present moment repertoires" to denote here/now relational responding when needed, particularly when discussing nontechnologically the process of intervention strategies. When considering case conceptualization, however, I will use the phrase "here/now repertoires," given the need to establish intervening variables to develop comprehensive analyses (see also Callaghan & Follette, 2020).

Theoretical Foundation

Relational frame theory (RFT; Hayes, Barnes-Holmes, & Roach, 2001) posits that deictic relational frames incorporate responding to contextual cues signaling I/here/now repertoires as opposed to you/there/now or I/there/then relations. Often this emphasis on responding to here/now contextual cues is established or denoted as "present moment" or "mindfulness" repertoires. Such constructs are often defined as nonjudgmental attention toward the present moment (e.g., Kabat-Zinn, 2015).

Present moment repertoires can be considered anything a person does that shifts their attention to here/now contextual cues across a range of contexts and stimuli. A shift (or discrimination) may be established by verbal stimuli or rules, or may be established by other arbitrary physical objects. The goal is the orientation toward here/now repertoires, as opposed to repertoires that reinforce there/then relations.

We may also consider here/now repertoires that help us label our own subtle experiences in our day-to-day lives, including what we may think or feel at various moments in space and time. For instance, self-management practices that target documenting specific environmental events, like what happened before and after a specified behavior or event, may help orient a person toward their own subtle experiences (or notice physiological changes or thoughts/feelings without attempting to change or modify the events; see also Bishop et al., 2004).

Other practices, such as antecedent strategies to practice alternative repertoires (often triggering or previously paired with the "mindless" or targeted repertoire), have been shown to have positive impacts on shifting toward here/now. Research conducted to date supports present moment interventions as effective strategies to assist parents with fully immersing themselves in the present (or here/now repertoires), thus reducing reliance on reactive repertoires, which in turn make it possible for parents to alleviate some of their stress-related behaviors (e.g., Singh et al., 2006). In this way, present moment repertoires can be arranged to help reduce parental stress and increase quality of life for the parent as well as their families.

Some have argued that by enhancing parental engagement in here/now repertoires, there is a reduction in a reliance on more reactive or avoidant repertoires (including punitive discipline practices). Take, for example, a parent who struggles with taking their child to the grocery store, as the child is likely to have a tantrum inside. The parent may report only aspects of the child's tantrum when asked about other environmental stimuli (i.e., where are you in the store, what happened just before the tantrum started, how did you feel before the tantrum started, etc.). Rather than attend to multiple aspects of the environment, the parent may instead focus their attention solely on the child's behavior and therefore may respond with a reactive repertoire such as yelling, limit setting, or other presumed fixes. The parent may see the child cry and throw a tantrum in the store and immediately react by yelling, "Stop your crying right now" or by simply taking the child out the store without verbally saying anything to the child. In both instances, the parent reacts to the stressor or aversive situation (i.e., the child's tantrum) rather than pausing and taking note of the environment, such as their feelings and thoughts or current wants or needs.

In contrast, if the same parent practices here/now responding, they may be able to notice other aspects of the environment, including their own feelings and thoughts when the child cries in the store. Doing so may enable them to engage in an alternative repertoire, such as calmly redirecting their child to a rule (e.g., "I know it is hard right now because you want X; let us both take a moment to breathe together"). The parent may also contact a change in what is important in that moment; the items needed in the store may have been important, but perhaps the tantrum becomes more important, thus changing the strength of the various reinforcement schedules operating in the environment. Both repertoires may result in the parent leaving the store before getting all necessary items, but the flexibility and the appetitive control of the alternative repertoire is a key distinction. Furthermore, the stressful event itself (the child's behavior) may not go away or change. How the parent responds to each event in each moment as it unfolds, however, is the target in present moment work.

Similar real-world experiences can be brought into parent training sessions to establish and practice shifting perspective toward here/now repertoires. The key within this component is to determine whether the parent can engage in flexible and focused attention on stimuli in the current environment, both aversive (unpleasant or unwanted) and appetitive (preferred or reinforcing). Such repertoires can be considered "home base," or the place to which parents can return when life gets off track (cf., K. G. Wilson, 2021). Said another way, the here and now (i.e., the "present moment") is always here, always now. Each moment is another opportunity to practice shifting perspectives to environmental stimuli. If parents are not engaging in active shifting awareness or attention toward multiple stimuli in the current environment, they may struggle to do so in more naturally aversive environments.

Getting Started

Prior to any intervention, it is critical to identify data collection and assessment strategies for the targeted repertoire. Psychometric assessment tools such as the Mindful Awareness Attitude Scale (Brown & Ryan, 2003) may be valid and reliable measures to include as part of a multidimensional layering strategy and may be helpful as a case conceptualization tool. Other data collection systems, such as self-reported Likert scale measures on the parents' experiences when shifting from I/there/then to I/here/now repertoires, can be helpful to consider or to use to determine how often they practice any of the selected interventions. Similar data may also be useful in determining the effects the interventions or strategies had on the believability or intensity of the parents' experiences when practicing or engaging in here/now repertoires.

It is important to consider your data collection approach and how here/now repertoires will be captured within the approach selected. Using information provided in chapter 4, be sure to consider whether the selected here/now repertoires will be targeted in other components (e.g., flexible perspective taking) or as a stand-alone repertoire. In this way, you may establish a measurement system that can better capture both the selected here/now repertoire as well as other components.

Next, it is critical to determine the here/now repertoire that will be targeted. Each parent will require their own unique training approach, which may change due to the targeted repertoire (e.g., shifting attention vs. identifying thoughts or emotion states) or goal of parent training (e.g., parent support vs. parent implementation). For instance, some present moment intervention strategies like Soles of the Feet (i.e., Singh et al., 2003) may target repertoires that are challenging for parents to engage in due to exposure to potentially aversive environments or stimuli.

Take, for example, the parent who finds an aspect of the behavior plan difficult to engage in during more intense situations (or when the magnitude of the conditioned aversive stimuli increases). In this context, it may be appropriate to help the parent shift their attention to here/now relations in order to learn alternative ways to respond in the presence of conditioned aversives. However, this intervention may not be effective for parents who tell you that they do not agree with your plan, and that is why they struggle with providing reinforcers noncontingently (or without requiring that the child engage in any specific behavior). In this case, the issue for the parents is not a lack of flexible here/now repertoires per se but rather a distinction in worldview between the parents and the behavior analyst. This distinction sometimes gets lost, and it is important to return to this delineation during case conceptualization, particularly as we focus our parent training on parent collaboration.

Finally, we want to stay committed to our philosophical roots and avoid midlevel terminology as best as we can. Often, when we talk about present moment repertoires, particularly ones that directly relate to subtle behaviors that are only directly observable to the parents, we may inadvertently use mentalistic constructs or hypothetical constructs as though they are directly observable events. Or, due to their subtle nature, we may only rely on parental self-report and omit possibilities of directly observable corollary events and behaviors. Instead, we should always return to our operational definitions to ensure we omit the use of hypothetical constructs, circular definitions, and explanations or definitions appealing to events that occur at different levels of analysis. If we stay committed to this practice, then we may agree that here/now repertoires can include what the parents say to themselves or others, and what they do in appetitive and aversive environments.

Assessment Considerations

With assessment strategies, it is imperative to look at the range of assessments at your disposal (e.g., indirect, direct, naturalistic, experimental) while considering the parents' current here/now repertoires. Do the parents already engage in here/now repertoires, reliably and across contexts and situations? If so, what do these behaviors look like, and what conditions are these behaviors more or less likely to occur in? If not, what do the alternative I/there/then or you/there/now repertoires look like? Direct observations and descriptive analyses can be helpful for you to not only determine operational definitions but to also establish with data how frequent or salient the repertoires are for the parents prior to treatment.

There are different evidenced-based present moment targeted protocols, such as Soles of the Feet (Singh et al., 2003) or Mindful STOP (Phang et al., 2014), that can be useful for shaping here/now repertoires. Such protocols or formal treatment programs can be useful when conducting baseline and before/after snapshots on outcome measures. For instance, the Soles of the Feet exercise (described in the next section) can be used as a baseline or pretest by reading the steps out loud to determine how or whether the parents respond. Dichotomous data can be converted into percent correct, to determine how many steps the parents engaged in prior to training (see also the baseline phase conducted in A. N. Wilson et al., 2014).

We may consider here/now repertoires in other ACT-related assessment strategies, such as tolerance assessments, flexibility assessments, reinforcer assessments, and so on. Rather than focusing on here/now repertoires as a stand-alone response class, we may consider how such repertoires may work alongside or in tandem with approaching, orienting, or pivoting toward more appetitive environments and reinforcers. Finally, it may be easy for some parents to orient their attention to their child's behaviors when in the privacy of their own homes, but when the child engages in the same behaviors out in the world (e.g., in the store or at the movies), the parents may struggle to persist in engaging in present moment repertoires. It would also be beneficial to consider the setting where the here/now repertoires occur.

Here/Now Relational Intervention Strategies

In the beginning of any intervention, lots of hype or expectations by either the client or the clinician can make starting sessions somewhat unnerving. Here/now exercises, such as breath work and related centering activities, can be beneficial for both the clinician and the parents to connect with their own here/now repertoires before starting the session. For this reason, consider building in a here/now exercise to start every session, even for just a few moments, in whatever modality or structure is best suited for you and the parents.

Consider the parents' current here/now repertoires before intervention begins, and before each individual intervention session. When you interact with the parents, or when the parents are implementing the behavior intervention plan, what do you notice? Where is their current level of here/now engagement? If you notice more emphasis on I/there/then or you/there/now, starting with a more explicit here/now activity (e.g., Soles of the Feet or other step-by-step training protocol) may be most beneficial for the parents.

Intervention strategies to increase here/now repertoires range from metaphorical paradoxes and thought exercises to practicing and rehearsing adaptive or flexible repertoires targeting here/now attention and responding. Thousands of present moment metaphors are readily available and easily acquired through a simple Google search (see also Stoddard et al., 2014, for a book with metaphors and exercises for each ACT component). Rather than provide an array of metaphors, let's look at a few evidenced-informed strategies to target here/now repertoires within parent training settings.

Soles of the Feet (SoF). Nirbhay Singh and colleagues developed a meditation-style protocol to teach present moment repertoires, dubbed "Soles of the Feet" (SoF) given the attention to one's awareness of their feet (Singh et al., 2003). Research on SoF to date suggests the protocol is effective for children, adolescents, parents, and caregivers across a range of presenting symptoms and target repertoires (e.g., Singh et al., 2006; Singh et al., 2014; Singh et al., 2017; Singh et al., 2019; A. N. Wilson et al., 2014). This protocol is easily adaptable to whatever environment you are working in and can be applied with parents using these steps (modified from Fuller & Fitter, 2020):

1. Sit or stand naturally, with a straight spine.

2. Tilt your head slightly forward, with your chin tucked slightly toward your throat.

3. Keep your eyes slightly open or close them lightly.

4. Touch the tip of your tongue to your upper palate, near the front of your mouth (no data).

5. Place your hands on your lap or on your legs, whichever is more comfortable.

6. Move your toes, feel your shoes covering your feet or the texture of your socks, and feel the curve of your arch (no data).

7. Breathe evenly by inhaling for three or four counts and exhaling for three or four counts.

8. Focus your attention on the flow of your breath (no data).

9. When you realize that your mind has wandered away, gently refocus your attention on the flow of your breathing (no data).

10. Once you are calm, you can walk away with a smile on your face or respond to the incident with a clear, calm, and concise verbal behavior; open your eyes or look toward me and let me know you are calm.

To establish a working baseline, read each step aloud to the parents, and see whether or how they respond. Observe the parents' behavior and indicate whether each parent engages in the step with accuracy (+) or not (-). After you read all ten steps, total the number of steps accurately completed (for each parent) and divide by the total number of steps, then multiply by 100 to get a percentage. Some of the steps are not possible to directly observe (i.e., focus your attention on the flow of your breath, step 8; notice your mind wandering and refocus your attention, step 9), and should not be incorporated into the calculation for percent completion. These items are noted with "(no data)."

After baseline, we may go about training the parent in the steps of the chain through various modalities, including use of shaping, modeling, and rehearsal. Work with the parents to engage in the SoF steps with a high degree of accuracy and independence to establish mastery (however defined). Next, exposure probes can be used, where a potentially aversive stimulus is presented to allow the parents to practice the SoF steps independently.

Mindful parenting. As an exercise to help parents practice here/now repertoires, use basic prompts to help them notice the five senses while doing common parenting tasks. This helps parents practice shifting their attention to various stimuli within the environment (see also Andrews et al., 2021, for a similar component used during parent training). Any behavior that is involved in "parenting" can be targeted for this intervention.

When working with a parent, have them start by selecting an action, behavior, or task that they do regularly—for example, getting meals ready, preparing for bed, dropping or picking up their children, or supervising playdates. Next, work with them to break down the chosen action or routine into smaller steps. For example, if a parent selects mealtime, they may start by asking their child to help them make dinner, followed next by walking into the kitchen, pulling out the ingredients for the meal, washing fruits or vegetables, preparing meat, opening canned goods, getting out pots and pans to prepare the meal, cooking the meal, and so on.

After all steps are identified, instruct the parent to focus on each of the actions or steps individually: noticing the smells and how they change throughout the prepping process; noticing what the food feels like in their hands, what the pots and pans feel like; noticing what their child is doing to "help" them prepare the food, and so on. They may also use each step as a prompt to notice their breath. This approach can be useful for a range of parenting repertoires and can be helpful with orienting the parent's focus to the moment, as it directly relates to their repertoires as a parent.

Mindful STOP. This tool was established to reduce stress and enhance general health and well-being for medical students (Phang et al., 2014). STOP works as a way for individuals to "log in" or check in on their current level of present awareness through four basic steps:

1. STOP: Stop whatever you are doing. Allow your attention to return to what is happening right here, right now.

2. TAKE: Take slow, deep, breaths. Focus your attention to your breath, the rising and falling of your chest and lungs. Focus on your breath as you breathe in and out.

3. OBSERVE: Observe what is happening right here, right now. Focus on your senses. What do you see, hear, feel, and taste?

4. PROCEED: Proceed with your focus and attention on the full environment.

This intervention strategy can be presented to parents by providing them with the four steps and the rationale for their use. Using behavioral skills training, you can model the steps for the parents before having them rehearse the steps while you provide feedback. After training, the parents can be prompted to use the STOP technique between sessions and debrief with you about their experiences.

Noticing the Phone. Urge surfing metaphors highlight how experiential avoidance of urges to engage in a behavior (e.g., to drink a beer or to gamble) will, over time, increase the probability of the person engaging in said behavior. As a variation to urge surfing metaphors, Noticing the Phone can be useful within sessions to help parents practice shifting their attention across various aspects of connecting with here/now repertoires—that is, the five senses of experience: what do you see, hear, taste, feel, and smell? As we've discussed, we may not have direct access to subtle behaviors during sessions, so we need to bring something into the session to establish a similar effect. The best thing I have found to establish such evocative effects has been the mobile phone and to have the parents practice not picking their phone up or looking at it when it rings or pings.

To do this exercise, instruct the parents to practice their present moment repertoires (i.e., noticing breath and bodily sensations, and how they change over time) the next time their phone rings or pings. The parents should notice the urge to pick up the phone and answer, and note how that urge shifts depending on the caller, whether they leave a message, whether they send follow-up text messages, or whether a different message or notification occurs; you get the idea! This exercise lends itself nicely to giving parents specific ways to rehearse shifting their attention from the current context to a specific stimulus (i.e., the phone). This activity can be practiced throughout the day and can be debriefed at follow-up sessions for shaping and generalization.

Family-friendly moments. As parents become more familiar with their own shifting attention and here/now repertoires, help them expand their practice to include their children and maybe other family members, as appropriate. Every moment they are with their children is a moment to practice present moment repertoires or specific activities. In my experience, creating ways for parents to connect with their families using here/now activities is best when we consider the family's unique needs and current strengths. Helping parents plan family events or habits (such as a family dinner or game night) can be one way to help incorporate fun activities with present moment repertoires.

The Quiet Game (e.g., Kasson & A. N. Wilson, 2017) can be a fun way to get their children involved. The goal is to get players to sit in silence for a specific period of time, and the winner or winners get a prize at the end. (In the research study, we gave a single chocolate candy to students who were silent during the interval.) When implementing in session, this game can be adapted to fit the needs of the child and parents. To begin, ask their child to close their eyes or lie down while the parents model the skill. Start a timer and tell the child to see how long they can stay quiet. The parents can use the time to connect with their child, helping their child with staying quiet, practicing still bodies, etc. This is a great opportunity to make it fun for everyone and to practice attending to what is happening right here, right now, rather than a specific goal (i.e., everyone must be still and quiet for five minutes).

Another breathing exercise, Mindful Mountain, can be used as an activity for both parents and child. (Mindful Mountain is a play on the mountain yoga pose.) To do it, the parents and child stop what they are doing, place their hands at their sides and stand tall. While circling their arms over their heads, they inhale until they can no longer breathe in. They pause briefly, then exhale while circling their arms back to their sides. The exercise can be repeated as many times and for as long as wanted or needed.

Family-friendly here/now activities can easily be created or adapted from solo activities to allow the parent-child relationship to develop naturally. Common everyday behaviors, like eating and drinking, can be targeted as a way to practice contacting the here-and-now aspect of the activity. For instance, a parent and child may sit down together and use all five senses to experience their lunch or snack before putting a single bite of food into their mouth. Parents can use the time to notice how their child may experience the same food in different ways, which can, generally speaking, be helpful for parents to begin to engage in more flexible perspective taking.

Using Here/Now Emphasis with Other Components

In my clinical practice, I have found that here/now repertoires are essential for any other work in the ACT model. Think about it this way: how can we expect our clients to attend to conditioned aversive stimuli or engage in flexible perspective taking if they do not first orient to here/now aspects of the context? Given this, it is critical that we embed some aspect of present moment work when targeting other ACT components. When practiced in conjunction with here/now repertoires, simply adding a phrase such as "What do you notice when...," or "Take a moment to get grounded by taking a few breaths," or "Where do you feel X when you notice Y" can be an easy way to embed present moment work within other components.

More explicit approaches to combining with other components can and should consider the goal of the component and the presenting repertoires of the parent. For instance, a common experiential exercise to enhance acceptance is Willingly Cold, where clients are asked to submerge their hand in a bowl of ice water. This exercise helps clients contact their own private experiences in the presence of an unwanted or unpleasant situation (i.e., their hand in ice water) and practice alternative repertoires to avoidance—for example, rather than pull their hand out immediately, how long can they leave their hand in the water? What do they do to prolong the time in the water? While on the surface the exercise focuses on acceptance, in order to help shift one's focus to the current environment or context, here/now repertoires must also be engaged in. To embed this into other components, we can have the parent put their hand in the ice water and ask the parent to debrief what they experienced without any instructions or deliberate attempts to change or control the situation. Cross-component questions should be targeted to ensure a thoroughgoing approach to using ACT, and you can incorporate questions such as these:

- Where did you feel it? Did it change over time? How was it the same or different? (Component: flexible perspective taking)

- What did you do to get through the discomfort? (Component: experiential acceptance)

- Did you notice anything that you did to try and change or control the situation? Did it work? (Component: flexible perspective taking)

- How did you stay engaged in what you were doing? Did you align with your goal in the beginning? (Component: values-based patterns of action)

These questions can be useful to help drive the conversation and get a sense of how experiential avoidance and related repertoires occur for the parent. When you ask the parent to do it a second time, set up the situation differently: this time, ask them to practice their here/now repertoires when their hand is in the cold water to see whether they can leave it in longer (sometimes they do, sometimes they do not).

Another way to combine here/now repertoires with other components is to embed here/now prompts in the first part of the session and/or the exercise itself. For instance, before doing a values map (see chapter 10 on values-based patterns of action), consider helping the parent engage in here/now repertoires first by prompting the parent through a brief here/now exercise, such as a breathing exercise, noticing their sense experiences, or other cues prior to starting the activity.

Conclusion

When taken together, present moment or here/now repertoires help us align our behaviors and our attention back toward what we want in our life and what we want our life to be about. I have found in my own clinical practice and research on ACT to date that, without a thoroughgoing present moment repertoire, other ACT targets (such as values-based patterns of actions or experiential acceptance) are harder to strengthen.

Repertoires that are not aligned with the here and now are often described as rigid, inflexible, or "mindless," essentially any other topography that helps the parents connect with past/future or there/then relationships (rather than focus attention on here/now relations). Repertoires that are under the control of past or future contingencies of reinforcement and/or punishment are not the same as attention to environmental contingencies per se. Repertoires that are under the control of past or future contingencies are often maintained by verbal rules about environmental outcomes that happened there/then and those that may happen in the future. However, verbal rules about contingencies are not the same as behaving according to currently functioning environmental contingencies. This distinction is important when considering present moment strategies, as they signal the importance of learning by doing rather than learning by way of verbal stimuli (or rules).

For instance, telling a parent "Instead of focusing on what happened yesterday, just focus on what is happening today" may provide an environment that can shape the parent's behavior in the moment. However, the parent may establish new rules provided by the behavior analyst that may not always align with the current environmental contingencies, and the subsequent rule-governed repertoire will be insensitive to changes in contingencies. In this way, we should always refrain from providing the parent with new rules; instead, we should establish the training environment to support the parent with learning new repertoires by doing and behaving.

All parent training should start with a foundation for here and now repertoires. My personal favorite is the Soles of the Feet, which can easily be modified to fit any clinical situation and population. I have found that exercises like SoF, with clear step-by-step protocols, can be very helpful for some parents, particularly those who like to get their child involved. Find alternatives to your favorites to better support the needs of the parents and family system! And come back to present moment repertoires often, as a refresher or to teach novel ways to orient oneself to the here and now.

Clinical Application

Now we turn our attention to how to put this together and apply it in clinical practice.

Parent: Shannon, 24-year-old single mother residing with her parents

Child: JT, 3-year-old male diagnosed with intellectual delay

Behavior Analyst: Miguel, BCBA-D for two years, just opened his own ABA company

Goal: Shannon will implement the ignore-and-redirect procedure in the behavior plan with 90% fidelity.

Assessment and Baseline Observations

Prior to training, Shannon reports that she finds it cruel to ignore JT when he cries. When he screams at her or really gets going and it impacts how he can breathe, she must respond and talk to him to calm him down. She reports that she just cannot *not* respond to him. During direct observations, Miguel observed her ignoring and following the plan when JT started to scream and cry, but every time JT got louder and started to struggle to breathe, she would stop following the plan and immediately attend to him and physically console him until he stopped crying. Miguel hypothesized that Shannon stopped ignoring the behavior to escape from the aversiveness of the situation/context.

Treatment Selection and Implementation

Miguel selected Soles of the Feet and modified the protocol for Shannon to focus on her hands instead of her feet, per Shannon's request. (She didn't like feet and didn't want to think about feet, including her own.) The SoF protocol was conducted three times by the analyst reading aloud the steps and observing Shannon's behavior. She engaged in about half of the steps independently prior to training. Miguel began intervention by reading aloud the steps while modeling the targeted response for Shannon. He and Shannon continued in this way about two or three times per session for four total sessions. Next, Miguel started to only read aloud the steps, providing corrective feedback to Shannon contingent on her engagement in each target response, fading over time to remove the vocalization of each step. Next, Miguel would role-play with Shannon, and arrange situations for Shannon to practice implementing the redirection procedure. Miguel then set up role-play situations for Shannon to practice while her parents were in the room, as she often reported difficulty in following the plan while her parents were watching her. During all role-plays, Shannon would practice engagement in the SoF steps throughout various contexts and situations.

After a few sessions, Miguel began using a family-friendly moment, targeting the Mindful Mountain for both Shannon and JT. Miguel first worked with Shannon on how she could adapt the game to be beneficial for her and JT. They modified the mountain activity, whereby each time they raise their hands up above their heads, they each would say something that they see, hear, feel, or taste. Miguel used behavioral skills training to teach Shannon how to use the exercise with JT, before coaching Shannon and JT through the activity during a stand-alone session. After a few observations and feedback sessions with Shannon, this activity was added to Shannon's data collection packet for between sessions. One question related to her use of the Mindful Mountain activity was added to Shannon's weekly self-monitoring tracker, and her responses to that question were discussed during coaching sessions.

Parent: Ray

Child: Kay, 9-year-old female, engages in property destruction for parental attention

Behavior Analyst: Kristi, BCBA for five years, new to the agency

Goal: Ray will engage with Kay at least once every 30 minutes, by chatting with her about preferred topics, discussing future or past preferred events, participating in an activity with her (watching television, doing homework), or engaging in related positive interaction.

Assessment and Baseline Observations

Ray reports that he doesn't implement his daughter's plan because he can't just stop what he is doing to attend to her. Kristi and Ray first worked to establish a variety of activities that he and Kay could do together and then determined how to schedule their work/school week and therapy schedule. She also helped him track how often Kay continued to engage in property destruction and what happened before and after each event.

Ray has been observed to interact with Kay and to adhere to their planned schedule for activity time. However, Kay will persist with trying to get Ray to play with her throughout the week, particularly on days that are not planned for an activity time with her dad. While Ray agreed to a 20- to 30-minute interval when he would spend a few minutes talking and interacting with Kay before returning to whatever he was doing, his adherence to this intervention is minimal. During observations, Ray completes this aspect of the behavior plan about 60% of the time when opportunities arise, and weekly data suggest that he completes this schedule less than half of the time. When given a calendar reminder or use of environmental modifications like timers, he completed the plan at similar rates. It was hypothesized that Ray does not give Kay his attention on the variable time schedule due to competing contingencies (there are other reinforcement schedules that are maintaining his behavior).

Treatment Selection and Implementation

Kristi selected the Mindful STOP intervention to assist Ray with contacting what was important to him in the moment. Every time he heard the signal to attend to Kay for a few minutes, he practiced the STOP steps. The STOP protocol was first conducted by reading aloud the steps and observing Ray's behavior. During three of these assessment probes, Ray engaged in some of the steps independently (all except "observe") and followed through when prompted to notice his senses. Next, Kristi arranged training sessions for Ray to practice the STOP steps when he heard a timer go off (the same sound as he hears for the attention protocol for Kay). During these sessions, Ray did less than half of the steps independently, and during each opportunity, he engaged in repertoires to escape or avoid the task by talking to Kristi about what they were doing and how to finish the session rather than engage in the STOP steps. This training setup was conducted for four total sessions before steady state was observed.

Kristi then faded out her reading and modeling of the STOP steps as Ray's independent engagement increased, before embedding times for Ray to practice the STOP steps with Kay. Kristi observed and coached Ray during real-plays with Kay using STOP as a pivot strategy to help Ray find a stopping point in his work and shift his attention to Kay for a few minutes. Kristi first selected watching television and, in particular, brief YouTube clips on preferred topics for both Kay and Ray to then talk about with each other. Ray would start the trial by doing other things, and when the timer would go off, he would find a stopping point to join Kay to watch videos online. Kristi would coach Ray depending on the situation, fading her prompts over time as Ray was successful in pivoting from work to engaging with Kay.

Checklist for Clinical Practice

Use this checklist to help you engage parents in present moment interventions.

☐   I can connect what I plan to do during sessions with the articulated parent training goals.

☐   I have identified and operationalized here/now repertoires for the parent(s).

☐   I can connect here/now repertoires with the overall goal of my parent training program.

☐   I have selected and established a valid data collection system for here/now repertoires.

☐   I have established a single or multimodal data collection system that incorporates here/now repertoires.

☐   My assessment data can be used to determine the effectiveness of the here/now intervention.

☐   I have selected an evidence-based approach to teaching here/now repertoires.

☐   I have arranged my parent training sessions to include evidence-supported interventions for here/now repertoires including aspects of behavioral skills training (i.e., instructions, modeling, rehearsal, and feedback).

☐   I take data each time I work with parents on here/now repertoires.

☐   I use the data collected to make data-based decisions.

CHAPTER 8

Using ACT in Clinical Practice
Flexible Perspective Taking

As discussed in chapters 1 and 2, there is a substantial reliance on midlevel terms to describe ACT processes, which may limit a consensus about functional definitions of traditional ACT components (see also Assaz et al., 2018; Foody et al., 2014). We may successfully circumnavigate this by moving away from chasing intervention strategies, and instead focus on molecular and molar aspects of parent topographies or repertoires that limit engagement in flexible and values-driven repertoires. By making this adaptation, we arrange our analysis toward patterns of actions that are flexible (*defusion* alternative) and align with here/now repertoires and shifting perspectives (*self-as-context* alternative).

This chapter will combine traditional ACT components of *defusion* and *self-as-context* into a single component that establishes flexible perspective taking. From a functional contextual framework, perspective taking is a relational repertoire that aligns with I/here/now functional contexts and functional relations. The main question within this component is the extent to which the parent responds to changing environmental contexts, particularly verbal stimuli, in a flexible or inflexible way. Said another way, flexible perspective taking considers not only the parent's deictic repertoire (I/here/now vs. there/then relations; see also chapter 2) but also how the parent interacts with verbal stimuli, including rules.

Theoretical Foundation

Returning to a singular component requires us to reconsider parent response patterns to incorporate relational and contextual functions. Combining *defusion* and *self-as-context* into a single component is not a new or novel idea. The early inception of ACT was often referred to as *comprehensive distancing*, where a primary goal was to teach clients to observe verbal stimuli (like thoughts or rules) and engage more directly with naturally occurring contingencies in the environment (Zettle, 2016). I have often heard ACT speakers and workshop presenters tell stories about how the two components came out of this idea—practicing observing verbal stimuli (*defusion*) and speaking about one's experience with verbal stimuli (*self-as-context*). Combining into a single emphasis on flexible perspective taking allows us to explore the range of flexible and rigid repertoires.

There may be some contexts where rigid response patterns are not necessarily detrimental in and of themselves and may serve an adaptive function. For instance, adhering to the rule "come to a complete stop at stop signs" may generally result in lower tickets or accidents. However, in an emergency, it may be more prudent to roll through, depending upon other variables, like oncoming traffic, pedestrians, and how important it is to get to the hospital. The extent to which the parents can shift their perspective from I/here/now and I/there/then will influence their adherence to following the rule. This adaptability of rule following may become problematic over time, particularly if established relational repertoires access escape or avoidance in the moment that produces a negative outcome or consequence long term.

As Assaz and colleagues (2018) point out, if stimulus functions are not sensitive or salient in the current context, "their influence over behavior will become more generalized in different situations, further increasing the probability of fear and avoidance responses" (p. 408). The primary problem with conditional aversive stimuli is not that the person seeks escape or avoidance; it is that they may only seek escape or avoidance rather than engage in other repertoires to access other reinforcers (see also K. G. Wilson & Murrell, 2004; as discussed in Assaz et al., 2018).

Take an example of a parent, Jim, who struggles to connect with his son, Michael. Jim often reports how challenging it is that his son doesn't talk, and he often gets mad when Michael throws his body onto Jim's. The BCBA working on the case believes Michael's behavior is multiply controlled, which makes Jim even more angry, and he reports not having trust in the BCBA because she can't figure out why Michael throws himself onto people. After a few sessions, Jim no longer attends parent training, and when he does attend, he doesn't stay in the room with Michael very long. When asked to participate in a session, Jim often reports wanting to have positive interactions with Michael, but often resorts to talking to the BCBA about past events with Michael rather than spend time playing.

The conditioned aversive in this example is Michael (neutral stimulus that is paired with a painful outcome, i.e., getting hurt when Michael throws himself onto Jim), and perhaps, through stimulus-stimulus pairing, the BCBA may also function within the same coordinative relational network as Michael and other aspects of Jim's experience with pain. Jim also appears to engage in rigid perspective taking, focusing on there/then emphasis with minimal shifting to Michael's perspective. The problem is not that Jim avoids Michael or the parent coaching sessions or other aspects of conditioned aversive per se; rather, it is that avoidance is the *only* pattern of action Jim engages in (therefore, by definition, not a flexible repertoire).

While this example includes stimuli based on formal properties, similar response patterns may be established through a history of differential reinforcement with socially selected abstract stimuli. Social environments reinforce verbal cues (i.e., contextual cues) that signal to the individual the discriminated response likely to be reinforced. In the example of Jim, verbal statements such as "Michael is worse today than he was yesterday" may signal a functional relation that today (here/now) is worse than (relational contextual cue of comparison) yesterday (there/then relations). If yesterday was bad, and today is worse, then patterns of actions that align with escape or avoidance of Michael may be more probable or likely to occur, even if Jim has yet to see or experience Michael that day. In this way, generalized operants based upon relational and functional contexts (i.e., arbitrarily applicable relational responding) help the individual arrange the world through verbal contextual cues, resulting in exponentially larger repertoires that relate to other generalized functional relations or contexts (i.e., relating relational networks; see also McEnteggart, 2018). The goal of our intervention, therefore, is to help parents respond to verbal stimuli in a way that is sensitive to contextual variations and considerate of one's current and long-term values.

As stated, the problem is not that we derive relations or that we engage in escape or avoidance patterns. The problem arises when those repertoires are persistent or regularly emitted, regardless of the long-term consequences. Given this, our goal will be to target shifting repertoires to both appetitive and aversive aspects of the environment, including verbal stimuli. We can think about environments as being *context limiting* or *context broadening*, both of which maintain and support arbitrarily applicable relational responding (AARR; see also chapter 2). There are different ways AARR can come to have limiting functions, that is, reducing access to reinforcers to a few functional relations. For instance, some derived relations may be a result of a discriminative function following differential reinforcement and eliciting functions after having a near-death experience while driving a rental car on a two-lane highway. After a near-death experience, the social community may tell you never to drive on that road again, which may be generalized to avoid all roads, not just the road you had the accident on. The avoidance repertoire may also function within relational contexts such as driving entirely or riding in vehicles at all. In this example, repertoires may, over time, narrow and subsequently reduce access to only a single reinforcer.

As you can see, there are different ways that humans come to establish AARR or generalized verbal operant repertoires. To date, there has been debate around how to best approach interventions or conceptualization of mechanisms of change for rigid AARR repertoires, specifically due to the many ways repertoires are established (i.e., respondent and operant conditioning). Assaz and colleagues (2018) proposed a way to conceptualize *defusion* to account for variations in acquisition of AARR across three different behavioral processes. Their approach will be used and modified to incorporate a focus on perspective taking to align within the newly established component (i.e., flexible perspective taking).

The first behavioral process is respondent extinction or habituation (Assaz et al., 2018). We would consider respondent extinction or habituation processes when conditional aversives are believed to maintain the target repertoire. Intervention strategies that target habituation or respondent extinction have been effective when target repertoires are established in this way (Hayes et al., 2011). For instance, silly word repetition activities or word repetition exercises (e.g., Titchener's deliteralization exercise, 1916; adapted in the Milk, Milk, Milk exercise in Hayes et al., 2011) can be used, where the parent is asked to repeat out loud in a funny voice the content of their thoughts or other verbal rules. Doing this over time helps reestablish the words as words (i.e., abstract verbal stimuli) rather than as their referents (i.e., moments in time, objects or places, people, etc.). The mechanism of change here is somewhat unclear, as it is possible that repeated presentation of the conditioned or neutral stimulus (i.e., the word that is repeated) is sufficient to decrease the strength of the stimulus. Or, through the repeated presentation, the conditioned response is replaced by a new response. While the exact mechanism of change may be unclear, there is no doubt that repeating the verbal stimuli can reduce the stimulus functions in the moment and over time.

The second behavioral process to consider is differential reinforcement of alternative behavior. Repertoires established through operant conditioning processes (i.e., schedules of reinforcement and/or punishment, shaping, imitation, etc.) can be effectively targeted through multiple schedules that target response acceleration (i.e., reinforcer provision following engagement in alternative behaviors) and response stagnation or deceleration (i.e., schedule targeted for the presenting problem or targeted repertoire). While behavior analysis has a long-standing history of defaulting to extinction schedules as a response reduction strategy, there is new evidence that suggests this approach is not the only schedule that can have deceleration effects (e.g., Vollmer et al., 2020).

This idea can be meaningful when we work with parents, particularly as we start to think beyond extinction and punishment schedules. As we think about ways to move beyond these schedules when using differential reinforcement, we can reconsider other processes like the matching law (i.e., Herrnstein, 1974) when selecting schedules for response deceleration. The *matching law* posits that two concurrently available reinforcement schedules will establish equal rates of responding. Let us consider this first in a more basic demonstration, through a computer game of sorts that we ask adult participants to play. This game isn't like most computer games, as it only has two shapes to interact with: a black circle and a black triangle. Participants play the game by clicking on either the circle or the triangle for money. In the first phase, selecting the circle provides $1 on a fixed ratio 5 (FR 5) reinforcement schedule (i.e., after the fifth selection of the circle, the participant gets $1 added to their bank), whereas selecting the triangle provides money ($1) on a fixed ratio 5 (FR 5) reinforcement schedule (i.e., after the fifth selection of the triangle, the participants get $1 added to their bank). Here, participants should respond equally across circles and triangles, given the reinforcement rate is the same across concurrently available schedules (i.e., each schedule pays out after 5 instances of behavior).

In phase two, the schedules change. Now, selecting the circle results in $1 after fifty clicks (i.e., FR 50 reinforcement schedule), while selecting the triangle results in $1 after every three clicks (i.e., FR 3 reinforcement schedule). In this phase, we would expect participants to shift their response allocation and select more triangles than circles. Why? Because participants can earn more money for engaging in fewer shape selections by selecting the triangles. We may also play with the various schedule parameters that will influence the extent to which the matching law still holds, including differing the amount of money (from $1 to $100), the shapes (from nonarbitrary to arbitrary), and the response requirement.

While this phenomenon has been demonstrated over many years and across multiple research labs (see also Davison & McCarthy, 2016), what is new and exciting is how this concept plays as an alternative to extinction schedules. If we consider the matching law when arranging our differential reinforcement procedures, we may decide to keep the target behavior on a lean reinforcement schedule while we arrange the alternative repertoire to function on a dense and low-effort schedule. For instance, when applying this with parents, we may decide that each time the parents shift toward here and now repertoires, aligning both their verbal behavior as well as their overarching patterns of actions, we will provide a range of reinforcers on dense schedules (e.g., FR 1 or FR 2 reinforcement schedules). We may also decide that repertoires targeted for deceleration (i.e., perseverating on past events) will not be subjected to extinction, but rather will be reinforced on a FR 10 or FR 15 schedule (to the extent that we can control the provision of the identified reinforcer). In this way, we can continue in our commitment to establish appetitive and reinforcement-rich environments over punitive or coercive ones.

The third behavioral process targets the context around the verbal relations and introduces new cues to "act as alternative functional contexts and directly diminish functional transformation" (Assaz et al., 2018, p. 411). Said another way, this process establishes new contexts that introduce new functional cues to signal the availability of reinforcement. To date, there have been two types of functional contexts established in the literature: recontextualizing thinking as narrative (i.e., descriptive autoclitics) and recontextualizing of thinking as spatially distant (i.e., creating space between you and your thoughts/feelings). These processes establish new contextual cues that compete with current contextual cues, and through transformation of stimulus functions can alter response allocation.

Getting Started

Since the goal of flexible perspective taking component is twofold (i.e., verbal stimuli that function as conditioned aversives and parental observation of their own behavior in real time), you will want to first conceptualize the selected targeted behaviors in this way. We know that rules can be helpful, and when followed or adhered to over time, they may become insensitive to changing environmental contingencies. Our job is to figure out what those verbal stimuli are within various functional contexts, and the extent to which parents can flexibly shift and notice their own behavior as it occurs in real time (i.e., here/now).

That job can be very cumbersome or daunting if we attempt to figure out these contextual variables without a clear conceptualization and corresponding data collection strategy. As is emphasized in other chapters, the selected data collection strategy should be sensitive enough to support your case conceptualization so that a functional context promotes deictic framing or conditioned aversive responding. This approach will more than likely result in the reliance on self-report in addition to directly observable data. How will you measure the parents' engagement in perspective taking? What behaviors or repertoires do you observe the parents engaging in during treatment implementation that align with rigid rule following or flexible rule following? It will be important for you to consider the parents' degree of flexibility from one functional relation or functional context to the next, which can be helpful in determining the parents' strengths as well as deficits.

During this process, consider how your target repertoire aligns with other repertoires targeted within the model. For instance, how do the parents engage in experiential avoidance? Is that somehow aligned with inflexible perspective taking? How are you operationalizing the parents' present moment (here/now) repertoires? You may find that some of these repertoires, like experiential avoidance and inflexible perspective taking, align topographically. But there may be parents whose experiential avoidance does not look similar to inflexible perspective taking. Establishing thoroughgoing conceptualizations of experiential avoidance and inflexible patterns of actions will help you in the long run. This should also be a component you return to during case conceptualization.

Another important consideration is the parent and family culture. Given that the social community is responsible for provision of reinforcement for rule following and other alignment between the person's behavior and contextual cues, it will be important to understand the family culture and worldview before making clinical decisions about parental repertoires that are maladaptive, problematic, or rigid. Take, for example, the parents that have different expectations for their son than they do for their daughter. They allow their son to make a mess in the playroom without requiring him to pick up his toys when he is done, but they require their daughter to clean up everything even if she is not the one to make the mess.

If we stop here in this observation, and don't become curious or ask follow-up questions, we may decide to help the parents implement house rules equally across both children. However, if we consider the family cultural selections, we may ask the parents to share with us why they require different levels of follow-through across their children. By doing so, the parents may share that they are not concerned about their son doing chores or cleaning up his toys; after all, no other man in their family does that nor will their son be expected to do that when he is older. This example highlights how critical it is for us to include the family's cultural orientation and practices in our treatment planning.

Assessment Considerations

The primary goal of flexible perspective assessments is to determine how sensitive the parents are to contextual variations. The main question in this component is whether the parents hold lightly to words and phrases, or do those words and phrases function as a conditioned aversive (and therefore they hold them tightly, not demonstrating sensitivity to contextual changes)? What are those verbal stimuli and corresponding repertoires or patterns of actions? How do those verbal stimuli impact the degree to which the parents engage in here/now deictic framing?

It is helpful to begin by establishing a functional relation between the environment (and particularly the verbal stimuli) and the target repertoire. Do the parents engage in inflexible perspective taking to escape a specific stimuli or functional context? What about the verbal stimuli—what words or phrases function as conditioned aversives? These questions can be answered through use of both indirect and direct assessment approaches rather than relying on a psychotherapeutic or "talk therapy" approach.

For instance, during the initial paperwork and consent process, a parent may report to you that she believes she is a bad mom whenever her child has a meltdown. Then, when conducting your intake assessments, you notice that the parent reports similar verbal stimuli, saying phrases like "I am always a bad mom when…" and "I can't worry about my husband when my child is awake." Next, you may decide to do a naturalistic observation, where you observe the parent and child interacting in a few different contexts and times of day (i.e., mealtime and free time). During your observations, you notice that across all functional contexts, the parent engages in a handful of responses to her child but with no real variability in her responding. Each of these contextual observations can be established as a descriptive analysis to help you get closer to a hypothesis about possible maintaining functional context and relations. The next step would be to conduct a naturalistic functional analysis (as appropriate) and to then test your hypothesis. (For additional context on how to conduct assessments, see chapter 6.)

It may also be prudent to consider how the parents' inflexible repertoires have been established to determine which approach to take during intervention. Unfortunately, this process is not black and white, and there isn't a single assessment strategy to use to determine that Parent A's behavior is a result of respondent conditioning while Parent B's behavior is a result of operant conditioning. Instead, it is up to you to determine what is potentially maintaining a parent's inflexible repertoires due to the way the parent talks about their experiences and the verbal stimuli you bring up and ask them to interact with. Take, for instance, the mom who reports believing she is a "bad mom" and can't do anything right. You may notice that when the mom states the aversive thoughts (i.e., "I am a bad mom" or "I can't do anything right") that she also engages in corollary avoidance patterns (i.e., biting her nails, pacing, crying, etc.). This doesn't necessarily mean that the verbal stimuli were established as conditioned aversives through respondent conditioning only; instead, it may mean that the content of the parent's thoughts may have conditioned aversive functions. These may benefit from respondent extinction and differential reinforcement as intervention strategies. Through direct observation, we can begin to narrow down potential conditioned aversives and use simple functional analyses (i.e., control condition and single test condition) to provide empirical support for our generated hypothesis.

There are different ways we may assess for perspective taking repertoires. This could be as simple as asking parents probe questions, anything from "If you were your child and your child were you, how do you think you'd feel?" to "Imagine yourself earlier in the week when you felt you were struggling—what was that like? If you slow down and notice yourself in that moment, what do you notice, feel, experience?" Or you may consider use of psychometric assessments to get a sense of the parents' initial or baseline repertoires pertaining to *defusion* or *self-as-context*.

Finally, you may establish an assessment of sorts from your observations and assessments within other ACT components. For instance, when conducting a present moment assessment, you may notice a parent report the same or similar types of rules or verbal stimuli (i.e., "I can't do what you want me to do when I get overstressed" or "I know my child does this on purpose— he is trying to push me off the edge" or "I should be doing a better job at parenting my child; this is why you are here so that you can tell me exactly what I should do"). Any of these statements may be a helpful starting point. These rules might be observed and considered in the assessment process to determine the parent's responses across various functional contexts. It is when you hear similar statements repeatedly throughout a session or over time that you will want to get curious as to how those rules may function across contexts.

Flexible Perspective-Taking Interventions

Intervention goals within *self-as-context* and *defusion* involve reframing thoughts/words as an ongoing process through deliteralization (exposure, habituation) activities, differential reinforcement, and recontextualizing verbal stimuli. Taking the same model described earlier (i.e., Assaz et al., 2018), we can consider our intervention strategies as dependent on how we hypothesize the rigid rule following and/or perspective taking is currently functioning.

When considering respondent extinction processes (like habituation or desensitization), word play interventions are the most common. Titchner's deliteralization (adapted from Hayes et al., 2011), for instance, is the common psychological strategy to have the parent repeat the verbal stimuli that function as conditioned aversive stimuli out loud as fast as they can, as slow as they can, or in a different tone of voice (such as singing, using a funny voice or accent, etc.). After each round of exposure (i.e., having the parent repeat the words for 30 seconds), ask the parent how the word or phrase changed—what do they notice that is different after repeating it? The goal is to have them identify other aspects of the experience beyond the referent (the thing the word means or points to), such as how it feels to say the word, the various sounds they hear, and so on. You may also instruct parents to write down the thoughts or phrases repeatedly; the goal is the same—to recontextualize the stimulus functions associated with the verbal stimuli.

In contrast, we may use interventions to disrupt the link between the verbal stimuli and patterns of action through use of differential reinforcement. Any activity that requires the parent to contact a known conditioned aversive stimulus and emit a different response typically evoked by the stimulus can be considered in this behavioral process. Moving Toward or Away can be an activity through which you help parents notice their own behavior with their child while differentially reinforcing moving toward rather than away from their child. Start by asking the parents to imagine the last time they interacted with their child and felt like they were struggling. Ask them, "Notice what was going on, where you were, what your child was doing. What were you doing or feeling?" Then ask the parents how they moved away from their child, metaphorically or literally. What was the aspect of the environment they were seeking to get away from? Next, see whether the parents are willing to move toward whatever was aversive at the time. Practicing this repertoire of noticing moving away in order to practice moving toward can start first as a thought exercise (i.e., Imagine a time when...), and can progressively move into practicing with the child after the parents begin to emit alternative responses in the presence of the aversive stimuli.

A fun differential reinforcement activity is Taking Your Mind for a Walk (adapted from Hayes et al., 2011), in which parents are instructed to notice their thoughts while taking a walk. As the parents notice their thoughts, help them to shift their focus to here and now aspects—that is, what do they feel, what do they see, what is in the environment that is contrary to the content of their thoughts? As the walk continues, have the parent kindly and gently thank themselves for the experience. For instance, the parent who has the thought *I have too much stuff to do to waste my time doing this nonsense* can be prompted to say out loud, "I am having the thought that I have too much stuff to do, and I'm taking it with me as I continue to do X" or some version of the alternative response. (In this instance, it is the additional verbal behavior, "I am having the thought that…and I am taking it with me.") In my practice, I have found it helpful to have the parent talk aloud during the first few walks. Over time, I help the parent start to fade the talk-aloud portion toward more silent and independent practice. This can also be incorporated into session challenges to help the parent practice between sessions.

Interventions that recontextualize thinking as either narrative or spatially distant from the self will include any activity or exercise that targets a reduction in function transformation. Recontextualizing thinking as a narrative helps recontextualize the content of thoughts that do not correspond to all environments. For instance, the activity Control Is the Problem (adapted from Hayes et al., 2011; Dixon & Wilson, 2014) can be helpful for recontextualizing thoughts as narratives rather than the content of the thoughts. Start by telling the parents, "For the next 30 seconds, whatever you do, do not think about chocolate cake [or any other neutral stimuli]." Repeat the instruction—"Don't do it, don't think about chocolate cake"—every 5 to 10 seconds throughout the interval. At the end of the interval, ask the parents whether they thought about chocolate cake. Everyone who engages in this activity will think about chocolate cake, as it is in the rule of what not to think about, so we must start there in order to engage in other relational frames such as distinction or opposition. Next, tell the parent, "For the next 30 seconds, think about whatever you want," and repeat the instruction—"Think about whatever you want"—every 5 to 10 seconds throughout the interval. At the end of the interval, ask the parents whether they thought about chocolate cake; sometimes people do, sometimes they don't. The goal here is to notice the difference between these two conditions (i.e., don't think about X, think about whatever you want).

Finally, tell the parents, "For the next 30 seconds, whatever you do, don't raise your hand," and repeat the instruction—"Don't do it, don't raise your hand"—every 5 to 10 seconds throughout the interval. At the end of the interval, ask the parents what that was like to be told what not to do and whether they did it or not. A quick note here about this step: Be ready for some parents to raise their hand. I have done this exercise in a plethora of contexts with a range of populations, and there is always someone who finds it reinforcing to go against the instruction (i.e., raise their hand). Be ready in case the parent responds in similar ways and meet them with kindness and curiosity.

At the end of the interval, have the parents reflect on their experience. I typically end this activity with some variation of the following:

> Did you notice that when told what not to think, you thought it? When you were told to think about whatever you wanted, maybe you still thought about it, but it wasn't as strong or as often. But when you were told what not to do or what pattern of action to avoid, you didn't do it. Maybe it is not about controlling our thoughts or other internal experiences. Maybe it is what we do with those experiences, how we relate to those experiences. What if you allowed your thoughts to be as they are, while continuing to do the thing that gets you the life

you want? What is it like to notice having thoughts that are different from what you do—that is, different from your actions?

Recontextualizing thinking as spatially distant, on the other hand, helps establish distance between the parents and the conditioned aversive stimuli that leads to reduced stimulus control. Examples in this process include those that establish the parents as separate from their subtle experiences (i.e., thoughts and feelings) and that establish additional spatial distance between the conditioned stimuli and their perspective about the stimuli. For instance, the Baggage Claim (modified from Dixon & Wilson, 2014) is an activity that can be tailored for parents. Here, parents are instructed to imagine themselves at the baggage claim, watching bags drop onto the conveyor belt slowly passing by. Ask them to notice what it is like watching bags drop one by one, looking for their bag, but not finding it. Next, instruct the parents to see whether they can place each thought or feeling they have on the bag as it drops in front of them and then watch the thought go off into the distance with the bag. What is it like to watch their thoughts leave and go away? Do the thoughts come back? Do they change? Do they notice a struggle to put the thought on the bag? Each type of question helps establish various stimulus functions around establishing contextual cues for engaging in alternative repertoires to the conditioned aversive.

Using Perspective Taking with Other Components

Flexible perspective taking can easily be combined with other ACT components. At the very least, it can be considered through probes or other forms of observations to establish or continue to establish known conditioned aversives and the extent to which they continue to elicit the conditioned response or evoke the targeted operant response. Helping parents shift their perspective, to notice their own behavior in real time, is effective at increasing other repertoires, including present moment or here and now repertoires, values-based patterns of action, and attending or approaching the conditioned aversive.

For instance, flexible perspective taking can be combined with acceptance and values-based patterns of actions using the Parent You Want to Be activity (modified from Stoddard & Afari, 2014). Here, start by asking the parents, "If you could wave a magic wand, how would your life be different? How would your parenting style or approach be different?" Similar questions can be asked to identify areas of their life that are appetitive or reinforcing, while also identifying aspects of their life that perhaps are aversive or unwanted. Then, ask the parents to imagine behaving in accordance with the way they want their life to be: "What do you see yourselves doing and where? What are people's responses to you? How does your child respond to you when you do X vs. Y?"

Another activity is Passengers on the Bus (Hayes et al., 2011), in which the parents are asked to imagine driving a bus on a highway that can only head north (toward values) or south (away from values). They are the driver, and while they can decide which direction to head, they cannot decide which passengers get on the bus. Once passengers get on the bus, they stay on: there is no dropping off passengers along the way. Passengers function like thoughts, memories, feelings, and so on, and they get loud (or quiet) depending on the context. Have the parents notice what it is like to imagine themselves driving their bus in the direction they are headed. As you go through the activity, ask the parents what passengers (thoughts and feelings, experiences or memories, etc.) are on their bus. Passengers serve as a metaphor for various conditioned aversives in the parents' experience, so be sure you know a general history before starting the activity. The idea is to expose the parents to the various passengers while they practice driving north (i.e., continue to engage in patterns of actions that are alternatives to the conditioned response).

Like other components, family-friendly moments can also incorporate flexible perspective taking. For instance, the Jumble Jar Game (also discussed in chapter 10) can be infused with flexible perspective taking activities. The Jumble Jar Game incorporates short sentence starters, or "jumbles," that can be read aloud and answered by family members and is a fun way to build positive relationships. You may start using this activity with parents and the family and embed perspective taking exercises during the parent coaching sessions.

First, begin by asking the parents to think about the last time they played the game with their family. Ask them to notice what they experienced while they played. Can they attend to I/here/now while shifting back toward I/there/then? Can they attend to how they felt and experienced the game in relation to how their child experienced the game (shifting between I/there/then and you/there/then)? Did their child say something that evoked certain reactions? If so, what did that look like? How did their behavior during the game align with here/now repertoires or other ACT-consistent repertoires (i.e., experiential acceptance, here and now emphasis, values-based patterns of actions)?

Conclusion

Flexible perspective taking as a treatment component can be assessed and influenced through three primary intervention considerations: deliteralization (exposure, habituation) activities, differential reinforcement, and recontextualizing verbal stimuli. By avoiding midlevel terminology, we not only ensure that we adhere to our scope of competence, but we also facilitate more specified treatment interventions.

The main idea within this component is that rigid rule following and inflexible patterns of actions often result in escape or avoidance. Using a single component here helps us establish not only how the parents respond to various rules or verbal stimuli, but also how their own verbal behavior and reinforcement histories influence their inflexible and flexible patterns of actions. We will never completely suppress previously established conditioned responses. However, we may be successful in finding ways to establish new networks and patterns of actions that compete with the reinforcement schedules associated with how the parents respond to rules and other relational networks.

Clinical Application

Parent: Molly (biological mother) and Chrissy, partners for seven years. Molly is the primary parent involved during parent training.

Child: Juan, 8-year-old diagnosed with attention deficit disorder and autism

Behavior Analyst: Dorothy, three years of BCBA experience

Assessment and Baseline Observations

During intake, Molly expressed concerns around her son lying about his video gaming and other things he does online. Both she and Chrissy report they had to "give in" to Juan's request to have a computer in his room, and since then, he does nothing but stay up late playing video games online. Juan has also been observed recently using profanity both online while gaming and with others around the house and at school.

Molly and Chrissy suspect Juan has social media accounts, even though they have tried to limit his use of apps like TikTok and Snapchat. Molly reports that she "can't keep going like this, it is a major issue in my marriage. I would rather just ignore it, and deal with whatever we have to as we have to, but Chrissy thinks we should remove everything from his room—no phone or computer—and give it back to him once he starts acting right." Molly also reports feeling ashamed and embarrassed by her son's use of profanity, often saying that "I just can't believe it. What happened to my little sweet boy? I can't help but think that some of this is my fault."

Dorothy asks Molly to complete the 6-PAQ as part of the intake process, and finds that Molly scores low in defusion, self-as-context, committed action, and present moment, while scoring moderately in acceptance and values subscales. Next, Dorothy goes through the parenting triangle with Molly and establishes that Molly relies on ignoring most of the issues she faces with Juan. Sometimes she relies on limit setting, as she reports taking away his TV time after dinner. Molly reports minimally providing reinforcers to Juan without requiring he do something particular or specific first.

Dorothy also asks Molly to record some of the times during the day that she reports are problematic, including bedtime and after-school routines. Dorothy watched all recordings given to her, and collected descriptive ABC data as appropriate. Next, Dorothy followed up with naturalistic observations during the period after school, and observed the confrontation and arguments reported by Molly and Juan. After analyzing the collected naturalistic observation data, Dorothy hypothesized that Juan's persistence in video gaming served a dual function: escape from household tasks or interaction with family members and access to social attention. Molly's behaviors were hypothesized to have a dual function: access escape from aversive situations or stimuli and access to alone time.

Treatment Selection and Implementation

Dorothy selected a respondent extinction exercise (modification of "I can't stand up and go to the door") for Molly's inflexible perspective taking and conditioned responses to Juan's behavior. Dorothy began by instructing Molly to repeat the phrase "I can't stand up and go to the door." As Molly began to state the phrase out loud, Dorothy prompted Molly to stand up and go to the door while she continued saying the phrase out loud. This activity was conducted at the beginning of each parent training session for the first few weeks. After a few weeks, Dorothy changed the target of the activity to Molly's specific inflexible rules (i.e., "My son can't get addicted to video games" or "I am a horrible mother for allowing him to say those words").

After a few sessions, Dorothy decided to use the Baggage Claim activity. Dorothy began by instructing Molly to use the breathing exercises targeted in earlier sessions (i.e., SoF chain). Next, Dorothy asked Molly to imagine she was at a baggage claim, watching bags drop onto the conveyor belt. Molly was instructed to place her thoughts or feelings or any other sensation that arose for her onto each of the bags and watch it continue off into the distance. Dorothy then spent time asking Molly to notice what it was like to place each thought or feeling on the bags and whether the thoughts came back, whether they changed, and whether she noticed a change in her struggle with the thoughts and feelings after placing them on the bags. Molly reported having difficulty letting go of her thoughts or feelings, stating that she didn't really put them on the bags. Dorothy returned to this activity for three additional sessions before Molly reported more ease in placing the thoughts on the bags and watching them continue on the conveyor belt.

Checklist for Clinical Practice

Use this checklist to help you engage parents in flexible relational responding.

☐ I have identified and operationalized flexible and inflexible relational responding for the parent(s).

☐ I can connect flexible relational responding repertoires with the overall goal of my parent training program.

☐ I can connect what I plan to do during flexible relational responding interventions with the articulated parent training goals.

☐ I have established potential rules that are rigidly adhered to by parents.

☐ I have selected and established a valid data collection system for flexible relational repertoires.

☐ I have established a single or multimodal data collection system that incorporates flexible relational responding.

☐ I have selected an assessment and data collection system to determine which flexible responding intervention to use.

☐ I have established a rationale for why I will use respondent extinction, differential reinforcement, and/or recontextualizing thinking as narrative or spatially distant.

☐ I have a plan to take data each time I work with parents on flexible relational responding.

☐ I can use the data collected to make ongoing data-based decisions.

CHAPTER 9

Using ACT in Clinical Practice
Experiential Acceptance

As mentioned in chapter 2, the concept of experiential acceptance is central to establishing repertoires of openness to the here and now. Experiential acceptance as a repertoire incorporates any approach response (or the absence of an escape response) that refrains from attempts to change or control stimuli or events (Blackledge & Drake, 2013). As such, acceptance repertoires are incompatible with experiential avoidance (EA) repertoires, or behaviors that attempt to change or control private experiences (such as thoughts, feelings, bodily sensations) even when doing so results in further behavioral harm (Hayes et al., 1996). At a basic level, experiential avoidance can be thought of as repertoires such as running, fighting, or hiding, so long as the behavior results in escape or avoidance from unwanted private experiences.

This chapter provides an overview of how to consider assessment and intervention strategies to shape experiential acceptance repertoires that can be emitted as alternatives to experiential avoidance. I will select a few acceptance-based interventions that are of minimal response effort for you to establish and conduct and that can easily be intertwined with other components during parent training. According to Kelly Wilson (2021), the central question within acceptance is the extent to which clients approach difficult aspects of the moment when valued living calls for it. For parent training contexts, we will adapt this question in this way: Are the parents willing to accept aversive aspects of the here and now and continue to implement the treatment plan or other patterns of actions that align with their values as parents?

Theoretical Foundation

Experiential avoidance behaviors and repertoires do not have to "look a certain way" per se. Instead, they are determined not based on the topography, but on the functional relationship between the behavior and the environment. Sometimes experiential avoidance repertoires are very subtle and difficult to directly observe by more than one person. In parent training contexts, we may consider subtle repertoires that are observable only to the parents by way of establishing *corollary repertoires* (i.e., other conjunctive behaviors the parents engage in, during similar moments in time that they report engaging in EA). For example, having the thought *I am a bad mom, I should just leave the store; I can't do this right now* may not be directly observable to other people. However, what is directly observable is the mom's change in other repertoires before and after the presentation of an unpleasant or unwanted experience or change in environmental conditions (i.e., when the child screams or cries).

Experiential avoidance repertoires are response topographies that are established within a functional relationship between specific environmental conditions, in particular the removal or prolonged delay of an unwanted event or stimulus. Escape and avoidance repertoires over time may come to have a narrowing effect on emission of novel repertoires, meaning they reduce the variability of response topographies to running, hiding, or fighting (see also K. G. Wilson, 2021).

In chapter 7, we discussed a parent who was struggling to take her child to the grocery store. Let us return to that situation for illustrative purposes. The parent reports struggling to take her child to the grocery store, as the tantrums are too much for her to deal with. The mom reports that every time the child throws a tantrum in the store, she responds, "Stop your crying, or we will leave the store"—and they inevitably leave the store without any groceries. When asked what she experiences in those situations, the parent may respond, "Well, I know that I am a horrible mother and all the people staring at me know this, that I knew this would happen, it always does; I need to leave and get out of here." Leaving the store puts physical space or distance between the parent and the aversive condition, even if the child continues to cry once out of the store.

The parent may engage in experiential avoidance even before getting into the store or before her child starts to cry by trying to suppress, ignore, or change her subtle experiences (i.e., thoughts about how bad the store trip will be, feelings about previous experiences, bodily sensations, and so forth.). When the parent physically leaves the store, she shifts to inflexible repertoires to access immediate reinforcers (i.e., removal of the aversiveness of the child's crying, the negative social attention of others).

If over time the pattern continued, the EA repertoire could begin to generalize to other situations or unwanted experiences. If EA was reinforced in the store with the child's screaming, it may also be reinforced when the child throws her food in the restaurant or when, rather than screaming, the child spits at her mother in the store. Further, the parent may also start to avoid talking about her child's behavior with friends and family in order to avoid further unwanted experiences and events. However, each time EA repertoires are used to access an immediate reinforcer (i.e., removal of the unpleasant or unwanted event), the parent further delays the forthcoming presentation of a larger reinforcer (i.e., valued living).

Experiential avoidance has been shown to be correlated with a range of concerning outcomes, including parental psychological inflexibility (Hayes et al., 2013), stress, and low levels of quality of life (Lloyd & Hastings, 2008; Shea & Coyne, 2011). Further, parents with high experiential avoidance have been found to be more likely to use ineffective parenting styles, including severe discipline (Brown et al., 2015). Experiential avoidance may also occur for parents when implementing behavior intervention plans, particularly if the intervention plan has high response effort or operates in opposition to the parents' perspective or worldview.

Intervention strategies that target experiential avoidance often include emphasis on experiential acceptance. When we consider noncolloquial definitions of experiential acceptance, most of the time other constructs like tolerance, surrender, or resignation to coercive control are also coordinated and included. As Russ Harris (2009) puts it, sometimes we mistakenly consider acceptance as an act of "gritting your teeth and putting up with it" (p. 134). If we just hold on tight, we can get through whatever unwanted or unpleasurable situation we experience; if we accept the unwanted thing now, maybe things will improve in the future.

However, acceptance repertoires within an ACT model do not align with this stance per se. Instead, acceptance repertoires are those that align with broadening repertoires in contexts that may have aversive stimulus features such as punishers or the loss of reinforcers.

For instance, when a child is sick and needs medical attention or surgery, being fully present in the hospital room may be incredibly painful and aversive for the parents. However, being physically and emotionally available to their child during that time may also provide longer term reinforcers for the parents (and the child) even if they are not fully contacted until a much later time. The degree to which the parents are willing to be open to the painful stimuli in the moment and continue to approach it (i.e., staying in the room, omitting from distractions like social media or TV shows) signals the extent to which the parents actively choose acceptance (Blackledge & Drake, 2013).

The important feature to identify is the distinction between the parents' EA repertoires and the parents' approach or *acceptance-based repertoires*. These two repertoires must be defined for each parent and be derived specifically from direct observations. It is important to clarify here that verbal report is not the same as directly observing the parents' behaviors. Distinguishing between these repertoires (experiential avoidance vs. experiential acceptance) is key.

The goal within experiential acceptance is to target approach repertoires—that is, willingness to experience aversive stimuli or events—as an active alternative to experiential avoidance and similar repertoires maintained by escape or avoidance. Similar to here and now repertoires, you can see how it may be hard for parents to stay committed to engaging in repertoires that align with their values if they don't fully agree to be willing to approach punishing or aversive stimuli. Acceptance is an ongoing and dynamic repertoire that supports selection of behaviors that result in larger later consequences rather than behaviors that result in immediate consequences that are sometimes not helpful or reinforcing long term.

Getting Started

As discussed in chapter 7, the here and now relational emphasis chapter, the first step when getting started is to identify data collection and assessment strategies that can be used to determine effectiveness of the intervention selected. For instance, how will you measure the parents' experiential avoidance and approach or acceptance repertoires? What behaviors or repertoires do you observe the parents engage in during treatment implementation? Can the parents talk about the plan and implement the plan with you there but not in other settings? Questions such as these help establish firm behavioral operational definitions and measurement systems, which will enable you to later examine the effectiveness of the intervention to influence change.

When first exploring EA repertoires as functioning within treatment nonadherence contexts, it is important to delineate issues pertaining to the behavior plan itself. The parents may escape engaging in the plan if the plan itself has a high degree of response effort, immediate response cost, or removal of reinforcers, or if the effects of the child's behavior from implementation of the plan are too punitive for the parents. For instance, let's say a parent tells you that the screaming just got too loud, and they couldn't deal with it anymore. Before concluding that the parent is avoiding the plan, think about how or whether the intervention plan for the child's screaming behavior can be modified or adjusted to attenuate for parental responding to thin schedules of reinforcement.

Another consideration is the parents' active engagement in willingness as an alternative to EA repertoires. *Willingness* can be defined as the active engagement in behaviors that result in accessing reinforcers that are not necessarily immediately available or reinforcers that are established through negative reinforcement. As discussed in chapter 2, the main premise within an ACT framework suggests that it is normal for humans to engage in strategies to remove or avoid unwanted events (i.e., EA repertoires), and therefore the target should be to emphasize willingness as an alternative to EA. Willingness, as a response class, includes any repertoire that necessarily involves the parents contacting the punitive or aversive stimuli and actively choosing to engage in a different repertoire (i.e., acceptance repertoire). Said another way, willingness is the openness to and active engagement with an unwanted experience or stimuli without struggling with it or trying to change or control it. In this way, one parent's willingness repertoire will not necessarily match in topography with a different parent's willingness but will in terms of function of the repertoire itself.

Finally, it is important to consider risk/reward ratios of EA repertoires, particularly given the insidious nature of EA repertoires. As such, it is critical to stay within your scope of competence when selecting and designing stimulus avoidance assessments or other assessments that may expose the parents (in some capacity) to potentially aversive stimuli.

Assessment Considerations

The primary goal in this component is to assess not only the avoided content of the environment or experience (i.e., stimulus objects, people, events, etc.) but also the avoidant repertoire engaged in by the parents (i.e., experiential avoidance repertoires) and how the parents escape or avoid an unwanted stimulus or experience. Further, we want to assess the extent to which the parents already engage in experiential acceptance and what stimulus conditions are more likely to evoke acceptance repertoires. To begin, determine the extent to which the parents actively engage in approach or experiential avoidance repertoires. The goal is to determine what it being escaped or avoided, and how the stimuli are being escaped. Consider assessing the *what* and the *how* of EA. Do the parents already engage in experiential acceptance repertoires? If so, what does the response class look like, and what conditions are more and less likely to evoke the repertoire? Do the parents engage in EA repertoires? If so, what private experiences are the parents avoiding? What environmental conditions evoke EA repertoires?

Next, assess how the parents engage in experiential avoidance: Do they leave the area (elope)? Do they hide (avoid specific stimuli within the environment)? Do they fight (engage in alternative repertoires that are aversive in nature in order to access immediate changes in the environment)? Indirect observations may be a helpful place to start, depending on the topography of EA repertoires for the parents, and can be very useful in the subsequent development of direct observations and descriptive analyses.

While there are numerous evidence-supported psychometric tools that have been developed to target "acceptance," one in particular that is relevant to our discussion around parent coaching is the Parental Acceptance Questionnaire (6-PAQ; Greene et al., 2015). The 6-PAQ is an eighteen-item assessment that measures parental psychological flexibility and has been shown to have high internal consistency and reliability. While the tool is somewhat new, it has also been validated with a Spanish sample and is also available in Spanish (Flujas-Contreras et al., 2020). Other acceptance psychometric tools do exist, but extreme caution is advised given that there is no "gold standard" of what acceptance as a construct is, and as a result, there is a lack of evidence to support an optimal measure (see also McAndrews et al., 2019, for a systematic review of acceptance psychometric measures). In other words, these measures may be helpful with identifying areas to target or explore with the parents, but should never be considered the primary dependent measure in our clinical practice.

Descriptive or direct observation assessments can also be useful when determining what is being avoided and how the parents are accessing avoidance. One approach is through *stimulus avoidance assessments*, where stimuli within the environment that may have aversive functions are identified and systematically arranged in a hierarchy (e.g., A. N. Wilson et al., 2014). For instance, asking the parents to report what happens before and after the (already established) avoidance repertoire can be a starting point for establishing a hierarchy of aversive stimuli.

Next, the parents consolidate and narrow down the various stimuli and/or conditions that may evoke avoidance repertoires. Then, each stimulus or condition is written on an index card or the equivalent (e.g., sticky note or computer paper). The index cards are then used as items when conducting a multiple stimulus without replacement rank order assessment, where parents are asked various questions about the index cards, and asked to rank order the cards depending on the question. For instance, you may consider asking the parent to "order the cards based on which ones make you engage in X [target behavior] the most" to establish a potential avoidance hierarchy. After a hierarchy is established, the events that were ranked as least evocative or least likely to result in engagement in the target behavior can be used first as ways to help bring aspects of the aversive environment into sessions to help the parent actively start to practice experiential acceptance.

After identifying parental treatment nonadherence and avoidant repertoires, another helpful assessment strategy is to determine the breaking point at which the parents may switch from engaging in treatment adherence and shift into avoidant and/or treatment nonadherence repertoires. *Breaking points* are anytime two concurrent reinforcement schedules are in effect and the person stops engaging in one behavior to engage in a different behavior, often as a result of changing magnitude, quality, or immediacy of the change in reinforcement schedule.

In a clinical exploratory study, A. N. Wilson and Gratz (2016) used progressive ratio schedules (or reinforcement schedules with increasing response requirements; Roane, 2008) to determine the response rate requirement upon which a functional communicative response would cease and the target response would be emitted. Within a parent training context, similar environmental arrangements can be established with a little creativity and planning. For instance, take the parent who reports that her son yelling at her makes her engage in avoidant repertoires the most. The analyst may consider a progressive ratio schedule to provide the parent with access to escape from implementing the treatment plan, following treatment adherence. The key here is ensuring enough repeated exposure or availability to engage in treatment adherence, so low-frequency events may not be appropriately assessed through this approach.

Remember, the key with acceptance-based assessments is to arrange the environment to establish (a) what the parents are avoiding (i.e., stimuli) and (b) how the parents are accessing escape or avoidance (i.e., response topography). Combining indirect, descriptive, and synthesized assessments will bolster your ability to determine a functional relationship between environmental conditions and parental engagement in experiential avoidance.

Acceptance Interventions

When thinking about how to select and implement acceptance-based activities, it is important to consider the parents' current EA and approach or acceptance repertoires before intervention begins. Consider the earlier discussion around the insidiousness of EA repertoires, and ask yourself these questions: *For these particular parents, what do their EA repertoires look like? How intense or severe are their EA repertoires?* If you notice more deficits than strengths within the acceptance repertoire prior to training, consider starting with more explicit acceptance-based exercises or activities in another environment or situation outside of the parent-child dyad and treatment implementation plan. When considering acceptance interventions, consider the goal of each session and the overarching goal of treatment in general.

Differential reinforcement of other, alternative, and low rates of behavior. At
a basic level, acceptance interventions involve two repertoires and reinforcement schedules: a *target repertoire* (or experiential avoidance repertoires: running, fighting, or hiding, etc.) is targeted for slower acceleration or deceleration, while an *alternative repertoire* (or acceptance repertoires: approaching, interacting with, physical contact with, etc.) is subjected to reinforcement schedules targeted for acceleration. In parent training contexts, you more than likely already use differential reinforcement schedules to increase parental adherence to treatment implementation. The distinction here is on a different repertoire or response class. Rather than focus only on the implementation skills (or treatment implementation), you would

shift focus on parental engagement in flexible repertoires in environments that have previously elicited EA repertoires.

Take, for example, the parent who has completed behavioral skills training and can implement his child's behavioral treatment plan, but recently has been asking the behavior analyst to do it instead. The parent repeatedly will say to the analyst, "I can't do what you are asking, if you could just do it for me this time" or "I'm just not ready to do this." Sometimes the analyst helps the parent by jumping in and showing him how to implement the plan, while at other times, the analyst may try to prompt the parent through the behavior intervention plan. Although perhaps well-meaning, by intermittently reinforcing the parent's escape repertoires, the analyst may also inadvertently strengthen the target repertoire (i.e., behavioral inflexibility or experiential avoidance).

When implementing a differential reinforcement procedure for acceptance repertoires, it is prudent to begin to shape these alternative repertoires in reinforcement-rich environments. Acceptance repertoires such as verbal statements like "This is really hard, and I am scared to mess it up, but okay, I'm willing to at least do two minutes of it," and perhaps the subsequent patterns of action, should be reinforced on multiple and dense reinforcement schedules. Reinforcement should also be functional, meaning we will need to provide escape as appropriate for engaging in the newly acquired alternative repertoires.

Shaping flexible repertoires.

Many different ACT metaphors and experiential exercises have been established and validated as effective strategies at shaping flexible, acceptance-based repertoires. One common focus in this component is the willingness of the parents, or the self-report of the acceptability of the conditioned aversive. We will help parents establish their own operational definitions for their willingness scale for their own targeted acceptance topography or repertoires. Using a Likert scale (0 = not at all willing, 2 = somewhat willing, to 4 = extremely willing), establish various activities and situations that require the parents to engage in a new behavior or repertoire that is somewhat hard or aversive in order to gauge their willingness, and keep track of their responses over time.

For example, the Willingly Cold Ice Challenge (modified from Hayes, 2005) brings practice engaging in willingness repertoires in real time. To begin, place a bowl of ice water in front of the parent and have them start by taking a few present moment breaths. Ask the parent to rate their willingness to put their hand in the bowl for as long as they feel comfortable with. After ranking, have the parent place their hand into the bowl while you set a timer. As soon as the parent pulls their hand out of the bowl, have them rank their willingness to put their hand immediately back into the bowl. There should be a difference in willingness ratings, or they would still have their hand in the bowl. By removing their hand, they are reporting "not at all willing." If the parent reports no difference in willingness, consider including a visual representation of the willingness scale or similar training considerations for accuracy of parental responding.

Next, talk with the parent about what they did in order to keep their hand in the water for as long as they did. See whether they are willing to put their hand in the bowl again, but this time to practice some of their favorite acceptance or present moment activities (e.g., here/now activities or Soles of the Feet steps before or while their hand is in the bowl; see also chapter 7). Consider instructing the parent to rate their willingness to do the activity again before they put their hand back into the bowl.

Sometimes a parent may keep their hand in longer the second time, and sometimes they may pull their hand out sooner. The goal here is not to increase the duration of time, but rather the parent's experience with their hand in the water while they were actively engaging in alternatives to removing or avoiding something that was unwanted or somewhat uncomfortable. There is no criterion or goal to reach, only to experience doing something potentially uncomfortable in a reinforcement-rich environment.

Distinction training. Another important consideration when targeting acceptance repertoires is the distinction between the targeted repertoire and related ones, such as compassion, empathy, or love. Experiential acceptance will look different for every parent, yet it will always include repertoires that move toward something aversive, such as bodily sensations, emotions, and other private experiences (see also Whittingham & Coyne, 2019).

Conjunctive repertoires, such as compassion, may align with experiential acceptance, but may not necessarily function as such. For instance, compassion may require being aware of and maintaining psychological contact with suffering, even though doing so results in the parents "rescuing" their child from their suffering by giving in (in the case of treatment adherence to access to tangibles) or by ignoring their child's emotional responding. Helping the parent distinguish between these repertoires through role-play, modeling, and corrective feedback will help arrange accelerating experiential acceptance repertoires.

Using Acceptance with Other Components

Acceptance can easily be embedded into any session that involves engaging in responses in the presence of aversive stimuli. Using the outcomes of the matrix (Polk et al., 2016) would be a good starting point, particularly when considering the parents' rules around the same aversive stimuli (i.e., flexible perspective taking) and their say-do correspondence between their values and externalized behaviors (i.e., values-based patterns of actions). Experiential avoidance repertoires can be identified on the matrix by aligning the bottom left quadrant (the subtle experiences that evoke experiential avoidance) to the upper left quadrant (the actions the parent does, defined as experiential avoidance). As such, interventions that seek to align parental engagement in experiential acceptance repertoires should align with movement from the bottom left quadrant to the upper right quadrant.

For instance, the exercise Saying No (Stoddard & Afari, 2014) targets a combination of present moment or here/now repertoires with experiential acceptance. You would instruct the parents to say no whenever they notice a sensation, thought, feeling, or similar private or subtle experience. As the parents continue to say no, see whether they can distinguish between physical sensations and thoughts/feelings aligned with resistance to sensations. You can general-ize this idea of saying yes or no during intervention plan training and modeling sessions.

Another option for shaping flexible experiential acceptance repertoires is a modified version of Man in the Hole (Hayes, 2005). In this exercise, ask the parents to think about how their struggle with treatment nonadherence is akin to being in a hole, and their attempts to get out of the hole align with the various attempts they've taken to try to change or fix the situation (or all the various topographies of behavior they've engaged in as part of their EA repertoire). Next, have the parents notice what they have been doing to get out of the hole (i.e., EA reper-toires). The paradox of the hole is that everything the parents have tried thus far results in a larger or deeper hole; it does not result in them getting out of the hole.

What if the way out of the hole was to drop the tools they've been using? What if the way out was the willingness to try something so novel and new that doing so may make them feel uneasy, vulnerable, or some other uncomfortable feeling? These questions can be helpful for parents to consider as they think about how they experience the willingness to drop whatever tools they are using inside the hole.

Some acceptance intervention strategies may not be as effective without identifying other repertoires or reinforcers for the parents. For instance, differential reinforcement schedules that are informed by the parents' identified values (or the larger later reinforcing aspect of their life) are more likely to be effective than schedules based on your clinical opinions only. Consider reinforcer assessments with values-based activities or stimuli to ensure motivation is established before any experiential acceptance work.

Conclusion

The goal within experiential acceptance is to assist parents to move toward unwanted immedi-ate events—particularly when doing so gets them closer to living in accordance with their values—rather than attempt to remove, control, or change the event (see also discussion in chapter 10). Within parent training contexts, the distinction between the experiential avoid-ance repertoires and experiential acceptance repertoires is paramount to acceptance-based intervention strategies.

Targeting willingness can be helpful when shaping alternative repertoires to experiential avoidance. By taking a layering approach, we can be cautious and systematic in how we collect data and how we subsequently use the data to inform us about how our intervention is working (or not). The willingness Likert scale and the provision of situations for the parents to actively engage in experiential acceptance are just a few examples of how we may use repeated measures as a layering strategy. We may also consider the single-subject design we use as another layering strategy.

Many of the acceptance intervention strategies discussed in this chapter focused on shaping and differential reinforcement. However, we can also consider how to align our prompts and corrective feedback statements with experiential acceptance. For instance, asking the parents to gauge their willingness prior to an activity or exposure to potentially aversive stimuli or events promotes experiential acceptance for the parents. Similarly, to facilitate correct feedback for the parents' engagement in experiential acceptance, we might say to the parents, "Wow, great job doing X. Approaching hard stuff is difficult, isn't it?! Do you think some of that relaxation stuff we do helped you today?"

Experiential acceptance, as an intervention goal, should be continued to be refined and redefined with input from the parents as well as from collected data and your clinical observations. As the parents gain new skills, and the parent-child relationship changes and begins to grow, the way in which experiential acceptance presents and/or persists (particularly during periods of thin or minimal reinforcers or appetitive environments) will also change and adapt. Our approach to parent training must therefore be adaptable and change as the needs of the parents shift. Returning to our definitions and measurement systems to target experiential acceptance and avoidance repertoires will be helpful in ensuring we adhere to conceptually systematic case conceptualization.

Clinical Application

Now we turn our attention to how to use acceptance intervention strategies in clinical practice.

Parent: Cynthia, 48-year-old married female

Child: Roman, 13-year-old male with ASD, traumatic brain injuries, and complex medical conditions

Behavior Analyst: Beth, BCBA-D for ten years, provides services in the school and at home

Goal: Cynthia will implement functional communication training to teach Roman functional ways to ask for access to tangibles with 90% fidelity and implementation timing (i.e., provide the targeted tangible item within 3 to 5 seconds of Roman's engagement in vocal approximation or sign).

Assessment and Baseline Observations

Cynthia has been working with the ABA agency for over ten years and has completed multiple rounds of ABA-informed parent training. Recently, she has been deviating from the intervention plan, as she reports an increase in her "worries" about Roman's future. She often reports to Beth, "I am worried about what happens to my child if he doesn't learn how to talk. Isn't there a point in time that if they don't learn it, they won't? Why can't you just teach him how to talk, then we wouldn't have the problems we have?" During direct observations, Beth observes Cynthia forcing Roman to vocally ask for things rather than reinforce vocal approximations or signed responses, as supported by Roman's behavior intervention plan. Beth also observed Cynthia chatting with family members and school staff and stating that when she makes him say the whole thing, she's ensuring that he doesn't have a future where he can't speak. Direct observations were collected over several days and across multiple contexts (home, school, and community).

During the matrix assessment, Cynthia identified three areas that showed up when she noticed herself moving away from the things she finds important in her life: fear of the future for Roman and running out of time. Each time these showed up for her, she reported an intense need to force Roman to talk and to use full physical guidance to help Roman complete a task. When taken together, Beth hypothesized that Cynthia was requiring Roman to vocally request using full sentences in order to avoid her verbal rules about Roman's future.

Treatment Selection and Implementation

Experiential acceptance was targeted and tracked using a 5-point Likert scale on willingness and exposure to low-to-moderate experiences requiring various degrees of willingness. The first exercise Beth used was Man in the Hole, and Cynthia monitored her willingness scale throughout the variations of the exercise, noticing how her bodily sensations shifted and changed with the different questions and paradoxes presented. Beth assisted Cynthia with labeling the type of tools she predominantly uses when parenting Roman: the shovel (when she physically forces Roman to do something) and the bucket (when she requires multiple responses from Roman before giving him the item). The tools, shovel and bucket, were also incorporated into flexible perspective taking activities—that is, asking, "What does it look like for you to drop the tools?"—and during parent training rehearsal and modeling sessions. For example, when Cynthia engaged in requiring multiple responses from Roman, Beth gently prompted her by saying, "Cynthia, is this the bucket tool?"

Similar experiential acceptance activities were used with Cynthia to help establish differences between acceptance and compassion for her son. Accepting Roman's language limitations were not the same as resigning herself to "he will never speak" nor were they symptoms of a boy needing "to be saved." Instead, Beth worked with Cynthia to help establish various response topographies that aligned with her parenting values and having compassion for Roman without necessarily reinforcing a challenging or maladaptive behavior. To Cynthia, compassion was when she would stop everything to make sure he would say the full word or phrase before she would give him the item; acceptance was requiring his response be at a level he was currently working at rather than where she wanted him to be. Compassion was giving him long explanations about why she had to make him talk; acceptance was understanding that sharing her experiences might inadvertently reinforce the wrong repertoire.

Parent: Patrick, 58-year-old married male with three children

Child: Shannon, 16-year-old girl, with epilepsy and learning delay

Behavior Analyst: Breanna, BCBA with fifteen years of experience

Goal: Patrick will ignore and redirect Shannon's rude verbal behavior with 90% fidelity

Assessment and Baseline Observations

Shannon recently began hanging out with new friends from school who, her parents believe, have influenced her to be disrespectful. Recently, Shannon has started to talk back to her parents whenever she wants to go out and they say no. She has started to push back on some of her medical needs, including not taking her medications daily, not adhering to her doctor's prescribed diet or lifestyle, and not attending doctor's appointments. She told her dad, Patrick, to "Eat shit and die" and sneaked out of the house after being told she was grounded. Patrick reports that Shannon's disrespect is out of control and says, "I am not going to ignore my child when she disrespects me. No way! There is no way that I am going to allow her to say that to me. What type of parent would I be if I allowed by daughter to disrespect me like that?" Patrick reports that when she makes him angry, he notices that he gets hot in his body and starts yelling. Sometimes his wife reminds him to calm down and that works; other times, nothing seems to calm him down. He acknowledges that engaging with Shannon goes against the behavior intervention plan, but he reports not having any control over what he does after she behaves that way.

Breanna began by conducting naturalistic observations and descriptive assessments when watching Patrick and Shannon interact during typical times throughout the week, including after school and mealtime. These assessments suggested Shannon's inappropriate verbal behavior was maintained by socially mediated negative attention and escape. Next, Breanna conducted a stimulus avoidance assessment to establish various behaviors emitted by Shannon that were potentially evocative for Patrick. Six different aversive events were established: Shannon raising her voice, using curse words, slamming doors, sneaking out, lying, and over-dramatizing her life (i.e., making things seem worse than they are). Each event was written on an index card, and Patrick completed the assessment three times to establish a hierarchy. Low aversive events were targeted first during SoF training, along with the use of the willingness scale. Moderate aversive events were targeted when Patrick was willing to practice with those events and when he responded with 80% accuracy.

Breanna hypothesized that Patrick's engagement in limit setting and punitive discipline approaches was to access escape and avoidance from unwanted events. Patrick's rigid rule fol-lowing (i.e., the strongly held belief he cannot be disrespected by his daughter) also resulted in his engagement in experiential avoidance, as evidenced through his immediate shift to yelling and punishing Shannon by grounding her and taking away her privileges.

Treatment Selection and Implementation

Treatment began with present moment and experiential acceptance–based interventions, including SoF and willingness scale. Patrick also completed the 6-PAQ a few times to start a conversation about his current level of acceptance toward various behaviors emitted by Shannon between parent training sessions. Items identified during the stimulus avoidance assessment were targeted through various SoF practice situations, giving Patrick a place to rehearse the newly established experiential acceptance repertoires.

Breanna also targeted parent-child interactions by working with Patrick and Shannon on fun activities they could do together throughout the week, regardless of what had happened earlier that day or week. This was an opportunity for Patrick to practice letting past events go and showing up fully to the activity with Shannon. Patrick would rehearse the SoF steps each session until he completed them with minimal prompts (or 80% accuracy). Patrick also com-pleted self-monitoring data throughout the week and tracked what he and Shannon did during the family-fun activity and how it went. This data was used to assess the extent to which Patrick adhered to completing the activity, particularly after Shannon engaged in a highly aversive behavior (such as when she slams the doors or sneaks out).

Checklist for Clinical Practice

Use this checklist to help you target experiential acceptance repertoires within parent training contexts.

☐   I can connect what I plan to do during sessions with the articulated parent training goals.

☐   I have identified and operationalized experiential acceptance and avoidance repertoires for the parents.

☐   I can connect the acceptance and avoidance repertoires with the overall goal of reducing parental treatment nonadherence.

☐   I have selected and established a valid data collection system for the parents' acceptance and/or avoidance repertoire.

☐   I have established a single or multimodal data collection system that incorporates acceptance and/or avoidance repertoires.

☐   My assessment data can be used to determine the effectiveness of the acceptance intervention.

☐   I know with a high degree of confidence that I have identified stimuli that evoke parental experiential avoidance.

☐   I have selected an evidence-based approach to teaching acceptance-based repertoires.

☐   I have arranged my parent training sessions to incorporate common and evidence-supported interventions for acceptance repertoires, including aspects of behavioral skills training (i.e., instructions, modeling, rehearsal, and feedback).

☐   I take data each time I work with the parents on acceptance repertoires.

☐   I have a plan to make data-based decisions.

CHAPTER 10

Using ACT in Clinical Practice
Targeting Values-Based Action

The term "values" is not a new concept within behavior analysis or other social sciences. Within behavior analysis, values are often used to describe a discrimination between a thing or certain variable and its reinforcing effect (Skinner, 1971). Values give purpose and meaning to our life. We can think of them as words that can be used to orient and align our here/now repertoires with high-quality yet delayed abstract reinforcers. A technological definition may consider values as rules or verbal stimuli that function as verbal motivating operations, which alter the reinforcing properties of the referents to the behaviors and repertoires engaged (Dixon et al., 2020; Paliliunas, 2021).

Said another way, values are "freely chosen verbally constructed consequences of ongoing, dynamic, evolving patterns of activity, which establish predominant reinforcers for that activity that are intrinsic in engagement in the valued pattern itself" (K. G. Wilson & Dufrene, 2009, p. 66). Values are *free* in a Skinnerian way, where such reinforcers are selected in and of themselves, not due to a concurrent negative reinforcement and/or punishment schedule. We can speak about values as verbal events that identify relationships between things and/or other verbal constructs and abstractions. These are shaped by our reinforcement histories, which align to what we categorize as a meaningful life. Values are inherently idiosyncratic and require a degree of insight into the nuances of the reinforcement and punishment histories of the individual and family.

The statement "I find meaning in being a loving and caring mother" may help bring aspects of the future into the here and now, particularly if the current environment does not signal such a reinforcement schedule (i.e., the identified reinforcer is not present and there is nothing indicating to the parent that the reinforcer is forthcoming or available). However, given the history of entailment and transformation of function between the reinforcing event of loving and caring for her daughter with the verbal stimuli ("I find meaning in being a loving and caring mother"), other smaller behaviors and repertoires that lead to similar conditions are paired with the verbal stimuli, bringing reinforcing aspects into the current environment.

For instance, a mother may have no issue with behaving in accordance with her value of loving and caring for her kids when they are sick, or hungry, or when they ask for help on their homework. She may find pleasure in creating handmade costumes for school dances or dress-up events and may understand the importance of resolving tense arguments or disagreements between her children. However, she may find it harder to orient herself to her parenting value when she comes home from work early and sees that her teenage daughter skipped school to hang out at the house with her boyfriend. The mother's parenting value does not show up or go away per se, but it may be more challenging for the mother to engage in behaviors that align with her parenting value depending on the environmental context.

From an RFT perspective, rules are verbal stimuli that evoke behaviors that are a direct result of a history of relational responding (Plumb et al., 2009; Paliliunas, 2021; Berkout, 2021). Verbal stimuli are abstract and arbitrarily applicable, meaning the stimuli can be anything that refers to objects, constructs, abstractions, or other things that are selected by the social community. For instance, the words "cat" and "gato" are used to refer to the four-legged domesticated mammal. Which word is used depends on the social community that is responsible for provision of reinforcers. As such, the person's use of the word "cat" and orienting one's behavior toward similar mammals upon hearing the word "cat" from others will be met with social reinforcers; in other communities, emitting the word "gato" and orienting one's behavior toward mammals with similar features as those paired with "gato" will be met with reinforcers.

In this way, values can be considered statements that have reinforcing effects due to specific relational frames, particularly hierarchical class memberships. *Hierarchical relational responding* refers to repertoires that are emitted because of stimulus classes related by membership, categorization, or attributions to other larger classes (Stewart et al., 2020). Take figure 10.1 as an example of a possible relational network for that same parent who values being a "caring and loving mother." The value statement here is "caring and loving mother," and the goals articulated by the mother include providing compassion and empathy to her children regardless of their behaviors and loving her children unconditionally. The values-based patterns of actions, or what she does that another person could observe that would result in such reinforcers, include practicing forgiveness, providing response-independent physical affection to her children, and telling her children daily that she loves them. If the parent engages in the articulated patterns of actions and if doing so aligns with reinforcers of "caring and loving mother," then we might conclude that the parent is behaving according to her values.

You can see how there are multiple functions that values and values-based patterns of actions take on. The first is the extent to which the parents can identify, construct, elaborate, and describe what is meaningful in their life. How well can the parents articulate what is important in their life? What is important to them as parents? The second is the extent to which the parents engage in patterns of action that either move them closer to what they find meaningful or further away from what is meaningful.

There is a third function, namely the extent to which the parents engage in correspondence between what they say they are going to do and what they do in a different moment in time (i.e., say-do correspondence; Deacon & Konarski, 1987). In values work, say-do correspondence can be a critical target, particularly to determine the workability of the value statement and the identified patterns of actions that result in reinforcement. Take, for example, a parent who says he values self-care and commits to doing 30 minutes of any self-care activity after his son goes to bed. The parent agrees to track what he does in a journal shared with the behavior analyst. Sometimes he reads a book or watches his favorite television show, and sometimes he

Example hierarchical relational network related to parental values

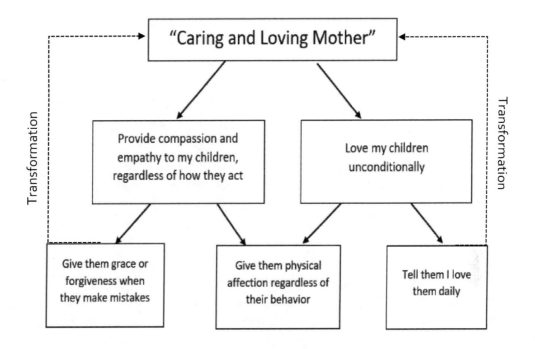

Note: Solid lines represent direct discrimination, and dashed lines represent derived transformation of function. Adapted from Paliliunas, 2021.

Figure 10.1

returns to his work and writes memos or legal briefs. His say-do correspondence is around 50%, or about half of the time his behavior aligns with what he said he was going to do.

When say-do correspondence is not occurring at moderate or high rates, there may be a mismatch between what the person says is important and what functions as important (or reinforcing), or there may be a mismatch in the environmental variables where discriminative stimuli may not be salient enough to signal the availability of a reinforcer. It is critical when targeting values that we establish reinforcement-rich environments, both within session (to support engagement in uncomfortable or new repertoires) and outside of sessions (in the natural environment). Accessing reinforcement-rich environments leads to more reinforcement-rich environments (K. G. Wilson, 2021).

Values work, at any level, is where we get to broaden the treatment focus beyond treatment adherence or parental nonadherence to treatment. Values work should never focus on whether the parent engaged in treatment adherence, because those skills can be better targeted elsewhere (i.e., flexible perspective taking and here/now repertoires). If we target treatment adherence as a value or even as a pattern of action that leads to a value, we can potentially arrange a coercive environment; we may also inadvertently limit the expansiveness that is someone's meaning in life. We want to establish contexts of possibilities, not contexts of limitations. Expanding our values work to other aspects of the parents' life, like finding joy and pleasure in life with their child and outside of their child, may result in the parents living a richer and more meaningful life.

Before embarking on values work with parents, an important distinction to make is the difference between values and goals. Goals are often things in the world that are tangible or achievable (Lundgren & Larsson, 2018), whereas values are abstract and not tangible or obtainable. For instance, parents may value their significant other and being a loving and caring parent, and they may set goals like getting married or changing their surname, or taking their child to the doctor, and so on. In this way, goals can be identified as important discriminations between what patterns of behaviors align with a value statement, but goals can never be values per se.

As in other chapters, I will use different phrases to help signify strict behavior analytic conceptualization terminology, as well as a loose translation of those processes. In this chapter, the term *values* will be used to denote verbally constructed motivations with a history of aligning with context-broadening environments. Use of this term is helpful when considering broader contextual situations and corresponding values-based actions. When considering case conceptualization, the phrase *verbal motivational operant* will be used to identify values-based identification and clarification. Similarly, *say-do correspondence* will be used to indicate the relationship between values statements or word-referent relationships with engagement in both micro and molar repertoires that align (or correspond).

Getting Started

An important starting point may be for us to look at our own values as they pertain to our commitment to engaging in unconditional positive regard for the parents and child throughout training. I have found that arranging environments of possibilities—where mistakes and "incorrect" behaviors are not met with punishment or extinction but support and discussion, and maybe sometimes humor or a moment of silence—yields more positive outcomes and results than more limiting environments.

Think about how you will remain committed to establishing and valuing appetitive environments for the parents to learn, grow, and develop. You may consider returning to values identification and clarification early and often when working with parents to ensure each session continues to support them toward a more meaningful life. Another commitment may be to focus on withholding judgment or evaluation on the parents' values—that is, to not inject your own values into the session. Take active reflection periods throughout your work with the parents, returning to this question about how to remain committed to establishing appetitive environments.

During the information-gathering stage, it will be helpful to establish the parents' perspective of their relationship with their child. This can also be helpful when determining parent-child values. Consider asking questions like these:

- What are your favorite activities to do with your child?

- Are these the same or different from your child's favorite activity to do with you?

- What about preferred activities with immediate family, friends, or neighbors?

- How does your child's state of being and overall wellness impact your parenting values or parent-child values?

- How do you generally interact with your child?

- How would you describe your relationship with your child?

Obviously, this is not an exhaustive list, and you should ask a range of questions to establish what aspects of the environment are either *context limiting* or *context broadening* (see also K. G. Wilson, 2021). Get curious as to how the parents go about teaching their child new skills. Noting ways parents already teach their child an array of new skills can be very valuable and, when considered early, may impact parental buy-in. These considerations can be targeted and measured using either a single or a multidimensional layering strategy.

Another important consideration is the parenting style. Do the parents use an authoritarian style, relying on strict rules and response cost (or loss of privileges)? Do they believe "kids will be kids" and engage in a more permissive or "gentle" parenting style? Or are they uninvolved? Knowing the parenting style and philosophy can be helpful when discussing alternative strategies to more punitive methods with the parents.

Assessment Considerations

At the most basic level, values assessments can incorporate any systematic attempt at determining which stimuli (either verbal or otherwise) are preferred and function as reinforcers. Preference assessments can and should be conducted often and can be as formal or informal as needed. Helping parents identify what they want their life to be about is the core of valued living, and preference assessments are basic ways we can attend to the values of the parents in the shifting environment of "now." The distinction here will be on how to go about implementing a preference assessment. Asking the parents, "What is important to you right now?" or "What fun thing should we do after our session today?" are easy, low-effort ways to assess for parental preferences. A rank order assessment is probably as formal as you need for most parents. Use your best clinical judgment as to when to use a more formal assessment to identify parental preferences.

Psychometric assessments, such as the Valued Living Questionnaire (VLQ; K. G. Wilson et al., 2010), may also be helpful to determine the parents' values and how their current patterns of actions align with their selected values (see also Barrett et al., 2019, for systematic review of values-based psychometric tools). For instance, the Parental Acceptance Questionnaire (6-PAQ; Greene et al., 2015), while established as an acceptance-based tool, includes ACT component subscales that can be helpful in establishing how the parents' values and acceptance repertoires align with how their child behaves. These three subscale items can be helpful for determining where to start with values:

- I can clearly state my values related to parenting (item 5)

- My actions as a parent are consistent with my values (item 10)

- I have clear parenting values that guide my interactions with my child (item 18)

Throughout the assessment process (both before and during intervention), parents may tell you about their subtle behaviors, such as how angry they were when their child did something last week or how anxious one of them became when their spouse dealt with the child's tantrums in public. These reports from parents can be considered signals of possible or shifting values in those moments. The way in which the parents speak to you and what they speak to you about may signal whether the parents are engaging in values-based patterns of action. Do you notice the parents are unwilling to fail and often retreat to a similar pattern of action that more reliably results in escape or avoidance from unwanted or unpleasant stimuli? When asked about their values, do they repeatedly say, "I don't know"? Or do they report what is important to them?

There may be other signals that the values may not be clearly functionable or articulated. For instance, the use of phrases or words that restrict or place limits on repertoires (i.e., have to, must, should, never, always, etc.), mismatches between values and patterns of actions, or correspondence between goals and engagement in behaviors may also signal value troubles. Such troubles often indicate possible values and inflexible repertoires that can be targeted within other treatment components (e.g., flexible perspective taking, experiential acceptance).

The matrix and the parenting triangle (see also chapter 6) are good assessments that can specifically target parental values. For instance, asking parents what is important about being a parent generally (molar repertoires) as well as right now, in the moment (micro repertoires, i.e., bottom right-hand corner of the matrix). Returning to this question regularly can be helpful when considering case conceptualization.

Say-do correspondence assessments will assist with establishing a baseline rate of how the parents do what they say they are going to do, particularly in relation to their articulated values. An easy assessment strategy here is to walk through something similar to figure 10.1. Begin by having the parents identify something they value about being a parent. Next, ask the parents to identify goal statements, or ways that demonstrate that value. Then, ask the parents to articulate an action pattern—something that others could see them do—that also aligns with their value. Drawing out the diagram with the parents' statements can be helpful to come back to, as values are more deeply explored, described, and tested. Finally, ask the parents to set a commitment goal to practice one or more of those identified patterns of action between sessions. Help the parents identify a small, reasonable, and obtainable goal. When the parents return and share their correspondence rate at the next session, it is important to maintain appetitive environments and avoid giving the parent corrective feedback on how to improve their correspondence.

Values-Based Action Interventions

As discussed, we can think about three primary functions of values and our work in values:

1. Identification and clarification of what the parents find important (i.e., labeling the value).

2. Identification and rehearsal of values-based patterns of actions (i.e., what they do to access what is important).

3. Correspondence between what the parents say they will do and what they do in that moment (i.e., say-do correspondence).

Given this, it will be critical to incorporate all three features in your values work with parents. Sometimes all three functions can be targeted in a single metaphor or activity, such as in Mapping Your Values (see below). At other times, you may want to isolate a feature so you can really spend time with it. For example, values clarification and identification can likely be articulated in 5 minutes, but imagine how much deeper you can go if you give it several 30-minute sessions. While the activities presented here will cover each of these features, it is important to determine each parent's unique presentation and situation in order to determine which feature should be emphasized throughout intervention.

Mapping Your Values (originally published in Dixon & Wilson, 2014, derived from Hayes, 2005). Modified for parents, this activity targets values identification and clarification, and can be extended to incorporate other ACT components to identify the parents' behavioral flexibility strengths and/or deficits. Start by having the parents identify two to three values across an array of value domains (e.g., family/parenting, relationship, career, education, civic responsibility, health/wellness, spirituality; see also the Valued Living Questionnaire for ten value domains articulated by K. G. Wilson et al., 2010). To align with treatment targets and scope of competence, be sure to have the parents focus on their parenting value domain as well.

After the parents identify two or three value domains, get curious about why those domains are important, without passing judgment or challenging what they find to be important or meaningful. If the parents discuss the domain more like a goal than a value (i.e., they identify important behaviors to engage in rather than an intangible thing or way of life), help them shift focus to why those behaviors are important and why they engage in those behaviors. You might say, for example, "I hear you when you say that you clean up the house and the play area for your child. I wonder, why is picking up your child's toys in the play area important? How does doing that get you closer to the life you want?" Once the parents identify values within each domain, you can combine the activity with other ACT components to understand conditions that may support or suppress the parents' patterns of actions.

For instance, flexible perspective taking can be incorporated to help understand what happens in the parents' life that stops them from living in accordance with their values. Ask the parents, "What gets in the way of you living consistently with (value)? What shows up that gets in the way of the life you want?" Instruct the parents to recontextualize the barrier outside of words or literal meaning and instead give the barrier a shape, color, or metaphorical connection. Once they establish something, explore their barrier with curiosity and reinforcers. This exercise can help rearticulate or clarify values and corresponding patterns of actions as well as identify and consider ways that verbal behavior (or other environmental conditions) can deter parents from engaging in values-based patterns of actions.

Take for example, a client I had early in my ACT practice. The client had articulated that health and wellness were important to him, but he struggled to work out or take care of himself. When working through this activity, he physicalized the barrier as the Alice in Wonderland bunny, singing "I'm late, I'm late, I'm late" with a larger-than-life version of a pocket watch. This barrier was stopping my client from aligning with his health and wellness values, as he "didn't have enough time to do everything he needed to do for work, school, and going to the gym." Identification of the barrier helped identify a stimulus to use during habituation exercises (i.e., flexible perspective taking) and with orientation of say-do correspondence (i.e., aligning verbal repertoires of what he would do when the barrier showed up in order to continue to behave in congruence with his values).

Biggest Little Things.
One thing I have noticed in my clinical practice is how often parents are hyperfocused on the "big" problems (e.g., their child's aggressive or destructive behaviors, how often their child lies to them or breaks a house rule, etc.) rather than being focused on aspects of their child and their relationship with their child that they find meaningful or reinforcing. The Biggest Little Things exercise was developed to help parents lean into the little aspects of their lives, to help them attend to what they value with their children and their relationship with their children, every moment of every day. Even in the presence of the "big" problems, there are "little" things that signal we are in congruence with our values. We may just need to look in specific ways to find them.

To begin, have the parents establish a free-play area for them to hang out with their child for a bit. Instruct the parents to interact with their child by playing or doing whatever they feel comfortable doing, noting that we will focus our attention away from correction-based procedures or implementing a rigid plan. Instead, we want to practice shifting our observations to how the child interacts with their world and how that impacts the parents. Throughout the observation, make a note for the parents when you see little things the child and parents do that may signal something of value. For instance, perhaps when the parents sit on the floor, the child gets close to the parents, takes the book out of their hand, and then runs away laughing. The parents, while trying to get the child to come back, are also observed laughing. You might say to the parents, "Did you notice that when you sat down at his level, he came over and took the book. Then what did he do? He laughed!" Starting small, helps the parents notice the little things and string together little behaviors that are important or meaningful to them.

Valued Living Log (modified from Stoddard & Afari, 2014). This activity can be easy to embed into your typical parent training programming. It can also be a useful tool to help collect data and analyze parental engagement in values-based patterns of actions between sessions. In my clinical practice, I have used this with clients as a homework type of activity, targeted to complete outside of sessions, and then discussed at the beginning and end of each session. In other clinical spaces, I have used this as a check-in of sorts, completed throughout the entire or majority of a session in groups and one on one. It can also be combined with other targeted ACT activities as appropriate. Across spaces, this tool has been helpful to establish all three features of values (values clarification, patterns of action, and correspondence between what we say and what we do when we experience different environments and life situations).

A Valued Living Log is a way for parents to reflect and track what they do each day that gets them closer to or further from their values. You can establish this activity in a variety of ways, so be sure to consider what approach would be most successful for the parents and child you are working with. Begin by meeting them where they are at. A Valued Living Log must feature the following variables:

- Verbal motivational operant(s): written tacts about appetitive environmental conditions

- Patterns of actions or activities: behaviors or repertoires, written out or open for parents to fill in

- Measurement system for patterns of actions and related repertoires: dimensions of behavior across any behavior engaged in by the parents and/or child

Once you determine each of those variables, instruct parents to track which actions get them closer to their values and how often they engage in them throughout the day. A common example is to target a single value and ask parents to track the patterns of actions they did each day, rating the difficulty of doing or the willingness to do each activity.

Pivoting One Degree (or Less). This activity is derived from a concept discussed by philosophers of science as *truthlikeness*, or goals that appear "true" or real even though they may in fact be false. Within a functional contextual framework, we may speak of "truth" as goals that work successfully; something is "true" insofar as it successfully works in the world. According to philosopher Graham Oddie (2013), the general idea is that there are some false propositions that are closer to aspects of truth than other (also false) propositions. We may be inclined to reject false propositions completely, but it is entirely possible to progress toward goals of truth through "a succession of false or even falsified" propositions (p. 541). In this way, the *truthlikeness* of an event can be considered the extent to which a goal or proposition works or gets closer to working.

We can apply this idea in our values work by thinking about our patterns of actions that either move us closer to or further from a life full of meaning and rich reinforcement. When we find ourselves moving away from our values, it may be overwhelming or require too much response effort to consider and engage in all the different things needed to get back in the direction of our values. What if there was a way to pivot to a very small degree back toward our values, even if doing so suggested some level of false proposition—just not *as false as* previous states or propositions? What if we can pivot in such a small degree, in any way, shape, or form, for us to inch ourselves closer to a vital and meaningful life? What if pivoting one degree (or less) got you closer to the things you want your life to be about?

This exercise can be helpful for parents who are stuck with "trying" to change or struggling to activate new patterns of actions. By recontextualizing their struggle and giving them permission to move in a direction that may not necessarily lead to the "truth proposition" (i.e., obtain the identified value), it may orient them in the general direction (i.e., obtaining environments closer to values but not yet accessing the value). This activity can also be adapted to target the extent of the pivot (one degree to two or five degrees) or what the pivot looks like—that is, what behaviors are aligned with less than a degree of pivot from those aligned with one or two degrees of pivot?

Take, for instance, a parent who tells you that they value having a meaningful relationship with their child, while also engaging in escape and avoidance when spending time with their child. If the goal for the parent is to lean into the here and now aspects of engaging with their child, pivoting even a fraction of a degree may look like the parent staying in the room (even though they may not interact with the child directly). The parent may also pivot in a small way that progresses from negative vocal statements toward neutral vocal statements (even though the goal may be to interact with positive statements).

Pivoting in this way may help facilitate behavioral activation toward a meaningful life, allowing the parent to begin to access reinforcement-rich environments. Doing so may also establish pivoting in larger segments, from one degree to maybe four or five degrees.

Family-friendly moments. Like other components, values work can be embedded into the family system. While families will have idiosyncratic value systems, the extent to which the parents' values align across valued domains or other environmental distinctions (e.g., having different parenting styles for each child) needs to be determined prior to implementing any family values work. It can be helpful to combine the selected interventions with other family targets (e.g., family dinner or game night as discussed in chapter 7).

The Jumble Jar Game (modified from Szabo et al., 2020) is a great way for parents and children to engage with each other while simultaneously sharing what they value and finding common experiences across family members. This activity can be done across a range of settings and contexts, but we'll discuss it as a game to play during mealtime to help develop familial connections while everyone is sitting around the table. It also can be helpful for families who struggle to keep their children at the table for the duration of the meal. Feel free to modify these steps to fit the needs of the family you are working with.

To start, each family member should write sentence starters, or "jumbles," on separate pieces of scratch paper or something similar, that can be read aloud and answered as a family. Jumbles should focus on aspects of what they find meaningful or valuable. For instance, jumbles targeting values may include these:

- Today, my biggest struggle was _____ and I enjoyed doing

  _____.

- I dream of doing _____.

- When I am in the dark, I feel _____.

- My favorite movie is _____ because _____.

- One thing I'd like to talk about with my family is _____.

- When nobody is watching, my favorite thing to do is _____ because

  _____.

- If I could wave my magic wand and change anything in the world, I'd change

  _____ because then I can

  _____.

Also consider embedding statements like "You get to avoid answering a question this round." Once all family members have written two or three statements, place all pieces of paper into a jar or container, and instruct each family member to pull out one piece of paper. When the family member completes the statement, parents can use that as an opportunity to ask further questions (i.e., "Wow, I didn't know your favorite movie was *Jurassic Park*! Do you want to go see the new one that is out in theaters?") or clarifying questions (i.e., "Hmm, I didn't know you saw *Jurassic Park*. Where did you watch that movie? Were you scared?"). Remind parents that the game should be reinforcing, so avoid questions that may suggest the child is somehow in trouble for sharing. Emphasize that they should always meet what their child says with curiosity and reinforcement.

Once parents start to notice little things in their life with their child that they find meaning in, there may be space to introduce a family version of Sweet Spot (modified from K. G. Wilson & Sandoz, 2008). Begin by asking parents to describe a sweet memory they have had with their family. As parents start to identify and describe the memory, prompt them to notice the various sensory details: What do they see? What are they feeling? What do they notice their child is doing or feeling/sensing? and so on. Connecting these "sweet spot" moments with other perhaps not-so-sweet moments helps the parents stay connected with their values and perhaps begin to shift focus to the sweetness in each moment. These sweet spots can also be established with the parent and child together, who go through the same process with each other, sharing a new moment while talking about a previously reinforcing moment.

This activity can also be adapted to work with families whose children may have limited verbal or vocal capacity. Even if a child does not vocally express themselves using complex words or sentences, we can still arrange the environment to help the parents and child experience an appetitive moment with each other. Consider having the parents sit close with their child, with something in hand that is a preferred item for the child and allows for child-directed play and interactions. Ask the parents to narrate their experience, sharing the sweet spot of the moment as it occurs, connecting with their child.

Using Values with Other Components

Values can be combined into regular ACT sessions and should be included to determine how or whether the parents are continuing to engage in patterns of actions that align with their stated values. Helping parents learn to enjoy their children, their family time, and other meaningful aspects of their life with their child is something that can be incorporated across all ACT components and should be targeted often, particularly in the beginning of intervention. Sometimes taking a moment to just be with their child—to play, laugh, or whatever the moment calls for—is overlooked by parents, as they struggle to juggle various responsibilities and demands on their time and attention. Establishing environments where the parents contact the here/now with their child and lean into the reinforcing aspects of just living in the world with their child is a great way to naturally embed values work.

Perhaps the simplest way to incorporate values into other ACT components is to return to values clarification and discrimination of values-based patterns of actions. Questions such as "What do you value here in this moment?" or "What did you do this week that aligned with being a loving mom?" can help orient the parents toward aspects of their values and corresponding patterns of actions. Any incongruencies or inflexible repertoires can be targeted as appropriate.

Conclusion

Just as present moment repertoires are the bedrock to sustaining most of the work we do in ACT, values are the bedrock to sustaining repertoires that align with a meaningful life. What does it mean for the parents and the family to live a meaningful life? The answer lies in our commitment to examine and engage in repertoires that result in a life we find (or articulate as) meaningful and important. This is the core work of values.

This chapter highlighted three important functions of values work from a behavior analytic perspective: values identification and clarification, patterns of actions that align with those statements, and the say-do correspondence between these networks. It is important to come back often to these three features throughout our work with parents. Values change, environments change. Parents will change their opinions, beliefs, and worldview. Our own acknowledgment and conceptualization of parental values must also change and evolve.

Finally, there is a space for values work by us as trainers. A potential barrier for new clinicians implementing ACT is engaging in novel repertoires in the presence of conditioned aversives (e.g., fear of messing up, struggle to "get the right metaphor," etc.). In this way, we may lose sight of the basic foundations for ACT, which is establishing and maintaining reinforcement-rich environments for the parents and families throughout training. Our own practice in flexible perspective taking as aligned to this shared value of arranging appetitive environments can be helpful to orient our own behaviors. We should also come back to how our own patterns of actions align with establishing and maintaining reinforcement-rich environments for the parents and their families when we conduct training. While this may not be directly related to our work with parents per se, it does help orient our own behaviors to ensure that we are implementing ACT in a way that is consistent within the overall model.

Sometimes the best way to help a parent connect with their values is to model values-based patterns of actions. How might we return to our own values-based practice? How might we continue to establish training environments that promote appreciation and contexts of possibilities rather than contexts of limitations? How can we stay committed to such a pursuit, even in the face of false propositions?

Clinical Application

Parent: Heather (adopted mom, goes by first name)

Child: Bell, 14-year-old female with chronic pain following a car accident

Behavior Analyst: Danny, BCBA for ten years, just started using ACT with parents

Goal: Heather will use reinforcement strategies, such as providing Bell noncontingent access to known reinforcers throughout the day. Heather will establish a healthy relationship with Bell by incorporating 30 minutes a day of doing activities selected by Bell.

Assessment and Baseline Observations

During the first intake session, Heather reports that Bell breaks the family rules all the time by using her phone 24/7, staying out past curfew, sneaking out of the house late at night, and posting inappropriate pictures on her social media pages. Danny used the parenting triangle to help determine Heather's parenting style and found that Heather relied heavily on limit setting and punishment and rarely used reinforcement-based strategies. Heather reported taking away privileges as the most frequently used discipline strategy. She used this anytime Bell would do something incongruent with "family rules" (i.e., lying, sneaking out or back in) or anything that Heather considered a demonstration of disrespect (i.e., yelling back at, making ill-humored jokes about Mom or Dad, breaking family rules). Heather also reported making Bell "work for the Wi-Fi password" to manage morning routines and would often ignore most of Bell's disrespectful behaviors to compromise with Bell.

Danny also conducted the matrix with Heather and Bell separately to help establish (a) whether parent-child values aligned or shared consistency and (b) to get an idea of repertoires to look for during observations. Heather reported her parenting values to include providing her children with a safe and loving home and having a meaningful relationship with Bell. She acknowledged that sometimes it was hard to support Bell in the way that aligns with what her therapists say, but it is important to her that Bell be successful in life, whatever that means for Bell. Heather also reported that she is exhausted and frustrated all the time, repeating quite often, "I try, and I try, but nothing really ever changes." When probed a bit further, Heather reported that she gets stuck in trying to do everything right, noting that "Nothing is working, things are getting worse," and others would know this because she never cooks dinner anymore (she is just too tired to do it, so the eldest cooks or they order takeout). She also reported that she yells more at Bell and takes away things that she never really considered were privileges (like the Wi-Fi password).

During observations, Danny watched Heather and Bell interact with each other on two occasions: family dinner time (both during meal prep and during the meal) and during family time (where Heather and Bell were asked to do whatever they would do together). Throughout observations, two general themes emerged from direct observation and corresponding conditional probabilities: Bell was more likely to engage in higher rates of verbal threats and inappropriate jokes to Heather when asked by Heather to complete an unwanted or nonpre-ferred task (e.g., help prepare dinner, set the table, or play a card game). Sometimes Heather would remove or change her directive to Bell, and other times she would persist and require Bell to complete the directive. During family time observations, Heather was unsure how to proceed or interact with Bell in a way that wasn't directive toward something for school, household chores, therapy next week, or something similar. There seemed to be a disconnect between Heather and Bell when there was not a specific topic or event to discuss.

Treatment Selection and Implementation

The results obtained during the matrix and parenting triangle confirmed Heather's value as a parent: *being a loving parent*. Danny also confirmed goal statements that move her toward being a loving parent: her children know they are safe and loved, and having a meaningful rela-tionship with Bell. From here, Danny confirmed with Heather two patterns of actions that aligned with being a loving parent: providing a healthy and filling end-of-day meal and speaking to Bell in a positive or neutral tone of voice. These functions of values (verbal statements, pat-terns of actions, and say-do correspondence) were reassessed throughout intervention and adapted as needed, contingent upon analysis.

Establishing a deeper relationship with Bell, outside of planning for future events or getting her to complete tasks around the house, was later targeted with input from Heather. This was tracked in her self-monitoring journal (i.e., type of activity, duration, and level of interaction/enjoyment by both Heather and Bell).

In the first values-based ACT session, Danny worked with Heather on the parenting triangle and established ways Heather could flip her triangle. Danny walked through each of the areas, helping Heather identify and commit to one or two behaviors in each section of the triangle. Heather agreed that limit setting (or removing Bell's access to the internet and spending time with her friends) will only be used when Bell runs away, sneaks out of the house, or engages in inappropriate or risky sexual behavior on social media. Danny worked with Heather on ways to use planned ignoring when Bell engaged in disrespectful behaviors, and established real-play situations for Heather to role-play and practice responding to Bell by getting curious and asking her questions about why she is behaving in those ways.

Danny conducted the Biggest Little Things exercise to help establish a deeper relationship. This was conducted in short intervals (no more than 5 minutes at a time) for three months. Short intervals were established to ensure that Heather would continue to access reinforcers through-out the entire interval; initial observations suggested that positive interactions between Heather and Bell lasted no more than 7 minutes (ranging from 7.20 minutes to 10.4 minutes). After each interval, Danny discussed with Heather things that he noticed: for example, when Bell seemed interested or when Heather arranged the environment in a way that Bell seemed to find appetitive. As Heather expanded her repertoire and orientation to not only here/now aspects with Bell but also in connecting with her value as a parent, the interval was lengthened, and fewer formal exercises were conducted as skills were transitioned into the natural environment.

Checklist for Clinical Practice

Use this checklist to help you engage parents in values-based patterns of actions.

☐   I have considered how I will remain committed to establishing and valuing appetitive environments for the parents to learn, grow, and develop.

☐   I have identified reinforcers that can be used to establish an appetitive environment for the parents.

☐   My data collection system is sensitive to gathering information about values statements (i.e., say), patterns of actions (i.e., do), and relative correspondence between each repertoire (i.e., say-do correspondence).

☐   I follow ethical standards or expectations when learning about family cultural dynamics.

☐   I am mindful not to impart my own beliefs and values onto the parents or family.

☐   I have aligned my assessment with my intervention plan.

☐   I have incorporated parental and child value systems (as appropriate) both to help the parents establish appetitive environments for the child and to ensure I can establish appetitive environments for the parent.

☐   I have established that the parents can identify and label what is important to them as parents.

☐   My intervention provides both response-independent and response-dependent reinforcement schedules for parental engagement in values-based patterns of actions.

☐   My intervention incorporates aspects of compassionate parenting techniques and repertoires.

☐   I model how to pivot one degree or less toward values throughout sessions. This may look like showing up honestly, laughing at my mistakes, allowing silence to be a therapeutic tool, and noticing when I "need to be an expert"—or it may look completely different.

☐   I consider the parents' values and values-based patterns of actions in every session, both as a stand-alone treatment component as well as something to return to when targeting other ACT components.

Acknowledgments

This book is the product of a community of people who have provided incredible support and encouragement along the way. I wish to first thank the families who opened their homes and trusted me to support them in their time of need. I am so thankful to the parents and caregivers who ventured with me as we explored new interventions like mindfulness, acceptance, and other alternatives to more traditional behavior modification. I am forever grateful for your willingness and commitment to live a vital and meaningful life, even when we didn't know what that meant or what that looked like. Without you, this book would not have been possible.

I also acknowledge the wonderful and hardworking graduate students and alumni who have volunteered their time in my research labs, assisting with various projects and disseminating our findings at conferences and beyond. I particularly want to thank my graduate assistants, Danielle Cohen and Jessica Turner, who helped in curating references used in the book.

I am indebted to my Saint Louis University family for all their unwavering support and friendship over the years. To my SWAT family (you know who you are): I cannot fully express my gratitude and thanks for all the support, kindness, and encouragement you give every day. To my dear friend Heather, you are a phenomenal clinician, and an even better human being— thank you for your love and guidance as I worked in a new way of thinking about ACT. Our conversations over the years directly influenced my clinical practice and how I came to think more deeply about interdisciplinary practice. Noelle Fearn, thank you from the bottom of my heart for trusting me and never doubting my (sometimes) crazy ideas or solutions, and for always providing me with the mentorship and guidance I so clearly needed. Without some of our conversations and your support, this book would have never made it from my brain onto paper.

To all the amazing women who have shaped my voice in behavior analysis, I cannot thank you enough for your love, mentorship, and friendship. Molly Dubuque, Kate Kellum, Paula Danquah-Brobby, Ruth Anne Rehfeldt—I am so honored to have you in my life. To the lovely Adrienne Fitzer, thank you so much for giving me a platform to test out some of the material presented in the book. Thank you, too, for the wonderful feedback and the intellectual discussions you were willing to have; I hope you can find some of the nuggets from our talks in the book!

Finally, to my mother, sister, aunt, and grandparents, thank you for always giving me grace and encouragement to write. To my spouse, who tolerated early morning writing sessions and the all-too-frequent *writers' hibernation* episodes that it took for me to finish the book. Your continued support helped me to write even when I questioned what I was doing. I cannot express the love that I have for you, and how thankful I am that we found each other on a sidewalk in Mississippi.

Case Study 1
The Manny Family

Note: Details in this case study have been modified to maintain confidentiality and to ensure anonymity of both the family and the clinical team. All names used are pseudonyms.

Case Context

Mr. and Mrs. Manny (i.e., Mom and Dad) self-referred for behavioral services for help with their son, Rayan. Parents self-identified as second-generation Pakistani American and resided in an urban area. They had three children, including a girl (18 years old living at college) and two boys (Rayan, 16 years old, and a 12-year-old living at home). Rayan was diagnosed with attention deficit/hyperactivity disorder (ADHD) and dyslexia. Rayan was prescribed medication to mitigate some of his ADHD symptoms, which he took inconsistently. Rayan was very involved with sports and played year-round hockey, seasonal soccer, and baseball at school.

Parents sought services for Rayan during his sophomore year of high school. Parents reported struggling with Rayan across a range of topics and settings. His grades fell to a C average after starting high school, which parents believed was a result of his "lack of trying" and "laziness." After school was also a struggle, as Rayan often refused to do his homework and would leave the house without permission or without letting someone know where he was going and when he would return. Rayan also started sneaking out of the house at night and got caught trying to come back inside, which parents believed was not his first time sneaking out.

Parents' primary concern was Rayan's lying. Rayan was reportedly lying all the time about everything, making it impossible for parents to know when he was being honest. Rayan's lying was becoming an issue between Mom and Dad, as evidenced by parents' tense interactions on how to best "handle it" when they discovered he had been lying. The school also reported issues related to Rayan's lying, and Mom was very concerned that the school treated him differently because of his lying.

Clinical team. The clinical team included an assistant behavior analyst assigned to Rayan's case and a behavior analyst assigned to parent training and support. The behavior analyst provided clinical supervision to a behavior technician, and as such was aware of Rayan's case conceptualization and intervention progress throughout treatment. The BCBA received ACT supervision by a BCBA-D once a month.

Funding considerations. Funding sources covered a flat amount that could be billed by the agency in whatever manner it wanted. This resulted in 30-minute parent training sessions (ten consecutive sessions and three biweekly booster and maintenance sessions) and 45-minute individual behavioral intervention sessions for Rayan (twelve consecutive sessions with five biweekly booster and maintenance sessions).

Intake

During intake, all consent paperwork and funder-related information was completed. Parents were given information about the different types of sessions they should expect, including observation sessions (either via web camera software or in person), parent coaching sessions (parents only, often targeting ACT intervention strategies), parent-child sessions (both the child and at least one parent or caregiver, targeting either implementation or parent support), and child-only sessions (that may or may not include ACT strategies).

After all required paperwork was completed, an open-ended interview was generated to get an idea of the presenting problem and potential goals for parent coaching and parent-child sessions, and to better understand the cultural and familial systems. The behavior analyst asked questions about the family dynamic, cultural considerations surrounding their religious traditions, and expectations of the team (e.g., no sessions were to be conducted after sunset during Ramadan). Finally, the behavior analyst asked questions about both Mom and Dad's physical, emotional, and behavioral health to establish a baseline or rationale for parental supports in addition to parent implementation of a behavior plan.

During this portion of the open-ended interview, Dad left the room and stated that Mom could answer for him. Mom reported high rates of stress, pain, and emotional discomfort because of the issues she faces with Rayan. She reported how she does not have a choice in how she parents Rayan. She reported agreeing with her husband about his approach to disciplining their children, including Rayan, and often stated that "Rayan shouldn't be treated differently than my [other children]." Mom also reported that Rayan is fortunate to have the house and school that he does, given what she and her husband went through at his age. She reported disappointment that Rayan doesn't "act like he should" by not showing how fortunate he is to have what he has. Before the end of the interview, Mom reported that the issues with Rayan have started to put a strain on her marriage, which in turn impacts her relationship with Rayan and Rayan's relationship with Dad. Mom stated that she wants a better relationship with Rayan but doesn't know how to "get him to listen" or "act right."

Assessment and Data Collection Strategy: Rayan

Results from the open-ended interviews were used to inform Rayan's behavioral intervention plan. First, both Mom and Rayan completed additional open-ended interviews on Rayan's engagement in lying (i.e., any stance where Rayan's statements or actions are not aligned with historical or future events, such as saying he will be home at 6 p.m. but showing up at 8 p.m. and stating he isn't late, that he is on time) and elopement without permission (i.e., any instance where Rayan leaves the house or area—park, mosque, grocery store—without telling an elder where he is going). Mom reported engagement in both repertoires were a function of escape or avoidance. Rayan's answers suggested engagement was multiply controlled (i.e., high engagement across environmental conditions including escape and avoidance, attention, and the rush of doing it). Results were used to determine parameters of naturalistic observations and further clarification of presenting concerns.

Next, natural observations were arranged after school, and the analyst observed the family virtually for an hour on two occasions. During observations, Rayan's engagement in lying (as contextualized by the conversation and if Mom was suggesting he was lying) was tracked via a descriptive assessment, where antecedent and consequential events were observed and recorded. Potential rules and statements that occurred during observations were also recorded to determine a pattern (i.e., Mom often stated, "You always do this, lie about absolutely nothing. What is with you?" or "Why do you do this to me and your family? Why do you disgrace us like this?"). Results were provided to the assistant behavior analyst on the team to inform further assessment and intervention considerations for Rayan.

Assessment and Data Collection Strategy: Parent Coaching

Results from the open-ended interviews were used to inform the assessment process. Given that Rayan's treatment plan was in development at the time of assessment, the analyst assessed for parental supports needed rather than focus only on parent implementation. Parent implementation was supported by the behavior analyst providing Rayan's treatment and was supplanted within parent coaching sessions later in treatment only as needed.

During the values assessment, Mom and Dad identified shared family values including living consistently with their religious values, being there for one another, communicating honestly and truthfully with each other, and showing respect—particularly for elders. Each value system was further clarified and articulated, including identification of patterns of actions that align with each value system. For instance, being there for one another was actualized by family members doing things for others without them needing to directly ask for it—like bringing the milk to the table for dinner or taking neighbors to mosque. Honest and truthful communication was very meaningful to the parents and was aligned with having meaningful conversations with their children and each other, even when the truth was hard to hear. This value was particularly important for parents, as they emphasized how frustrating Rayan's lying was for them.

The matrix was conducted during the second parent training session and was completed only by Mom. Mom identified the following as parenting values: children follow Allah, children know they are loved, and children are more successful than she and her husband. She stated her behavior aligned with these values all the time, as it was her responsibility to make sure her children did all these things. When asked what may get in the way of her parenting values, she initially reported that nothing would get in her way of parenting her children. After a few moments of sitting with the question, she reported that she fears Rayan isn't following Allah and how her husband may react if Rayan continues in his ways. She reported sadness that she failed Rayan as a mother, and how her fears and sadness were never there until he started high school. She was unable to articulate initially what she did when those things showed up; however, after two training sessions, she articulated that she "probably yelled more at Rayan" when she was worried about what her husband might do.

Targeted repertoires and measurement system. Results from the open-ended interviews and initial assessments (i.e., values assessment and matrix) identified two potential areas for parent support: flexibility in perspective taking and patterns of actions that align with parenting values. Given that Dad's attendance at parent training sessions was inconsistent, only Mom's behaviors were targeted.

Flexible perspective taking was measured by the behavior analyst at the end of every parent training session as (4) occurring for most of the session, (3) occurring for more than half of the session, (2) occurring only after prompts, (1) not occurring at all. Flexible perspective taking was also measured during probe and maintenance sessions as a total count, where each probe question resulted in a 1 (yes, the parent shifted perspective) or 0 (no, the parent did not shift perspective), and was calculated into a percentage by dividing the total number of yeses by the total number of opportunities, multiplied by 100.

Patterns of values-based actions were considered anytime Mom engaged in a specific pattern of action that aligned with her values. This repertoire was measured through parental self-report between sessions. The analyst trained Mom how to record how many times she engaged in a values-based pattern of action from the list established during the values assessment. Do-say and say-do correspondence was also tracked via self-monitoring by Mom, who made commitments during parent coaching sessions and tracked when she engaged in the specified action.

Finally, Mom was asked to monitor the time she spent with Rayan working on building their relationship and the activities they did together. Mom tracked this between sessions.

Ongoing assessment. After four parent coaching sessions, the parenting triangle assessment was conducted with Mom (see figure A.1, top panel). Mom jumped into the assessment by emphasizing all the things Rayan did wrong or "acts out" and how she and her husband discipline him. Most of Mom's parenting strategies relied on limit setting, either adding punishers (i.e., having to ride along to drop off a sibling, requiring attendance at community and school events) or removing privileges (i.e., taking away his phone, his computer and tablet, taking away his guitar and video games). When asked about rewards or things that Rayan is given or earns, she reported saying "thank you" and reminds him that he "isn't a bad boy—he just makes bad decisions." She also stated that Rayan is always allowed to play hockey, which is something that is never *not* an option for him.

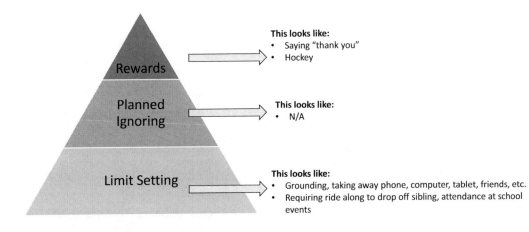

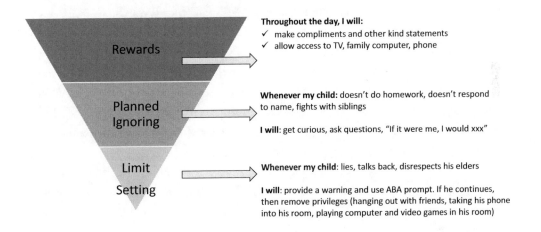

Figure A.1

Finally, flexible perspective taking probes were collected throughout parent coaching sessions. Flexible perspective taking probes were presented to Mom either when she was telling the analyst about an event that happened between sessions or within the session as a specific exercise or activity. For instance, Mom often spoke about an event between sessions where Rayan left the house without permission following an argument between him and Dad. The analyst asked Mom, "If you were in Rayan's shoes, how do you think you would feel after the argument?" During the first probe, Mom responded almost instantly, "I would never be in Rayan's shoes. I would have never argued with my father like he does." The analyst scored Mom's answers as either taking Rayan's perspective or not (her answer provided earlier was scored as not taking Rayan's perspective).

Implementation: Parent Coaching and Parent-Child Sessions

Parent coaching sessions started with general knowledge and overview of common ADHD symptomology (i.e., hyperfixation, excessive talking, acting quickly and without thoughtful planning or organization, etc.) and general behavior analytic concepts such as reinforcement, punishment, extinction, and skill acquisition.

After getting a better understanding of the dynamics between Mom and Rayan, the behavior analyst worked with Mom to slow down and work on building a relationship with Rayan. This started with parent-child sessions, where the analyst asked Rayan about his hobbies, things he liked to do with his friends and family, and one thing that he'd like to see happen at home with his Mom. Rayan articulated that he didn't understand why he couldn't have his phone in his room and wished that he could do that. This was brought up in future parent coaching sessions as a possible provision of a context-broadening environment for Rayan.

Next, the analyst focused on Mom's values and corresponding patterns of actions. The behavior analyst did a modified version of the Mapping Your Values activity, and specifically targeted Mom's parenting, family, and self-care values. Mom identified three specific repertoires that aligned with all three valued domains: (1) reading the Qur'an, (2) having "chats" with Rayan, just the two of them, and (3) getting enough rest each night (about 7 hours). These repertoires were included in the self-monitoring system, where Mom was asked to commit to at least one level of engagement in patterns of values-based actions.

The behavior analyst also targeted the Soles of the Feet (SoF) activity (see chapter 7), and trained Mom on the SoF protocol during a single session. At first, Mom could follow all steps when prompted to do so by the behavior analyst, but only completed about half of the steps when asked to complete the steps after setting up a somewhat aversive environment (i.e., imagining the last fight or incident that occurred between Rayan and her and her husband with the behavior analyst stating some of the hurtful things Rayan says to her during their fights). Mom was later prompted to use the SoF protocol throughout natural observations and parent-child sessions as appropriate.

The analyst conducted a range of exercises and activities targeting habituation, differential reinforcement, and recontextualization of thinking and feeling as spatially distant. For instance, a modified version of the sunset metaphor was used (Hayes et al., 2011), where Mom discussed what life would look like with Rayan if she approached their relationship the same way she experienced a sunset. Experiencing Rayan as a unique sunset, one that changes every time we experience it, is different than experiencing a sunset by breaking down all the various chemical reactions and processes or astrological realities that make the sunset the way that it is. This activity was embedded with experiential acceptance metaphors by asking Mom to rate her willingness to experience Rayan as a sunset, across various times of day and behaviors emitted by Rayan (i.e., Mom was willing to accept Rayan as a sunset if he got a failing grade on an exam, but was less willing to accept him when he lies or leaves the house without permission).

Similarly, habituation exercises targeted Mom's rigidity around specific things Rayan did, such as protesting or screaming "No!" at her. Using the Titchner's repetition activity (i.e., milk, milk, milk), Mom was instructed to imagine hearing Rayan scream "No!" at her while actively practicing here and now repertoires, such as connecting with her breath or following SoF steps. Other habituation exercises included adding phrases such as "I am having the thought/feeling that…" before labeling what she was experiencing when talking about fears and worries identified during the matrix assessment.

After a few parent coaching sessions, the parenting triangle assessment was used to further refine and enhance flexible perspective taking exercises, where Mom was asked about barriers that got in the way of her engaging in alternative parenting strategies, such as planned ignoring and limit setting. The behavior analyst walked through a "flipped triangle," where Rayan was afforded more reinforcing environments than punitive or depleted ones. The activity was presented with multiple ACT components to facilitate a discussion around some of the aversive stimulation experienced when asked to flip her triangle. Mom reported fear as one of the biggest barriers, and said it was "as heavy as she can hold." The behavior analyst used exercises to recontextualize thinking and feeling as spatially distant (i.e., creating space between Mom and her "fear" related to her parenting). Experiential acceptance was embedded into these conversations, by asking Mom about her willingness to stay within a "flipped" parenting approach. Mom established her own metaphor to help her connect the "flipped" parenting approach, by considering a "joy bucket of compliments." She could just "reach deep in the bucket" to come up with a compliment for Rayan. The activity became about statements or phrases that could fill the bucket; the behavior analyst returned to the bucket metaphor when conducting future parent-child sessions.

During maintenance probes, similar assessment data was collected, including parent self-monitoring data on engagement in values-based patterns of actions and flexible perspective taking, flexible perspective taking probes, and engagement in steps on SoF during exposure to aversive environments or situations. Results showed engagement in values-based patterns of actions increased following parent coaching sessions, while SoF completion remained steady at around 80% accuracy across opportunities (she often only took one or two deep breaths rather than the prescribed three or four).

Case Study 2
The Winter Family

Note: Details in this case study have been modified to maintain confidentiality and to ensure anonymity of both the family and the clinical team. All names used are pseudonyms.

Case Context

Mr. Winter (Dad) self-referred for behavioral services for help with his two children, Johnny and Sue. He and his ex-wife were recently divorced (within six months of referral), and he reported that, while they shared custody of the children, he was actively fighting for sole custody, given her history of neglect. Mr. Winter identified as a mixed-race male and resided in a rural area. Eight-year-old Johnny was diagnosed with autism around age 4, and had been receiving intensive in-home applied behavior analysis services for three years. Sue was 11 years old at the time of referral and was in the gifted program at school (after skipping third grade). Dad reported that Sue was very good with Johnny, and she often helped him during his ABA services, at school, and when they visited their grandparents. While Dad originally was referred for services related to Johnny, he also wanted tips for how to better interact with Sue, who was starting to talk back more.

Dad's primary concern was with Johnny. Dad was concerned that Johnny still wasn't talking in full sentences (Johnny could vocally respond with one- or two-word phrases for greetings, ask for preferred items, and jump into the pool). He was also concerned about Johnny's aggressive behaviors, which had gotten worse in the past year. Johnny had destroyed three couches in the same year by jumping on them, and had ripped down two screen doors when trying to access the family pool. Dad was very unhappy with the current ABA program, and often reported how "bad" Johnny's BCBA was. (He often would say, "If she was any good, she would figure out why he is doing these things.")

Dad was also looking for assistance with Sue, who he reported had recently started being more argumentative with him and stopped "being his little girl." She had her own opinions about things and would often tell him how he was wrong or "illogical." He reported that when they would fight, Sue would yell at him while running to her room.

Clinical team. The clinical team assigned to work with Johnny included a board-certified behavior analyst (BCBA) and two registered behavior technicians (RBT). Dad sought additional parent training services outside of the agency his son received ABA services. The parent training team consisted of a BCBA-D and a behavior analyst in training who provided two hours of training to the family per month for six months.

Funding considerations. Dad funded the parent training sessions on his own, and there were no funding constraints.

Intake

During intake, all consent paperwork and funder-related information was completed. Dad was given information about the types of sessions he should expect, including observation sessions (either via web camera software or in person), parent coaching sessions (parent only, often targeting ACT intervention strategies), and parent-child sessions (himself and one or both children).

After all required paperwork was completed, an open-ended interview was generated to get an idea of the presenting problem and potential goals for parent coaching and parent-child sessions, and to better understand the cultural and familial systems. During the interview, Dad reported that the family was not religious, and that he wasn't sure how to explain the family dynamics, particularly after the divorce. He reported how hard the divorce was on him and the kids, and he was unsure about what the "new" family dynamics were. The analyst asked questions about his physical, emotional, and behavioral health, to which Dad focused entirely on the divorce and how draining that was for him.

Given Dad's emphasis on his emotional struggles following his divorce, he was given information about how to access psychological services in his area, and special care was taken to ensure the services were covered by his insurance. This information was provided to him multiple times throughout services (see also chapter 3 for methods used).

When asked about primary concerns for Johnny and Sue, Dad reported that his biggest issue is with Johnny's aggressive behaviors. For Sue, Dad reported he didn't know why she was acting out, being disrespectful, or acting "like her mother."

Assessment and Data Collection Strategy: Parent Coaching

Results from the open-ended interviews were used to inform the assessment process. The team established clear boundaries around the topic of his divorce, and guidelines for how trainers would respond when he would speak about the divorce. Trainers never gave him any legal advice, nor did they coach him on how to secure sole custody. When he brought up how the divorce was impacting his emotional and psychological health, trainers reminded him of counseling services in his area and continued providing options that fit within his insurance requirements. This was done to ensure scope of competence and was clearly discussed throughout services.

Similarly, it was noted during intake that Dad was sometimes relying entirely on Sue to assist him with daily care of Johnny. To avoid asking Sue to help all the time, the trainers helped Dad find respite care from various agencies and support systems. This was embedded early during services to help establish parent-child interactions between Dad and Sue.

The matrix and values assessment were conducted and targeted Dad's parenting and relationships with Johnny and Sue. For Dad, the most important aspect of being a parent to Johnny was ensuring he was safe and could live independently when he grew up; being a parent to Sue was different and difficult for him to articulate immediately. It was important that she knew he loved her and that she respected him. He reported others would see this by him taking them to school (when they could just as easily take the bus), making their lunches and preferred meals, and playing together in the pool. Dad reported that a barrier to those values was his "temper," particularly with Sue. For both children, however, he reported that he behaved similarly: either he yelled and would ground Sue particularly, or he would make both children go to their rooms.

Next, trainers used the parenting triangle to determine what ways Dad used limit setting (or punishment strategies), planned ignoring, and provision of noncontingent access to reinforcers or reinforcing environments. Dad reported that for Sue, he relied heavily on reprimands, rule setting, and removal of privileges (i.e., no more swimming for the day/week depending on situation, no more iPad for a month after an intense argument, no special breakfast). These were operationalized and tracked during naturalistic observations and were observed as responses to instances when Sue was "disrespectful to Dad" (i.e., when she rolled her eyes, called him names, or made exaggerated gestural movements of head and hands).

When asked about ways that he may ignore aspects of Sue's behavior, Dad reported that he never really would say things to her when she interacts with Johnny (i.e., playing physically, taking away the iPad from him). For Johnny, Dad reported that he ignores a lot more than he wants to ignore, due to the ABA program he was "required to follow." Dad reported often how much he did not like Johnny's ABA services, and how angry he was at times after some of Johnny's sessions. He reported multiple times that "I don't care what they tell me to do; if it works, I'll continue to do it. But if it doesn't, I'm not going to do it."

Direct observation sessions occurred twice within one week, during which the family was observed in the evening and after school. During both sessions, a time-based descriptive assessment was conducted where the duration of each parent-child interaction was tracked in addition to tracking environmental stimuli and parent-child responses. Results suggested that Dad was more likely to interact with both children with negative affect and statements. Some of the initial presenting problems identified by Dad at intake were not observed, but general patterns of parent-child interactions helped established potential environmental contextual factors and subsequent targets for intervention.

Targeted repertoires and measurement system. Results from the open-ended interviews and initial assessments identified three potential areas for parent support: parent-child interactions, flexible perspective taking, and arranging appetitive home environment. Values-based patterns of actions were added following ongoing assessment. Data was collected and subjected to visual analysis throughout services. Dad reported that he was not interested in any self-monitoring or tracking of any kind between sessions, so only within-session data was collected.

Parent-child interactions were considered either positive (appetitive interaction, positive tone or affect), negative (punitive or coercive interaction, negative tone or affect), or neutral (question and answers for specific facts, e.g., "What time do you have Girl Scouts today?"). Interactions were observed and recorded using momentary-time sampling (1 minute) throughout 10- to 15-minute naturalistic observations.

Dad articulated his parenting values–based patterns of actions as allowing Sue some space to do what she wanted to do, speaking to Sue and Johnny in a positive or neutral tone/affect, and not yelling at the kids. Patterns of actions were tracked during naturalistic observations. Say-do correspondence was targeted to ensure Dad's actions aligned with the commitments he was making during sessions. Say-do correspondence was tracked during naturalistic observations as well as percent of opportunities.

Arranging appetitive home environment was first established with Dad and Sue to help identify what an appetitive home environment means for the family. They agreed that these important aspects were needed to establish an appetitive or context broadening environment: eating a preferred breakfast, eating family dinner with preferred meal, swimming in the pool, watching movies on family movie night, returning things to their respective place or home, and helping Johnny. Targets were tracked if they occurred or not during a naturalistic observation, and Dad was asked to report on how often each occurred during the time between sessions.

Ongoing assessment. Both the matrix and the parenting triangle were reassessed throughout training to align ACT interventions. During the second matrix, Dad reported that in addition to his temper, he noticed how Sue sometimes reminds him of his ex-wife (her mother) and he then gets mad. This information was helpful to target during here and now emphasis sessions. Trainers also gave Dad the 6-PAQ to help establish patterns of his perspective on his parenting and brought in some of the low scoring items into sessions (i.e., he scored low on "I can clearly state my values related to parenting" when asked specifically about Sue).

Naturalistic observations were conducted throughout services and functioned as an ongoing assessment strategy. The descriptive assessments were sufficient to determine hypotheses about potential maintaining variables for Dad's engagement in targeted repertoires. For instance, values-based patterns of actions, such as remaining in a positive or neutral affect when interacting with Sue, were targeted during the descriptive assessment. The clinical team did not initially observe these repertoires until after formal values and say-do correspondence training started.

Implementation: Parent Coaching and Parent-Child Sessions

Parent coaching sessions started with general knowledge about ASD symptomology across the life span and general behavior analytic concepts such as reinforcement, punishment, extinction, and skill acquisition. Parenting styles and environmental considerations (i.e., authoritarian parenting styles align with more punitive or context-limiting environments for Sue and Johnny) were also targeted during the initial coaching session.

The trainer worked with Dad to problem-solve how to put into place a more reinforcing or appetitive environment. The trainer helped Dad identify shared preferences for meals, identify homes or places for commonly used items around the house (including iPads, scissors, TV remote, etc.), and establish rules around allowing free access to the swimming pool (i.e., no swimming 30 minutes before or after eating, no swimming without an adult present, and pool closes at 9 p.m. are not the same as no more swimming because you did X or no swimming because I said so). Next, the trainer coached Dad on implementing each of these, one at a time, using differential reinforcement, modeling, rehearsal, and feedback.

Next, trainers attempted to use Soles of the Feet (SoF) with Dad. This was attempted in two parent coaching sessions, but given Dad's attitude and approach to doing it (i.e., eye-rolling, long drawn-out sighs), SoF was omitted on the third session and replaced with less informal here and now activities. A mindful eating activity was initially selected and conducted with Dad and Sue, where they were asked to eat a favorite snack while they focused on their five senses and slowly ate the snack one bite at a time. The Mindful Mountain activity was also used, where the trainer modeled various bodily shapes to take while practicing "mindful breathing." After Dad and Sue began to practice taking slow and deep breaths in various body shapes, the trainer modeled how anyone could ask for a Mindful Mountain pause. This was rehearsed for the remainder of the session and practiced as needed throughout subsequent sessions.

Trainers focused on interventions that could easily be targeted during family interactions, such as family dinner. Family dinner was an important aspect to both Dad and Sue, and trainers selected a modification of the Jumble Jar Game to start. Prior to implementation with the children, Dad worked with the trainer to go over how to use the game during mealtime and to role-play different scenarios using behavioral skills training. The trainer provided an array of possible responses when role-playing Sue to ensure Dad was given adequate rehearsal in the presence of appetitive and aversive situations. Dad played the game with both Sue and Johnny while the trainer observed and only prompted Dad on next steps or to engage in positive or neutral comments. This game was later adapted for Sue to more of a trivia type of game, in which each person wrote something about him- or herself and the others had to guess who the family member was.

Dad's values were also targeted, using information gathered from the parenting triangle and matrix assessments. The Mapping Your Values activity was conducted early during parent coaching sessions and was returned to often when values identification and correspondence weren't aligning. From the values map, Dad articulated that Sue's behaviors were the biggest barriers to him living his parenting values. The trainer targeted this barrier during various values-based patterns of action activities, including the Pivoting One Degree (or Less) activity. During this activity, Dad was encouraged to only think about pivoting his behavior less than one full degree. He expressed how doing so was somehow "too easy" or "not going to be enough," things that were subsequently brought up in other sessions targeting flexible responses and experiential acceptance.

Dad's experiential acceptance repertoires were targeted throughout services, with emphasis on shaping flexible repertoires. The first activity the trainer used was the Willingly Cold activity. The trainer started by first asking Dad to rate his willingness to put his hand in a bowl of ice water, to which his response was 0, that he was not willing. In discussing why, Dad reported that he didn't get why he had to put his hand in ice water, and that there was no way doing so was going to change his parenting approach. After establishing rationale for the activity, Dad reluctantly engaged in the activity with the trainer. In the first attempt, Dad reported low willingness; during the second attempt, Dad reported slightly higher willingness, and then pulled his hand out faster than the first attempt. This was very frustrating for Dad, who told the analyst how stupid the activity was because it didn't work. The analyst continued with the activity by asking Dad if the struggle with the ice water was the same the second time (when he approached it with slightly more willingness) as with the first (when he wasn't that willing to begin with).

A more successful experiential acceptance activity for Dad was the Man in the Hole activity. The trainer conducted the activity as a conversation, couched in his presenting concern of his relationship with Sue. For Dad, he resonated with the metaphor of the man in the hole and had a completely different response to it than the Willingly Cold activity.

Finally, the trainer also targeted flexible perspective activities that recontextualized Dad's thinking as spatially distant. In this way, the trainer helped Dad use phrases such as "I'm having the thought that..." and "I am currently feeling X and have the urge to...." Similarly, the Control Is the Problem activity was used to help Dad contact the difference between controlling our thoughts and feelings vs. controlling our physical actions. He later shared that he used this with Sue to help her with a problem she was having at school.

During maintenance probes, similar naturalistic observations were conducted, and data collected on the aspects of appetitive family environments (i.e., eating preferred meals, using the pool, watching films on family movie night, returning items to their home, and helping Johnny), as well as parent-child interactions, flexible perspective taking, and the say-do correspondence between Dad's identified values and patterns of actions between sessions. Results showed increased correspondence in stated parenting values and Dad's engagement in patterns of actions as well as establishing appetitive environments. Parent-child interactions between Dad and Sue improved over time, as evidenced by increased use of positive interactions overall with diminished use of negative interactions.

References

Andrews, M. L., Garcia, Y. A., Catagnus, R. M., & Gould, E. R. (2021). Effects of acceptance and commitment training plus behavior parent training on parental implementation of autism treatment. *The Psychological Record*, 1–17. https://doi.org/10.1007/s40732-021 -00496-5

Assaz, D. A., Roche, B., Kanter, J. W., & Oshiro, C. K. (2018). Cognitive defusion in acceptance and commitment therapy: What are the basic processes of change? *The Psychological Record*, 68(4), 405–418.

Baer, D. M., Wolf, M. M., & Risley, T. R. (1968). Some current dimensions of applied behavior analysis. *Journal of Applied Behavior Analysis*, 1(1), 91–97. https://doi.org/10.1901 /jaba.1968.1-91

Baer, D. M., Wolf, M. M., & Risley, T. R. (1987). Some still-current dimensions of applied behavior analysis. *Journal of Applied Behavior Analysis*, 20(4), 313–327.

Barnes-Holmes, Y., Hussey, I., McEnteggart, C., Barnes-Holmes, D., & Foody, M. (2015). Scientific ambition: The relationship between relational frame theory and middle-level terms in acceptance and commitment therapy. In R. D. Zettle, S. C. Hayes, D. Barnes-Holmes, & A. Biglan (Eds.), *The Wiley handbook of contextual behavioral science* (pp. 365–382). Hoboken, NJ: Wiley-Blackwell.

Barrett, K., O'Connor, M., & McHugh, L. (2019). A systematic review of values-based psychometric tools within acceptance and commitment therapy (ACT). *The Psychological Record*, 69(4), 457–485.

Baum, W. M. (1995). Introduction to molar behavior analysis. *Mexican Journal of Behavior Analysis*, 21(3), 7–25. https://doi.org/10.13140/2.1.2785.2481

Baum, W. M. (2018). Multiscale behavior analysis and molar behaviorism: An overview. *Journal of the Experimental Analysis of Behavior*, 110(3), 302–322. https://doi.org/10 .1002/jeab.476

Bearss, K., Burrell, T. L., Challa, S. A., Postorino, V., Gillespie, S. E., Crooks, C., et al. (2018). Feasibility of parent training via telehealth for children with autism spectrum disorder and disruptive behavior: A demonstration pilot. *Journal of Autism and Developmental Disorders*, 48(4), 1020–1030. https://doi.org/10.1007/s10803-017-3363-2

Bearss, K., Burrell, T. L., Stewart, L., & Scahill, L. (2015a). Parent training in autism spectrum disorder: What's in a name? *Clinical Child and Family Psychology Review*, 18(2), 170–182. https://doi.org/10.1007/s10567-015-0179-5

Bearss, K., Johnson, C., Handen, B., Smith, T., & Scahill, L. (2013). A pilot study of parent training in young children with autism spectrum disorders and disruptive behavior. *Journal of Autism and Developmental Disorders, 43*(4), 829–840. https://doi.org/10.1007/s10803-012-1624-7

Bearss, K., Johnson, C., Smith, T., Lecavalier, L., Swiezy, N., Aman, M., et al. (2015b). Effect of parent training vs. parent education on behavioral problems in children with autism spectrum disorder: A randomized clinical trial. *Journal of the American Medical Association, 313*(15), 1524–1533. https://doi.org/10.1001/jama.2015.3150

Behavior Analyst Certification Board (BACB). (n.d.). *BACB certificant data.* Retrieved July 1, 2021, from https://www.bacb.com/BACB-certificant-data.

Behavior Analyst Certification Board. (2020). *Ethics code for behavior analysts.* https://bacb.com/wp-content/ethics-code-for-behavior-analysts

Berkout, O. V. (2021). Working with values: An overview of approaches and considerations in implementation. *Behavior Analysis in Practice,* 15, 1–11.

Bishop, S. R., Lau, M., Shapiro, S., Carlson, L., Anderson, N. D., Carmody, J., et al. (2004). Mindfulness: A proposed operational definition. *Clinical Psychology: Science and Practice, 11*(3), 230–241. https://doi.org/10.1093/clipsy.bph077

Blackledge, J. T., & Drake, C. E. (2013). Acceptance and commitment therapy: Empirical and theoretical considerations. In S. Dymond & B. Roche (Eds.), *Advances in relational frame theory: Research and application* (pp. 219–252). Oakland, CA: Context Press/New Harbinger Publications.

Blackledge, J. T., & Hayes, S. C. (2008). Using acceptance and commitment training in the support of parents of children diagnosed with autism. *Child & Family Behavior Therapy, 28*(1), 1–18. https://doi.org/10.1300/J019v28n01_01

Bloom, M., Fischer, J., & Orme, J. G. (2006). *Evaluating practice: Guidelines for the accountable professional.* Boston: Allyn & Bacon.

Brehaut, J. C., Kohen, D. E., Raina, P., Walter, S. D., Russell, D. J., Swinton, M., et al. (2004). The health of primary caregivers of children with cerebral palsy: How does it compare with that of other Canadian caregivers? *Pediatrics, 114*(2), e182–e191.

Brown, F. L., Whittingham, K., & Sofronoff, K. (2015). Parental experiential avoidance as a potential mechanism of change in a parenting intervention for parents of children with pediatric acquired brain injury. *Journal of Pediatric Psychology, 40*(4), 464–474. https://doi.org/10.1093/jpepsy/jsu109

Brown, K. W., & Ryan, R. M. (2003). The benefits of being present: Mindfulness and its role in psychological well-being. *Journal of Personality and Social Psychology, 84*(4), 822.

Burrell, T. L., Postorino, V., Scahill, L., Rea, H. M., Gillespie, S., Evans, A. N., et al. (2020). Feasibility of group parent training for children with autism spectrum disorder and disruptive behavior: A demonstration pilot. *Journal of Autism and Developmental Disorders, 50*(11), 3883–3894. https://doi.org/10.1007/s10803-020-04427-1

Callaghan, G. M., & Follette, W. C. (2020). Interpersonal Behavior Therapy (IBT), functional assessment, and the value of principle-driven behavioral case conceptualizations. *The Psychological Record, 70*(4), 625–635.

Catania, A. C., Shimoff, E., & Matthews, B. A. (1989). An experimental analysis of rule-governed behavior. In S. C. Hayes (Ed.), *Rule-governed behavior* (pp. 119–150). New York: Springer.

Cihon, J. H., Ferguson, J. L., Leaf, J. B., Milne, C. M., Leaf, R., & McEachin, J. (2021). Acceptance and commitment training: A review of the research. *European Journal of Behavior Analysis, 22*, 1–21.

Cohn, L. N., Pechlivanoglou, P., Lee, Y., Mahant, S., Orkin, J., Marson, A., et al. (2020). Health outcomes of parents of children with chronic illness: A systematic review and meta-analysis. *The Journal of Pediatrics, 218*, 166–177.

Cooper, J. O., Heron, T. E., & Heward, W. L. (2019). *Applied behavior analysis* (3rd ed.). New York: Pearson Education.

Corti, C., Pergolizzi, F., Vanzin, L., Cargasacchi, G., Villa, L., Pozzi, M., et al. (2018). Acceptance and commitment therapy-oriented parent-training for parents of children with autism. *Journal of Child and Family Studies, 27*(9), 2887–2900. https://doi.org/10.1007/s10826-018-1123-3

Costa, A. P., Steffgen, G., & Ferring, D. (2017). Contributors to well-being and stress in parents of children with autism spectrum disorder. *Research in Autism Spectrum Disorders, 37*, 61–72. https://doi.org/10.1016/j.rasd.2017.01.007

Coyne, L. W., & Wilson, K. G. (2004). The role of cognitive fusion in impaired parenting: An RFT analysis. *International Journal of Psychology and Psychological Therapy, 4*(3), 469–486. http://www.ijpsy.com/volumen4/num3/95/the-role-of-cognitive-fusion-inimpaired-EN.pdf

Crnic, K. A., Gaze, C., & Hoffman, C. (2005). Cumulative parenting stress across the preschool period: Relations to maternal parenting and child behaviour at age 5. *Infant and Child Development: An International Journal of Research and Practice, 14*(2), 117–132.

Davison, M., & McCarthy, D. (2016). *The matching law: A research review.* New York: Routledge.

Dawson, G., Rogers, S., Munson, J., Smith, M., Winter, J., Greenson, J., et al. (2010). Randomized, controlled trial of an intervention for toddlers with autism: The Early Start Denver Model. *Pediatrics, 125*(1), e17–e23.

Deacon, J. R., & Konarski Jr., E. A. (1987). Correspondence training: An example of rule-governed behavior? *Journal of Applied Behavior Analysis, 20*(4), 391–400.

deCarvalho, R. J. (1991). *The founders of humanistic psychology.* Westport, CT: Praeger.

DeLeon, I. G., & Iwata, B. A. (1996). Evaluation of a multiple-stimulus presentation format for assessing reinforcer preferences. *Journal of Applied Behavior Analysis, 29*(4), 519–533. https://doi.org/10.1901/jaba.1996.29-519

Diaz-Salvat, C. C., St. Peter, C. C., & Shuler, N. J. (2020). Increased number of responses may account for reduced resurgence following serial training. *Journal of Applied Behavior Analysis, 53*(3), 1542–1558. https://doi.org/10.1002/jaba.686

Dixon, M. R., Hayes, S. C., Stanley, C., Law, S., & al-Nasser, T. (2020). Is acceptance and commitment training or therapy (ACT) a method that applied behavior analysts can and should use? *The Psychological Record, 70,* 559–579. https://doi.org/10.1007/s40732 -020-00436-9

Dixon, M. R., & Wilson, A. N. (2014). *Acceptance and commitment therapy for gambling disorders.* Carbondale, IL: Shawnee Scientific Press.

Dymond, S., & Rehfeldt, R. A. (2000). Understanding complex behavior: The transformation of stimulus functions. *The Behavior Analyst, 23*(2), 239–254. https://doi.org/10.1007/BF03392013

Edwards, G. S., Zlomke, K. R., & Greathouse, A. D. (2019). RUBI parent training as a group intervention for children with autism: A community pilot study. *Research in Autism Spectrum Disorders, 66,* 101409. https://doi.org/10.1016/j.rasd.2019.101409

Fisher, W., Piazza, C. C., Bowman, L. G., Hagopian, L. P., Owens, J. C., & Slevin, I. (1992). A comparison of two approaches for identifying reinforcers for persons with severe and profound disabilities. *Journal of Applied Behavior Analysis, 25*(2), 491–498. https://doi.org/10.1901/jaba.1992.25-491

Flujas-Contreras, J. M., García-Palacios, A., & Gómez, I. (2020). Spanish validation of the parental acceptance questionnaire (6-PAQ). *International Journal of Clinical and Health Psychology, 20*(2), 163–172. https://doi.org/10.1016/j.ijchp.2020.03.002

Fonseca, A., Moreira, H., & Canavarro, M.C. (2020). Uncovering the links between parenting stress and parenting styles: The role of psychological flexibility within parenting and global psychological flexibility. *Journal of Contextual Behavioral Science, 18,* 59–67.

Foody, M., Barnes-Holmes, Y., Barnes-Holmes, D., Törneke, N., Luciano, C., Stewart, I., et al. (2014). RFT for clinical use: The example of metaphor. *Journal of Contextual Behavioral Science, 3*(4), 305–313. https://doi.org/10.1016/j.jcbs.2014.08.001

Freeman, T. R., LeBlanc, L. A., & Martinez-Diaz, J. A. (2020). Ethical and professional responsibilities of applied behavior analysts. In J. O. Cooper, T. E. Heron, and W. L. Heward (Eds.), *Applied Behavior Analysis* (pp. 758–784). New York: Pearson Education.

Fuller, J. L., & Fitter, E. A. (2020). Mindful parenting: A behavioral tool for parent well-being. *Behavior Analysis in Practice, 13*(4), 767–771. https://doi.org/10.1007/s40617-020-00447-6

Gifford, E. V., & Hayes, S. C. (1999). Functional contextualism: A pragmatic philosophy for behavioral science. In W. O'Donohue & R. Kitchener (Eds.), *Handbook of behaviorism* (pp. 285–327). New York: Academic Press.

Gilbert, P. (2014). The origins and nature of compassion focused therapy. *British Journal of Clinical Psychology, 53*(1), 6–41. https://doi.org/10.1111/bjc.12043

Ginn, N. C., Clionsky, L. N., Eyberg, S. M., Warner-Metzger, C., & Abner, J. P. (2017). Child-directed interaction training for young children with autism spectrum disorders: Parent and child outcomes. *Journal of Clinical Child & Adolescent Psychology, 46*(1), 101–109. https://doi.org/10.1080/15374416.2015.1015135

Gould, E. R., Tarbox, J., & Coyne, L. (2018). Evaluating the effects of acceptance and commitment training on the overt behavior of parents of children with autism. *Journal of Contextual Behavioral Science, 7*, 81–88.

Greene, R. L., Field, C. E., Fargo, J. D., & Twohig, M. P. (2015). Development and validation of the parental acceptance questionnaire (6-PAQ). *Journal of Contextual Behavioral Science, 4*(3), 170–175. https://doi.org/10.1016/j.jcbs.2015.05.003

Gross, A. C., & Fox, E. J. (2009). Relational frame theory: An overview of the controversy. *The Analysis of Verbal Behavior, 25*, 87–97. https://doi.org/10.1007/BF03393073

Hahs, A. D., Dixon, M. R., & Paliliunas, D. (2019). Randomized controlled trial of a brief acceptance and commitment training for parents of individuals diagnosed with autism spectrum disorders. *Journal of Contextual Behavioral Science, 12*, 154–159.

Han, A., Yuen, H. K., Lee, H. Y., & Zhou, X. (2020). Effects of acceptance and commitment therapy on process measures of family caregivers: A systematic review and meta-analysis. *Journal of Contextual Behavioral Science, 18*, 201–213.

Harris, R. (2009). *ACT made simple: An easy-to-read primer on acceptance and commitment therapy.* Oakland, CA: New Harbinger Publications.

Harte, C., & Barnes-Holmes, D. (2022). The status of rule-governed behavior as pliance, tracking, and augmenting within relational frame theory: Middle-level rather than technical terms. *The Psychological Record, 72*(1), 145–158. https://doi.org/10.1007/s40732-021-00458-x

Hayes, L. J., & Fryling, M. J. (2019). Functional and descriptive contextualism. *Journal of Contextual Behavioral Science, 14*, 119–126. https://doi.org/10.1016/j.jcbs.2019.09.002

Hayes, S. C. (2005). *Get out of your mind and into your life: The new acceptance and commitment therapy.* Oakland, CA: New Harbinger Publications.

Hayes, S. C., Barnes-Holmes, D., & Roche, B. (Eds.). (2001). *Relational frame theory: A post-Skinnerian account of human language and cognition.* New York: Springer.

Hayes, S. C., Barnes-Holmes, D., & Wilson, K. G. (2012). Contextual behavioral science: Creating a science more adequate to the challenge of the human condition. *Journal of Contextual Behavioral Science, 1*, 1–16. https://doi.org/10.1016/j.jcbs.2012.09.004

Hayes, S. C., Hayes, L. J., Reese, H. W., & Sarbin, T. R. (Eds.). (1993). Varieties of scientific contextualism. Oakland, CA: Context Press/New Harbinger Publications.

Hayes, S. C., Levin, M. E., Plumb-Vilardaga, J., Villatte, J. L., & Pistorello, J. (2013). Acceptance and commitment therapy and contextual behavioral science: Examining the progress of a distinctive model of behavioral and cognitive therapy. *Behavior Therapy, 44*(2), 180–198. https://doi.org/10.1016/j.beth.2009.08.002

Hayes, S. C., Luoma, J. B., Bond, F. W., Masuda, A., & Lillis, J. (2006). Acceptance and commitment therapy: Model, processes, and outcomes. *Behaviour Research and Therapy, 44*(1), 1–25. https://scholarworks.gsu.edu/psych_facpub/101

Hayes, S. C., Strosahl, K. D., & Wilson, K. G. (2011). *Acceptance and commitment therapy: The process and practice of mindful change* (2nd ed.). New York: Guilford Press.

Hayes, S. C., Wilson, K. G., Gifford, E. V., Follette, V. M., & Strosahl, K. (1996). Experiential avoidance and behavioral disorders: A functional dimensional approach to diagnosis and treatment. *Journal of Consulting and Clinical Psychology, 64*(6), 1152–1168. https://doi.org/10.1037/0022-006X.64.6.1152

Herrnstein, R. J. (1974). Formal properties of matching law. *Journal of the Experimental Analysis of Behavior, 21*(1), 159–164. https://doi.org/10.1901/jeab.1974.21-159

Holmberg Bergman, T., Renhorn, E., Berg, B., Lappalainen, P., Ghaderi, A., & Hirvikoski, T. (2022). Acceptance and commitment therapy group intervention for parents of children with disabilities (Navigator ACT): An open feasibility trial. *Journal of Autism and Developmental Disorders.* https://doi.org/10.1007/s10803-022-05490-6

Howard, A. R., Lindaman, S., Copeland, R., & Cross, D. R. (2018). Theraplay impact on parents and children with autism spectrum disorder: Improvements in affect, joint attention, and social cooperation. *International Journal of Play Therapy, 27*(1), 56. https://doi.org/10.1037/pla0000056

Iadarola, S., Levato, L., Harrison, B., Smith, T., Lecavalier, L., Johnson, C., et al. (2018). Teaching parents behavioral strategies for autism spectrum disorder (ASD): Effects on stress, strain, and competence. *Journal of Autism and Developmental Disorders*, 48(4), 1031–1040. https://doi.org/10.1007/s10803-017-3339-2

Iwata, B. A., Dorsey, M. F., Slifer, K. J., Bauman, K. E., & Richman, G. S. (1994). Toward a functional analysis of self-injury. *Journal of Applied Behavior Analysis*, 27(2), 197–209. https://doi.org/10.1901/jaba.1994.27-197

Johnston, J. M., & Pennypacker, H. S. (2008). *Strategies and tactics of behavioral research* (3rd ed.). New York: Routledge.

Kabat-Zinn, J. (2015). Mindfulness. *Mindfulness*, 6(6), 1481–1483. https://doi.org/10.1007/s12671-015-0456-x

Kaminski, J. W., Valle, L. A., Filene, J. H., & Boyle, C. L. (2008). A meta-analytic review of components associated with parent training program effectiveness. *Journal of Abnormal Child Psychology*, 36(4), 567–589.

Kant, I. (1785/1959). *Foundations of the metaphysics of morals*. Indianapolis, IN: Bobbs-Merrill.

Kasari, C., Lawton, K., Shih, W., Barker, T. V., Landa, R., Lord, C., et al. (2014). Caregiver-mediated intervention for low-resourced preschoolers with autism: An RCT. *Pediatrics*, 134(1), e72–e79. https://doi.org/10.1542/peds.2013-3229

Kasson, E. M., & Wilson, A. N. (2017). Preliminary evidence on the efficacy of mindfulness combined with traditional classroom management strategies. *Behavior Analysis in Practice*, 10(3), 242–251. https://doi.org/10.1007/s40617-016-0160-x

Kazdin, A. E. (2013). *Behavior modification in applied settings* (7th ed.). Long Grove, IL: Waveland Press.

Kitchener, K. S., & Anderson, S.K. (2011). *Foundations of ethical practice, research, and teaching in psychology and counseling* (2nd ed.). New York: Routledge.

Lloyd, T., & Hastings, R. P. (2008). Psychological variables as correlates of adjustment in mothers of children with intellectual disabilities: Cross-sectional and longitudinal relationships. *Journal of Intellectual Disability Research*, 52(1), 37–48. https://doi.org/10.1111/j.1365-2788.2007.00974.x

Lovejoy, M. C., Graczyk, P. A., O'Hare, E., & Neuman, G. (2000). Maternal depression and parenting behavior: A meta-analytic review. *Clinical Psychology Review*, 20(5), 561–592.

Lundgren, T., & Larsson, A. (2018). Values choice and clarification. In S. C. Hayes & S. G. Hofmann (Eds.), *Process-based CBT: The science and core clinical competencies of cognitive behavioral therapy* (pp. 375–388). Oakland, CA: Context Press/New Harbinger Publications.

Luoma, J. B., Hayes, S. C., & Walser, R. D. (2007). *Learning ACT: An acceptance & commitment therapy skills training manual for therapists.* Oakland, CA: Context Press/ New Harbinger Publications.

MacKenzie, K. T., & Eack, S. M. (2022). Interventions to improve outcomes for parents of children with autism spectrum disorder: A meta-analysis. *Journal of Autism and Developmental Disorders, 52*(7), 2859–2883. https://doi.org/10.1007/s10803-021-05164-9

MacNaughton, K. L., & Rodriguez, J. R. (2001). Predicting adherence to recommendations by parents of clinic-referred children. *Journal of Consulting and Clinical Psychology, 69*(2), 262–270. https://doi.org/10.1037/0022-006X.69.2.262

Magnacca, C., Thomson, K., & Marcinkiewicz, A. (2021). Acceptance and commitment therapy for caregivers of children with neurodevelopmental disabilities: A systematic review. *Current Developmental Disorders Reports, 8*(2), 152–160.

Mak, M. C. K., Yin, L., Li, M., Cheung, R. Y. H., & Oon, P. T. (2020). The relation between parenting stress and child behavior problems: Negative parenting styles as mediator. *Journal of Child and Family Studies, 29*(11), 2993–3003.

Marr, M. J. (1993). Contextualistic mechanism or mechanistic contextualism? The straw machine as tar baby. *The Behavior Analyst, 16,* 59–65. https://doi.org/10.1007/BF03392611

Martens, B. K., Baxter, E. L., McComas, J. J., Sallade, S. J., Kester, J. S., Caamano, M., et al. (2019). Agreement between structured descriptive assessments and functional analyses conducted over a telehealth system. *Behavior Analysis: Research and Practice, 19*(4), 343–356. https://doi.org/10.1037/bar0000153

McAndrews, Z., Richardson, J., & Stopa, L. (2019). Psychometric properties of acceptance measures: A systematic review. *Journal of Contextual Behavioral Science, 12,* 261–277. https://doi.org/10.1016/j.jcbs.2018.08.006

McConachie, H., & Diggle, T. (2007). Parent implemented early intervention for young children with autism spectrum disorder: A systematic review. *Journal of Evaluation in Clinical Practice, 13*(1), 120–129. https://doi.org/10.1111/j.1365-2753.2006.00674.x

McEnteggart, C. (2018). A brief tutorial on acceptance and commitment therapy as seen through the lens of derived stimulus relations. *Perspectives on Behavior Science, 41*(1), 215–227. https://doi.org/10.1007/s40614-018-0149-6

McLaughlin, D. M., & Carr, E. G. (2005). Quality of rapport as a setting event for problem behavior: Assessment and intervention. *Journal of Positive Behavior Interventions, 7,* 68–91. https://doi.org/10.1177/10983007050070020401

Moore, J. (2010). Philosophy of science, with special consideration given to behaviorism as the philosophy of the science of behavior. *The Psychological Record, 60,* 137–136. https://doi.org/10.1007/BF03395698

Myers, S. M., Johnson, C. P., & Council on Children with Disabilities. (2007). Management of children with autism spectrum disorders. *Pediatrics, 120*(5), 1162–118.

Newsome, D., Newsome, K., Fuller, T. C., & Meyer, S. (2019). How contextual behavioral scientists measure and report about behavior: A review of JCBS. *Journal of Contextual Behavioral Science, 12*, 347–354. https://doi.org/10.1016/j.jcbs.2018.11.005

Nock, M. K., & Kazdin, A. E. (2001). Parent expectancies for child therapy: Assessment and relation to participation in treatment. *Journal of Child and Family Studies, 10*, 155–180. https:// doi.org/10.1023/A:1016699424731

Oddie, G. (2013). Truthlikeness. In M. Curd & S. Psillos (Eds.), *The Routledge companion to philosophy of science* (pp. 506–516). New York: Routledge.

O'Donohue, W., & Kitchener, R. (Eds.). (1999). *Handbook of behaviorism.* New York: Academic Press.

Oliver, A. C., Pratt, L. A., & Normand, M. P. (2015). A survey of functional behavior assessment methods used by behavior analysts in practice. *Journal of Applied Behavior Analysis, 48*(4), 817–829. https://doi.org/10.1002/jaba.256

Paliliunas, D. (2021). Values: A core guiding principle for behavior-analytic intervention and research. *Behavior Analysis in Practice, 15*(1), 115–125.

Pence, S. T., Roscoe, E. M., Bourret, J. C., & Ahearn, W. H. (2009). Relative contributions of three descriptive methods: Implications for behavioral assessment. *Journal of Applied Behavior Analysis, 42*(2), 425–446. https://doi.org/10.1901/jaba.2009.42-425

Phang, C., Keng, S., & Chiang, K. (2014). Mindful-S.T.O.P.: Mindfulness made easy for stress reduction in medical students. *Education in Medicine Journal, 6*(2). https://doi.org /10.5959/eimj.v6i2.230

Plumb, J. C., Stewart, I., Dahl, J., & Lundgren, T. (2009). In search of meaning: Values in modern clinical behavior analysis. *The Behavior Analyst, 32*, 85–103. https://doi .org/10.1007/BF03392177

Polk, K. L., Schoendorff, B., Webster, M., & Olaz, F. O. (2016). *The essential guide to the ACT matrix: A step-by-step approach to using the ACT matrix model in clinical practice.* Oakland, CA: Context Press/New Harbinger Publications.

Reddy, S. D., Negi, L. T., Dodson-Lavelle, B., Ozawa-de Silva, B., Pace, T. W., Cole, S. P., et al. (2013). Cognitive-based compassion training: A promising prevention strategy for at-risk adolescents. *Journal of Child and Family Studies, 22*(2), 219–230. https:/doi .org/10.1007/s10826-012-9571-7

Rekart, K. N., Mineka, S., Zinbarg, R. E., & Griffith, J. W. (2007). Perceived family environment and symptoms of emotional disorders: The role of perceived control, attributional style, and attachment. *Cognitive Therapy and Research, 31*(4), 419–436.

Roane, H. S. (2008). On the applied use of progressive-ratio schedules of reinforcement. *Journal of Applied Behavior Analysis, 41*, 155–161.

Roane, H. S., Vollmer, T. R., Ringdahl, J. E., & Marcus, B. A. (1998). Evaluation of a brief stimulus preference assessment. *Journal of Applied Behavior Analysis, 31*(4), 605–620. https://doi.org/10.1901/jaba.1998.31-605

Rogers, C. R. (1957). The necessary and sufficient conditions of therapeutic personality change. *Journal of Consulting Psychology, 21*(2), 95–103. https://doi.org/10.1037/h0045357

Rosenberg, N. E., & Schwartz, I. S. (2019). Guidance or compliance: What makes an ethical behavior analyst? *Behavior Analysis in Practice, 12*(2), 473–482.

Rovane, A. K., Hock, R. M., & January, S. A. A. (2020). Adherence to behavioral treatments and parent stress in families of children with ASD. *Research in Autism Spectrum Disorders, 77*, 101609. https://doi.org/10.1016/j.rasd.2020.101609

Sanders, M. R. (2012). Development, evaluation, and multinational dissemination of the Triple P-Positive Parenting Program. *Annual Review of Clinical Psychology, 8*, 345–379. https://doi.org/10.1146/annurev-clinpsy-032511-143104

Sanders, M. R., Kirby, J. N., Tellegen, C. L., & Day, J. J. (2014). The Triple P-Positive Parenting Program: A systematic review and meta-analysis of a multi-level system of parenting support. *Clinical Psychology Review, 34*(4), 337–357. https://doi.org/10.1016/j.cpr.2014.04.003

Sarokoff, R. A., & Sturmey, P. (2004). The effects of behavioral skills training on staff implementation of discrete-trial teaching. *Journal of Applied Behavior Analysis, 37*(4), 535–538. https://doi.org/10.1901/jaba.2004.37-535

Saunders, B. S., Tilford, J. M., Fussell, J. J., Schulz, E. G., Casey, P. H., & Kuo, D. Z. (2015). Financial and employment impact of intellectual disability on families of children with autism. *Families, Systems and Health, 33*(1), 36.

Schneider, K. J., Pierson, J. F., & Bugental, J. F. (Eds.). (2014). *The handbook of humanistic psychology: Theory, research, and practice.* New York: Sage Publications.

Shea, S. E., & Coyne, L. W. (2011). Maternal dysphoric mood, stress, and parenting practices in mothers of Head Start preschoolers: The role of experiential avoidance. *Child & Family Behavior Therapy, 33*(3), 231–247. https://doi.org/10.1080/07317107.2011.596004

Shireman, M. L., Lerman, D. C., & Hillman, C. B. (2016). Teaching social play skills to adults and children with autism as an approach to building rapport. *Journal of Applied Behavior Analysis, 49*, 512–531. https://doi.org/10.1002/jaba.299

Siegel, D. J. (2004). Attachment and self-understanding: Parenting with the brain in mind. *Journal of Prenatal and Perinatal Psychology and Health, 18*(4), 273.

Singer, G. H., Ethridge, B. L., & Aldana, S. I. (2007). Primary and secondary effects of parenting and stress management interventions for parents of children with developmental disabilities: A meta-analysis. *Mental Retardation and Developmental Disabilities Research Reviews, 13*(4), 357–369.

Singh, N. N., Lancioni, G. E., Medvedev, O. N., Sreenivas, S., Myers, R. E., & Hwang, Y. S. (2019). Meditation on the soles of the feet practice provides some control of aggression for individuals with Alzheimer's disease. *Mindfulness, 10*(7), 1232–1242. https://doi.org/10.1007/s12671-018-1075-0

Singh, N. N., Lancioni, G. E., Myers, R. E., Karazsia, B. T., Courtney, T. M., & Nugent, K. (2017). A mindfulness-based intervention for self-management of verbal and physical aggression by adolescents with Prader-Willi syndrome. *Developmental Neurorehabilitation, 20*(5), 253–260. https://doi.org/10.3109/17518423.2016.1141436

Singh, N. N., Lancioni, G. E, Winton, A. S., Fisher, B. T., Wahler, R., McAleavey, K., et al. (2006). Mindful parenting decreases aggression, noncompliance, and self-injury in children with autism. *Journal of Emotional and Behavioral Disorders, 14*(3), 169–177. https://doi.org/10.1177/10634266060140030401

Singh, N. N., Lancioni, G. E., Winton, A. S., Karazsia, B. T., Myers, R. E., Latham, L. L., et al. (2014). Mindfulness-based positive behavior support (MBPBS) for mothers of adolescents with autism spectrum disorder: Effects on adolescents' behavior and parental stress. *Mindfulness, 5*(6), 646–657. https://doi.org/10.1007/s12671-014-0321-3

Singh, N. N., Wahler, R. G., Adkins, A. D., Myers, R. E., & Mindfulness Research Group (2003). Soles of the feet: A mindfulness-based self-control intervention for aggression by an individual with mild mental retardation and mental illness. *Research in Developmental Disabilities, 24*(3), 158–169. https://doi.org/10.1016/s0891-4222(03)00026-x

Skinner B. F. (1945). The operational analysis of psychological terms. *Psychological Review, 52*, 268–277. https://doi.org/10.1017/S0140525X00027187

Skinner, B. F. (1953). *Science and human behavior*. New York: Macmillan.

Skinner, B. F. (1969). *Contingencies of reinforcement: A theoretical analysis*. New York: Appleton-Century-Crofts.

Skinner, B. F. (1971). *Beyond freedom and dignity*. New York: Knopf.

Skinner, B. F. (1974). *About behaviorism*. New York: Random House.

Skinner, B. F. (1981). Selection by consequences. *Science, 213*(4507), 501–504. https://doi.org/10.1126/science.7244649

Skinner, B. F. (1987). Whatever happened to psychology as the science of behavior? *American Psychologist, 42,* 780–786. https://doi.org/10.1037/0003-066X.42.8.780

Staddon, J. E. (1993). Pepper with a pinch of salt. *The Behavior Analyst, 16,* 245–250. https://doi.org/10.1007/BF03392632

Stewart, I., McLoughlin, S., Mulhern, T., Ming, S., & Kirsten, E. B. (2020). Assessing and teaching complex relational operants: Analogy and hierarchy. In M. J. Fryling, R. A. Rehfeldt, J. Tarbox, & L. J. Hayes (Eds.), *Applied behavior analysis of language and cognition: Core concepts & principles for practitioners* (pp. 198–213). Oakland, CA: Context Press/New Harbinger Publications.

Stoddard, J. A., & Afari, N. (2014). *The big book of ACT metaphors: A practitioner's guide to experiential exercises and metaphors in acceptance and commitment therapy.* Oakland, CA: New Harbinger Publications.

Sugai, G., Lewis-Palmer, T., & Hagan-Burke, S. (2000). Overview of the functional behavioral assessment process. *Exceptionality: The Official Journal of the Division for Research of the Council for Exceptional Children, 8*(3), 149–160. https://doi.org/10.1207/S15327035EX0803_2

Sun, X. (2022). Behavior skills training for family caregivers of people with intellectual or developmental disabilities: A systematic review of literature. *International Journal of Developmental Disabilities, 68*(3), 247–273.

Szabo, T. G., Richling, S., Embry, D. D., Biglan, A., & Wilson, K. G. (2020). From helpless to hero: Promoting values-based behavior and positive family interaction in the midst of Covid-19. *Behavior Analysis in Practice, 13,* 568–576. https://doi.org/10.1007/s40617-020-00431-0

Tarbox, J., Szabo, T. G., & Aclan, M. (2020). Acceptance and commitment training within the scope of practice of applied behavior analysis. *Behavior Analysis in Practice, 15,* 11–32.

Taylor, B. A., & Fisher, J. (2010). Three important things to consider when starting intervention for a child diagnosed with autism. *Behavior Analysis in Practice, 3*(2), 52. https://doi.org/10.1007/BF03391765

Taylor, B. A., LeBlanc, L. A., & Nosik, M. R. (2018). Compassionate care in behavior analytic treatment: Can outcomes be enhanced by attending to relationships with caregivers? *Behavior Analysis in Practice, 12*(3), 654–666. https://doi.org/10.1007/s40617-018-00289-3

Thomas, R., & Zimmer-Gembeck, M. J. (2007). Behavioral outcomes of parent-child interaction therapy and Triple P-Positive Parenting Program: A review and meta-analysis. *Journal of Abnormal Child Psychology, 35*(3), 475–495.

Thompson, M., Bond, F. W., & Lloyd, J. (2019). Preliminary psychometric properties of the Everyday Psychological Inflexibility Checklist. *Journal of Contextual Behavioral Science, 12*, 243–252.

Titchener, E. B. (1916). *An outline of psychology by Edward Bradford Titchener.* New York: Macmillan.

Törneke, N. (2010). *Learning RFT: An introduction to relational frame theory and its clinical application.* Oakland, CA: Context Press/New Harbinger Publications.

Törneke, N. (2017). *Metaphor in practice: A professional's guide to using the science of language in psychotherapy.* Oakland, CA: Context Press/New Harbinger Publications.

Vollmer, T. R., Borrero, J. C., Wright, C. S., Van Camp, C., & Lalli, J. S. (2001). Identifying possible contingencies during descriptive analyses of severe behavior disorders. *Journal of Applied Behavior Analysis, 34* (3), 269–287. https://doi.org/10.1901/jaba.2001.34-269

Vollmer, T. R., Peters, K. P., Kronfli, F. R., Lloveras, L. A., & Ibañez, V. F. (2020). On the definition of differential reinforcement of alternative behavior. *Journal of Applied Behavior Analysis, 53*(3), 1299–1303. https://doi.org/10.1002/jaba.701

Vostanis, P., Graves, A., Meltzer, H., Goodman, R., Jenkins, R., & Brugha, T. (2006). Relationship between parental psychopathology, parenting strategies, and child mental health. *Social Psychiatry and Psychiatric Epidemiology, 41*(7), 509–514.

Whiting, M., Nash, A. S., Kendall, S., & Roberts, S. A. (2019). Enhancing resilience and self-efficacy in the parents of children with disabilities and complex health needs. *Primary Health Care Research & Development, 20*, e33, 1–7. https://doi.org/10.1017/S1463423619000112

Whittingham, K., & Coyne, L. (2019). *Acceptance and commitment therapy: The clinician's guide for supporting parents.* New York: Academic Press.

Whittingham, K., Sanders, M. R., McKinlay, L., & Boyd, R. N. (2016). Parenting intervention combined with acceptance and commitment therapy: A trial with families of children with cerebral palsy. *Journal of Pediatric Psychology, 41*(5), 531–542. https://doi.org/10.1093/jpepsy/jsv118

Wilson, A. N., & Gratz, O. H. (2016). Using a progressive ratio schedule of reinforcement as an assessment tool to inform treatment. *Behavior Analysis in Practice, 9*(3), 257–260. https://doi.org/10.1007/s40617-016-0107-2

Wilson, A. N., Kasson, E. M., Gratz, O., & Guercio, J. (2014). Exploring the clinical utility of an aversive stimulus assessment to enhance a relaxation training model. *Behavior Analysis in Practice, 8*(1), 57–61. https://doi.org/10.1007/s40617-014-0035-y

Wilson, A. N., Kellum, K. K., & Jackson, M. (2021). Introduction to the special issue: Acceptance and commitment training in applied behavior analysis. *Behavior Analysis in Practice, 15*, 7–10. https://doi.org/10.1007/s40617-021-00645-w

Wilson, K. G. (2001). Some notes on theoretical constructs: Types and validation from a contextual behavioral perspective. *International Journal of Psychology and Psychological Therapy, 1*(2), 205–215. https://www.redalyc.org/pdf/560/56010205.pdf

Wilson, K. G. (2021, March 5–April 9). Using the ACT hexagon to promote psychological flexibility in applied behavior analysis. (Virtual workshop). ABACNJ. https://v3cer tificates.abacnj.com/course/kw-w21-dr-kelly-wilson-presents-using-the-act-hexagon-to -promote-psychological-flexibility-in-applied-behavior-analysis/start-course

Wilson, K. G., & DuFrene, T. (2009). *Mindfulness for two: An acceptance and commitment therapy approach to mindfulness in psychotherapy.* Oakland, CA: New Harbinger Publications.

Wilson, K. G., & Murrell, A. R. (2004). Values work in acceptance and commitment therapy: Setting a course for behavioral treatment. In S. C. Hayes, V. M. Follette, & M. M. Linehan (Eds.), *Mindfulness and acceptance: Expanding the cognitive-behavioral tradition* (pp. 120–151). New York: Guilford Press.

Wilson, K. G., & Sandoz, E. K. (2008). Mindfulness, values, and the therapeutic relationship in acceptance and commitment therapy. In S. Hick & T. Bein (Eds.), *Mindfulness and the therapeutic relationship* (pp. 89–106). New York: Guilford Press.

Wilson, K. G., Sandoz, E. K., Kitchens, J., & Roberts, M. (2010). The Valued Living Questionnaire: Defining and measuring valued action within a behavioral framework. *The Psychological Record, 60*(2), 249–272.

Yi, Z., & Dixon, M. R. (2020). Developing and enhancing adherence to a telehealth ABA parent training curriculum for caregivers of children with autism. *Behavior Analysis in Practice, 14*(1), 58–74. https://doi.org/10.1007/s40617-020-00464-5

Zettle, R. (2016). Contextual approaches to clinical interventions and assessment: An introduction to part III. In R. D. Zettle, S. C. Hayes, D. Barnes-Holmes, & A. Biglan (Eds.), *The Wiley handbook of contextual behavioral science* (pp. 275–286). Hoboken, NJ: Wiley-Blackwell.

Zettle, R. D., & Hayes, S. C. (1982). Rule-governed behavior: A potential theoretical framework for cognitive-behavioral therapy. In P. C. Kendall (Ed.), *Advances in cognitive-behavioral research and therapy* (Vol. 1, pp. 73–118). New York: Academic Press.

Zuriff, G. E. (1985). *Behaviorism: A conceptual reconstruction.* New York: Columbia University Press.

Alyssa Wilson, PhD, BCBA-D, is associate professor and department chair of applied behavior analysis programs at The Chicago School of Professional Psychology in Southern California. She received her PhD in rehabilitation with an emphasis on behavior analysis and therapy from Southern Illinois University, Carbondale. She splits her time between St. Louis, MO; and Los Angeles, CA.

Index

Real change *is* possible

For more than forty-five years, New Harbinger has published proven-effective self-help books and pioneering workbooks to help readers of all ages and backgrounds improve mental health and well-being, and achieve lasting personal growth. In addition, our spirituality books offer profound guidance for deepening awareness and cultivating healing, self-discovery, and fulfillment.

Founded by psychologist Matthew McKay and Patrick Fanning, New Harbinger is proud to be an independent, employee-owned company. Our books reflect our core values of integrity, innovation, commitment, sustainability, compassion, and trust. Written by leaders in the field and recommended by therapists worldwide, New Harbinger books are practical, accessible, and provide real tools for real change.

 **newharbinger**publications